THE YOUNG SCIENTIST
JETS · SPACEFLIGHT · ELECTRICITY

CONTENTS:

D1741620

PART 1/1
JETS

PART 2/33
SPACEFLIGHT

PART 3/65
ELECTRICITY

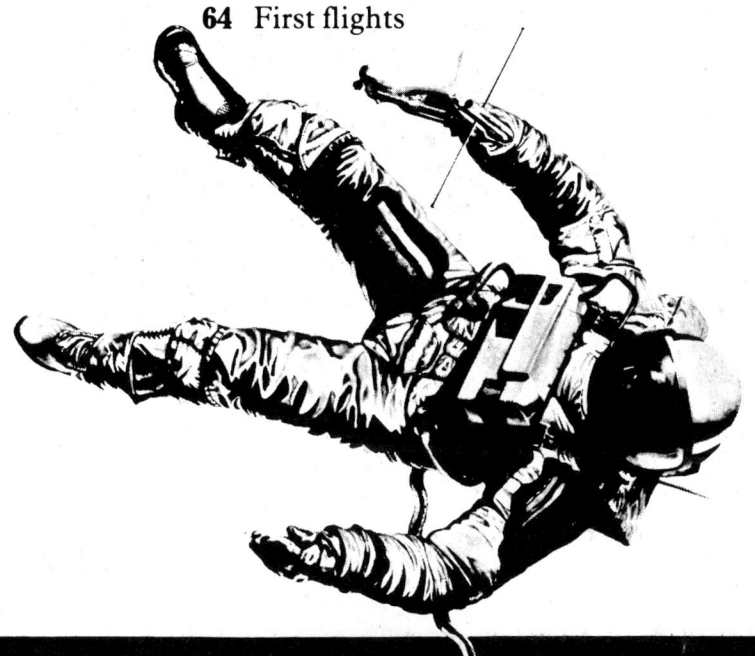

This book is made up from three titles in the Usborne Young Scientist series, originally published as Jets, Spaceflight, Electricity.

© 1978 Usborne Publishing Ltd

First published in 1978
Usborne Publishing Ltd
20 Garrick Street
London WC2E 9BJ

The name Usborne and the device are
Trade Marks of Usborne Publishing Ltd.

Printed in Italy

PART 1: JETS

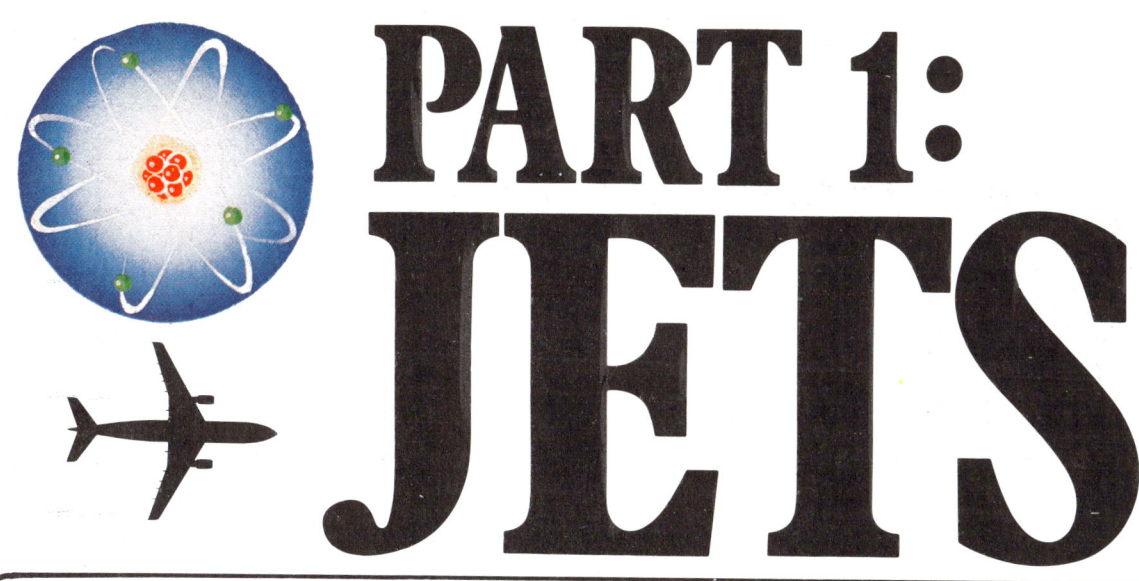

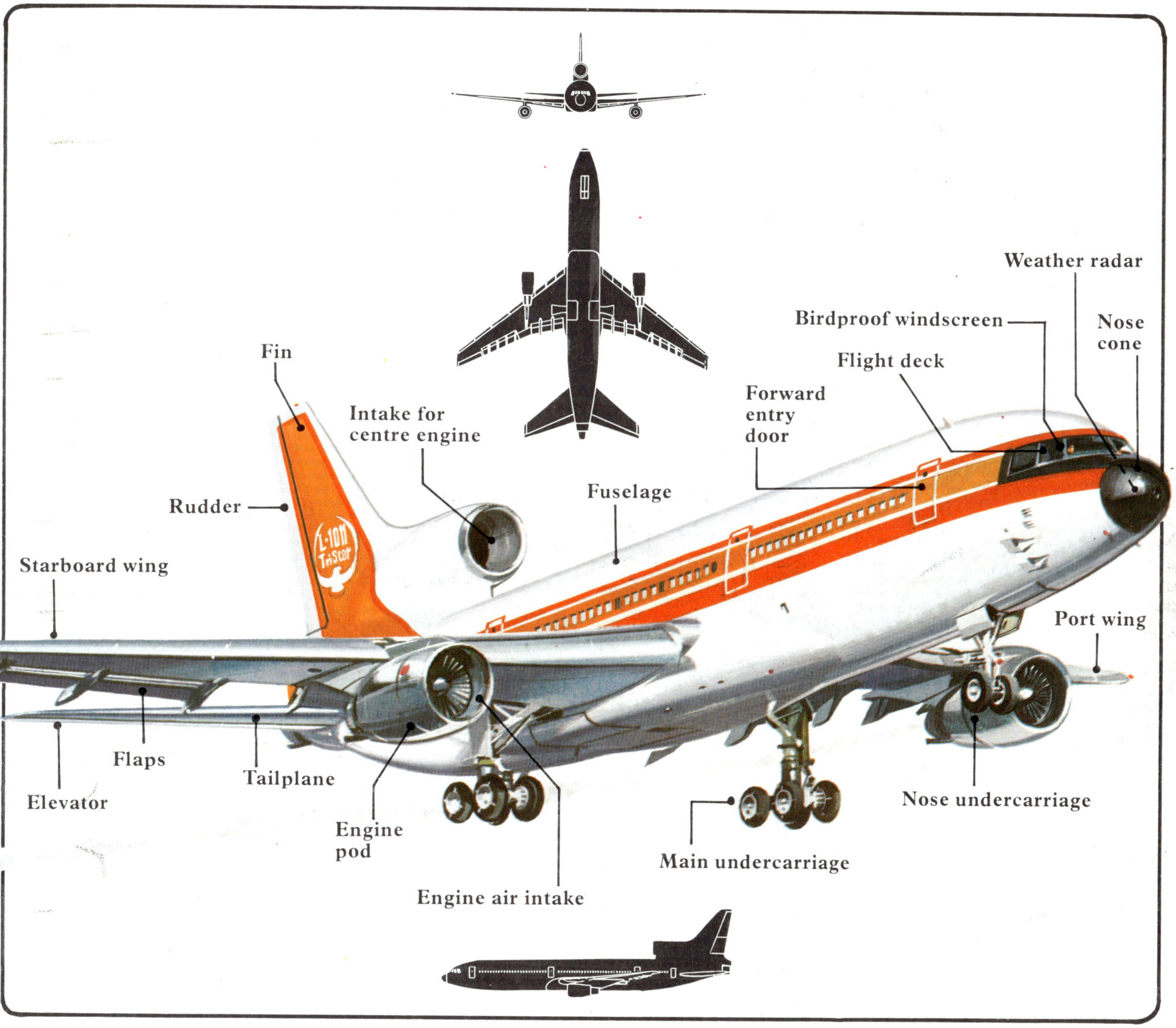
Weather radar
Birdproof windscreen
Nose cone
Flight deck
Fin
Forward entry door
Intake for centre engine
Rudder
Fuselage
L-1011 TriStar
Starboard wing
Port wing
Flaps
Tailplane
Elevator
Engine pod
Nose undercarriage
Main undercarriage
Engine air intake

CREDITS

Written by
Mark Hewish
Art and editorial direction
David Jefferis
Text editor
Tony Allan
Educational advisor
Frank Blackwell
Revised by Alan Wright

Illustrators
Derek Bunce, Gordon Davies,
Malcolm English, Phil Green,
Terry Hadler, John Hutchinson and
Michael Roffe

Revised and updated in 1982

The jets on this page are
Dassault Mirage F1Cs of the
Armee de l'Air, the French air force.

THE EXPERIMENTS

Here is a checklist of the equipment you will need for the experiments and things to do included in Part 1.

General equipment
Notebook and pencil
Ruler or tape-measure
Sticky tape
Glue
Scissors
Watch (preferably with a second hand)
Rubber bands

For special experiments
Action and reaction (p.5): Balloon

Air compression (p.6): Plastic detergent bottle
             Modelling clay

Glider (p.8): Drinking straw
       Sheet of stiff paper at least 22.5 cm. long

Aerodynamic lift (p.9): Sheet of paper, roughly 15 x 20 cm.

Wing section (p.11): Three sheets of A4 paper (21 x 29.8 cm.)

Artificial horizon (p.13): Plastic pot (an empty cream carton is ideal)
             Match with sharpened end

Sound power (p.19): Wide-necked glass bottle
             Sheet of polythene
             Sugar

Heat experiment (p.25): Two narrow-necked bottles
             Two drinking straws
             Modelling clay
             Ink
             Black and white paints

WEIGHTS AND MEASURES

All the weights and measures are metric. Here are some equivalents in imperial measures.

mm. = millimetre
(1 inch = 25.4 mm.)

cm. = centimetre
(1 inch = 2.54 cm.)

m. = metre
(1 yard = 0.91 m.)

km. = kilometre
(1 mile = 1.6 km.)

k.p.h. = kilometres per hour
(1,000 m.p.h. = 1,609 k.p.h.)

sq. cm. = square centimetre
(1 square inch = 6.45 sq. cm.)

sq. m. = square metre
(1 square yard = 0.84 sq. m.)

A hectare is 10,000 sq. m.
(1 acre = 0.40 hectares)

kg. = kilogram
(1 stone = 6.35 kg.)

A tonne is 1,000 kg.
(1 ton = 1.02 tonnes)

1 litre is 1.76 pints

°C = degrees Centigrade
(Water freezes at 0°C and boils at 100°C)

PART 1: JETS

ABOUT JETS

How do jet engines work? Why is there a bang when planes travel faster than sound? Why do jets leave vapour trails? Why do some planes have swing-wings?

Jets sets out to answer questions like these. It tells the story of the jet plane, from the beginnings in the 1930s to designs that are still on the drawing-board today. It explains the basic principles of jet flight. It describes what the most important instruments in an airliner cockpit are for, and how air traffic control works. It also covers such developments as supersonic airliners and vertical take-off, and the problems of noise pollution and jet-lag.

Jets also contains many safe and simple experiments that can be done at home with ordinary household equipment. They range from simple illustrations of scientific principles to projects like building a drinking-straw glider.

CONTENTS

THE FIRST JETS

It took a surprisingly long time for the jet engine to be invented, considering that the principle on which it works was known in ancient Greece. An inventor called Hero devised a sphere that was turned by escaping steam (see 1 below).

The idea of jet-propelled aircraft was first suggested in 1865, but the earliest planes to be built and flown were propellor-driven. Jet propulsion was not seriously considered again until 25 years after the Wright Brothers' first flight, when an English airman called Frank Whittle took up the idea.

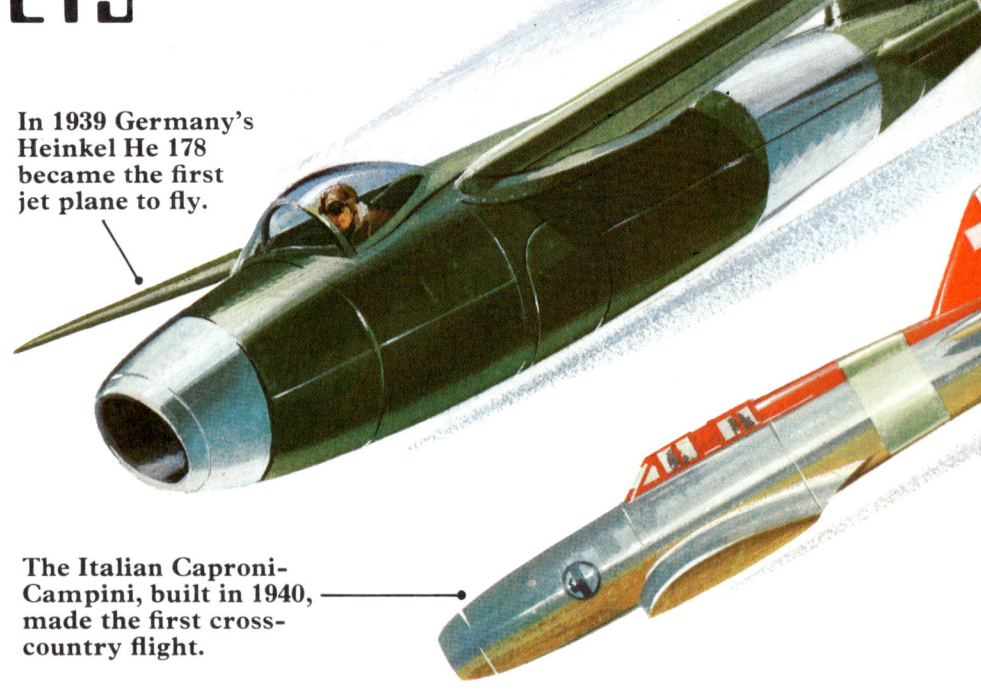

In 1939 Germany's Heinkel He 178 became the first jet plane to fly.

The Italian Caproni-Campini, built in 1940, made the first cross-country flight.

Hero's steam sphere

▲ Pabst von Ohain, a German physicist, designed the engine for the world's first jet plane.

After taking a degree at Göttingen University in Germany, he began building working models of gas turbines. In 1936 he was employed by the aircraft manufacturer Ernst Heinkel.

A year later he successfully tested his first jet engine. An improved version of it was installed in the specially designed He 178 test plane in 1939.

▲ Soon after dawn on August 27, 1939, Captain Erich Warsitz lifted the He 178 off the runway at the test base at Marienhe. He circled the airfield, then sideslipped in to land, completing the first jet flight ever.

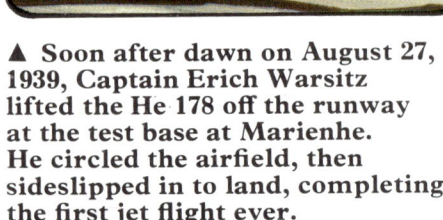

▲ On May 15, 1941, the E.28/39 took to the air for the first time, flown by Flt. Lt. P. E. G. Sayer. Whittle's engine gave the Squirt, on its first flight, a performance almost as fast as a Spitfire's, and it later reached 750 k.p.h.

▲ The V-1 flying bomb was an offshoot of the development of the jet engine. It was powered by a pulse jet that allowed 'gulps' of air to pass into the combustion chamber, where they were mixed with petrol and ignited.

▲ Heinkel's experience with the 178 led to the wood-framed He 162 Salamander jet fighter. It first flew in December 1944. Only 116 were built, though plans were made to build 4,000 a month. Few Salamanders flew in combat.

Britain's Gloster E.28/39 was the brainchild of Frank Whittle, who had worked for 12 years on jet engine development before its maiden flight in 1941.

The Bell XP-59A Airacomet brought the U.S. into the jet age in 1942. Its twin turbojet engines were developed from Whittle's designs.

▲ The Caproni-Campini made its maiden flight exactly a year after the He 178. In 1941 it flew from Milan to Rome, a distance of 470 km. It was a slow flyer, though, with a top speed of only 375 k.p.h.

▲ Frank Whittle began thinking about jet propulsion in the late 1920s, when he was at the Royal Air Force College, Cranwell.

The Air Ministry rejected his designs, but in 1935 a friend raised the money to back his work, and Power Jets Ltd. was formed.

Their first working engine ran on April 12, 1937, and in July 1939 the company was awarded a contract to build an engine for the experimental Gloster E.28/39 – nicknamed the Squirt.

▲ The Me 262 and Meteor twin-engined warplanes both went into service in World War 2, but they never fought one another. The Me 262 had swept wings – a development pioneered by German aircraft designers.

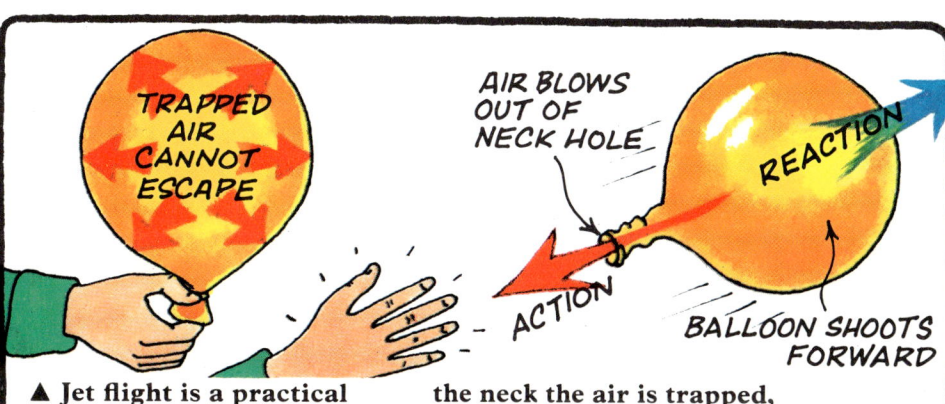

▲ Jet flight is a practical application of the Third Law of Motion, which states that for every action there is an equal and opposite reaction. Try it for yourself by blowing up a balloon. While you hold the neck the air is trapped, but when you let go it rushes out. This action causes a reaction, so the balloon shoots forward in the opposite direction to the air. Jet planes speed along in a similar way.

TURBOJET AND TURBOFAN

Early jet engines were pure turbojets. Air passing through them goes through four main stages. First it is sucked in through the intake. Then it is compressed. The compressed air is mixed with fuel and set alight. Finally the hot gases produced are forced back through the exhaust, driving the aircraft forward.

Some jets now use large fans to draw in more air. This kind of engine is called a turbofan.

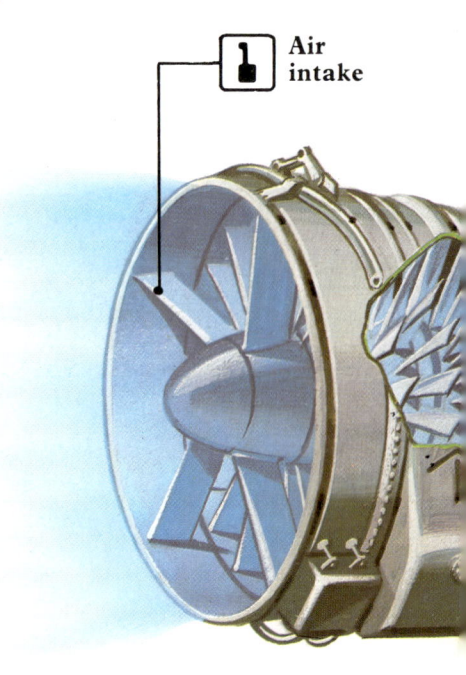

Air intake

Turbojet-powered Concorde

The turbojet shown opposite is the Rolls-Royce Olympus engine used in Concordes. Air entering the intake (1) passes through the compressor (2) – a series of vanes that pack it densely together. It is mixed with vaporized kerosene in the combustion chamber (3) and burned.

The hot gases this produces roar through the turbine (4), which spins round like windmill blades in wind, turning the vanes in the compressor as it goes . They then pass through a nozzle (5) into the afterburner (6), where more fuel is burned to provide extra thrust.

1 Air compression

Jet engines have compressors to pack as much air as possible into the combustion chamber. The amount of thrust an engine gives increases as more fuel is used, and the fuel needs oxygen in the air to make it burn—so the thrust depends also on the amount of air that is sucked in.

Cold air is best, as it is denser than hot air. But air heats up as it is compressed. Try pumping up a bicycle tyre. You will soon find that compression and friction combined have warmed pump and tyre up.

2 PLASTIC BOTTLE
PLASTICINE
TAPE-MEASURE

▲ This is a neat and simple experiment which shows just how powerful a force compressed air can exert. All you need is an empty plastic washing-up-liquid bottle, a piece of plasticine, and a tape-measure.

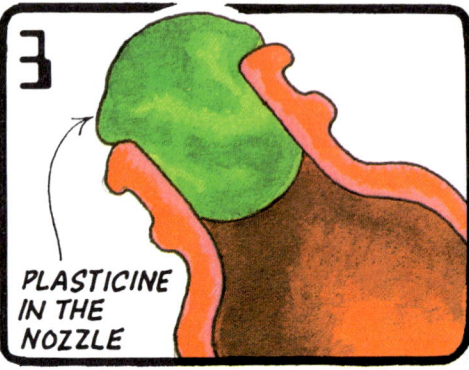

3 PLASTICINE IN THE NOZZLE

▲ Take the nozzle off the bottle, and ease a lump of plasticine into the neck. Make sure the seal is airtight by squeezing the bottle gently and listening for air leaks. Take the bottle outside or into a large room.

▲ Lay the bottle on the ground, then jump on it! The pressure of compressed air will blow the plasticine cork up to 20 m. away. Mark the spot where it lands, then see which of your friends can make it go furthest.

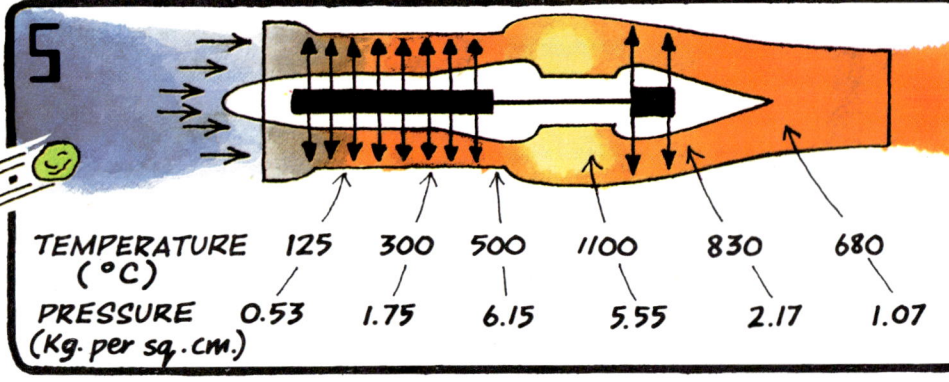

TEMPERATURE (°C)	125	300	500	1100	830	680
PRESSURE (Kg. per sq. cm.)	0.53	1.75	6.15	5.55	2.17	1.07

▲ This diagram shows what happens to the temperature and pressure of air as it passes through the Olympus turbojet of a Concorde flying at twice the speed of sound nearly 20,000 m. up. The compressors increase the air pressure more than ten times, so that as much as possible is crammed into the combustion chamber. The air temperature, which has steadily increased in the compressor, is doubled when the fuel ignites, while the pressure starts to fall.

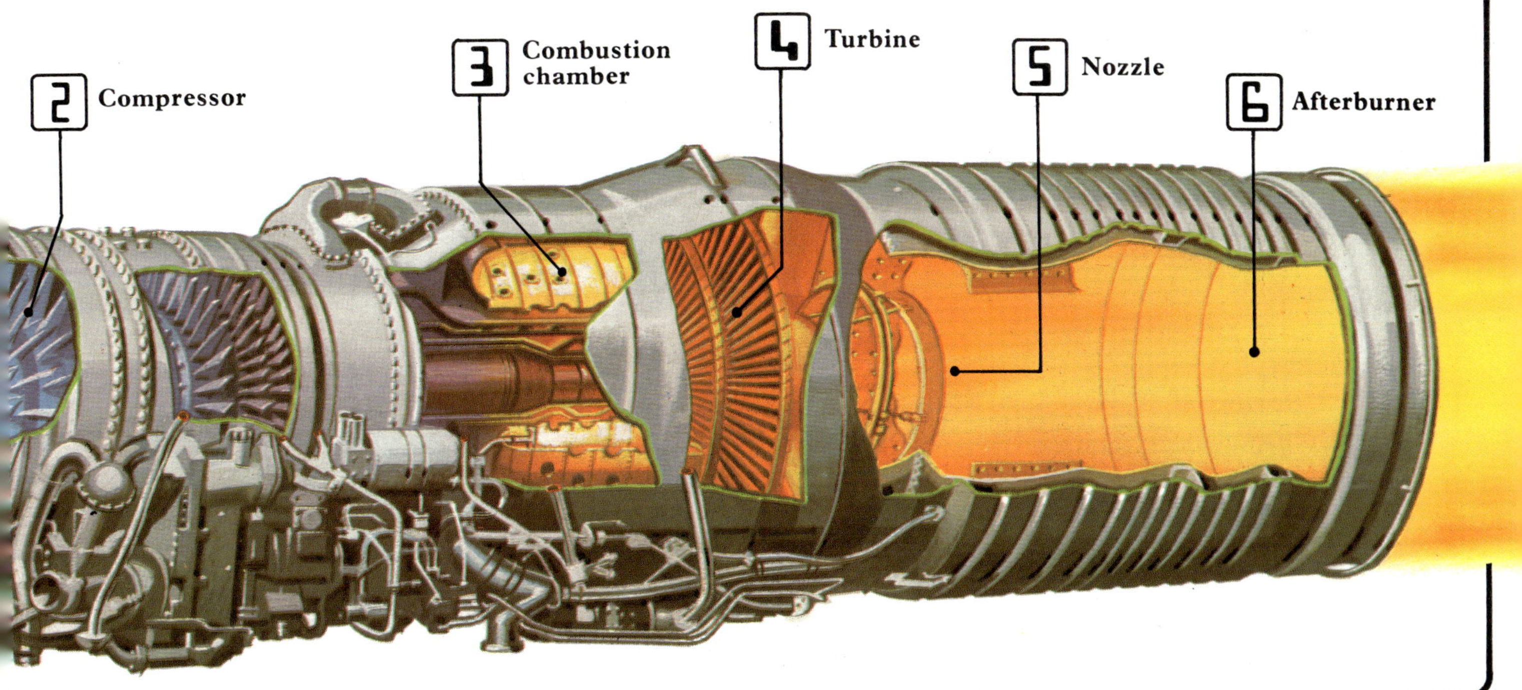

2 Compressor

3 Combustion chamber

4 Turbine

5 Nozzle

6 Afterburner

Turbofan-powered Lockheed TriStar

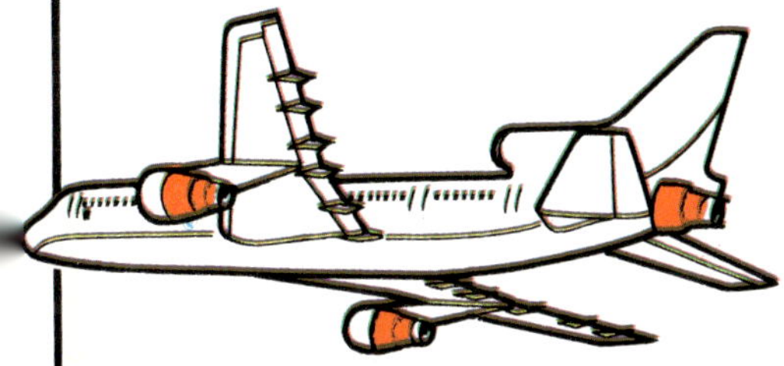

The Rolls-Royce RB 211 used in the TriStar is a turbofan engine. A turbofan is basically a turbojet with a big fan at the front or back. Most modern models use front fans. The fan (1) acts as a many-bladed propellor, drawing air into the compressor (2) just as a ventilator draws air into a room. The air then passes through the combustion chamber (3), the turbine (4) and the nozzle (5) as in a turbojet.

The 211 is a high-bypass-ratio engine, however. This means that a lot of the air (more than four-fifths of that entering the intake) is blown around the jet core. This air is not burned, but provides thrust as it blows back through the fan exhaust (6).

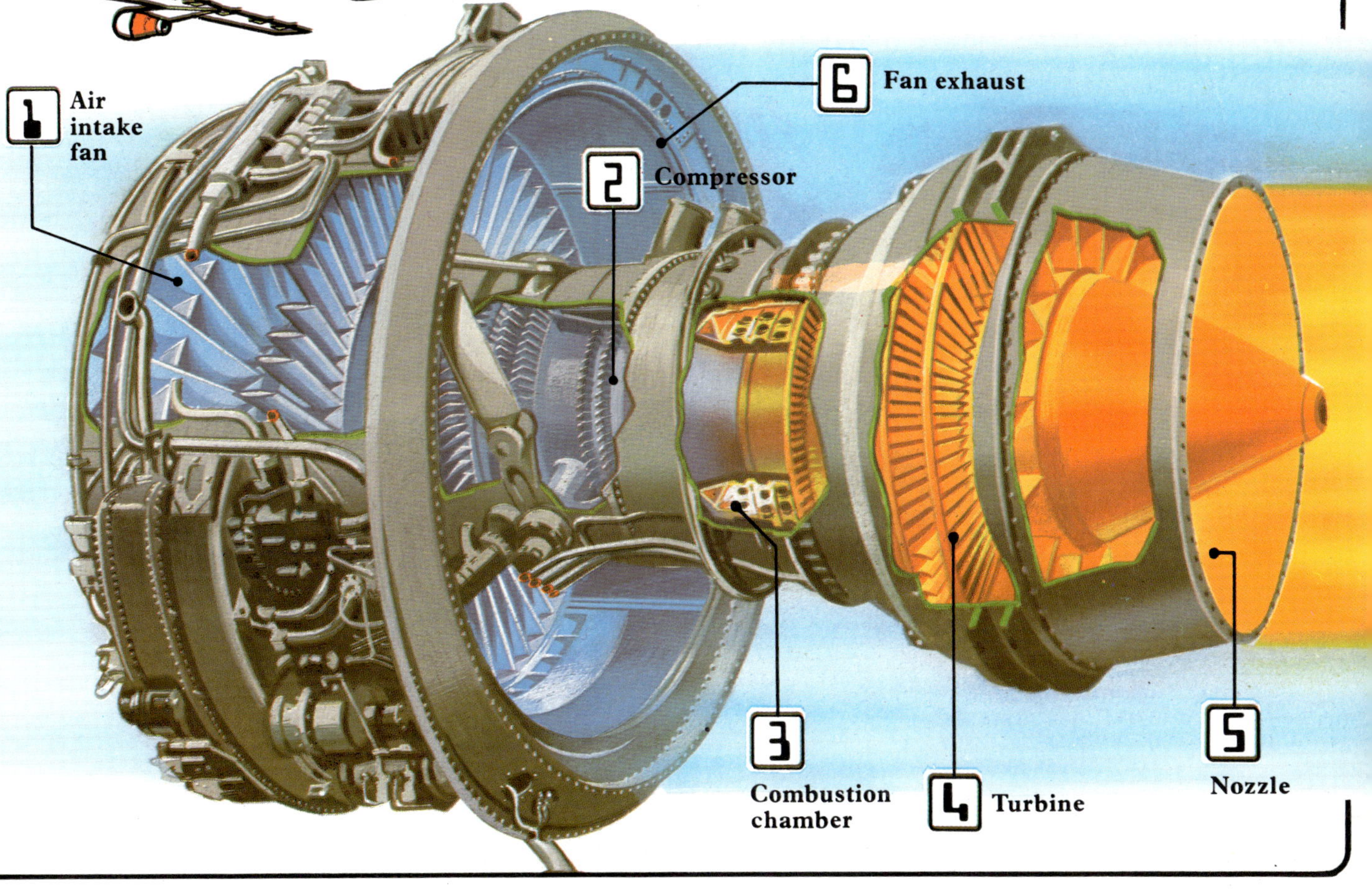

1 Air intake fan

6 Fan exhaust

2 Compressor

3 Combustion chamber

4 Turbine

5 Nozzle

HOW AND WHY JETS FLY

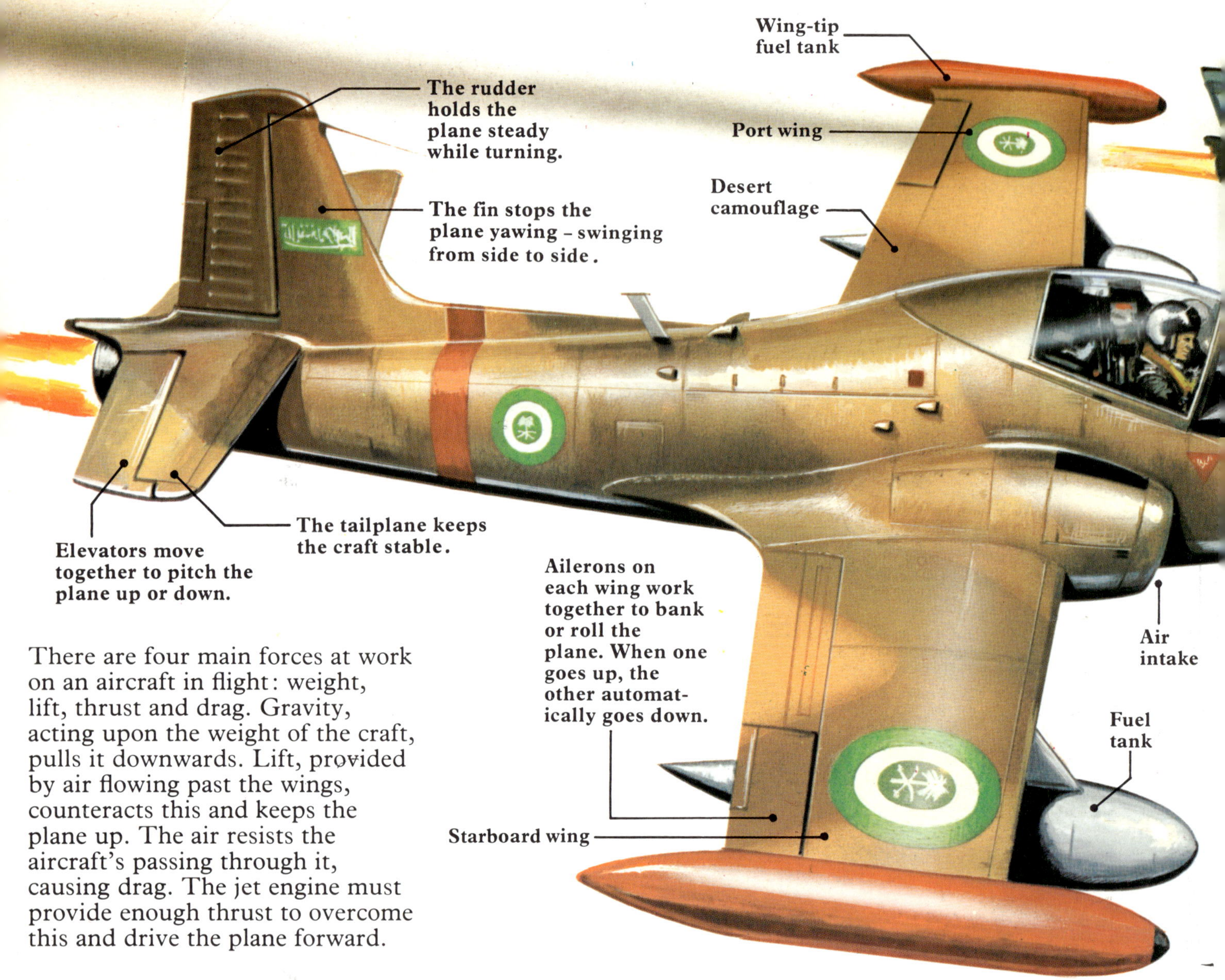

Wing-tip fuel tank

Port wing

Desert camouflage

The rudder holds the plane steady while turning.

The fin stops the plane yawing – swinging from side to side.

Air intake

Elevators move together to pitch the plane up or down.

The tailplane keeps the craft stable.

Ailerons on each wing work together to bank or roll the plane. When one goes up, the other automatically goes down.

Fuel tank

Starboard wing

There are four main forces at work on an aircraft in flight: weight, lift, thrust and drag. Gravity, acting upon the weight of the craft, pulls it downwards. Lift, provided by air flowing past the wings, counteracts this and keeps the plane up. The air resists the aircraft's passing through it, causing drag. The jet engine must provide enough thrust to overcome this and drive the plane forward.

How to make and flight-test your own aircraft

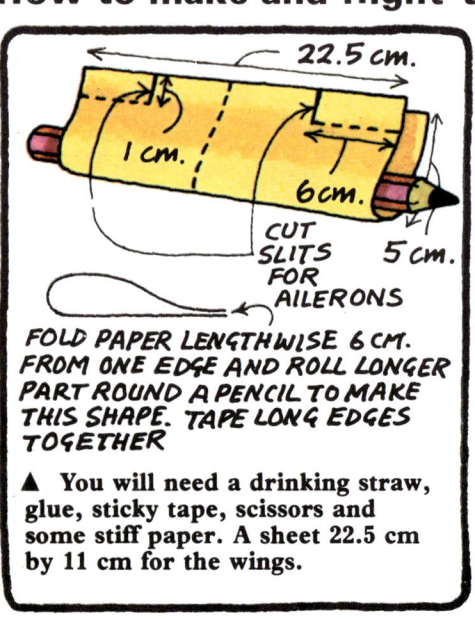

22.5 cm. 1 cm. 6 cm. 5 cm. CUT SLITS FOR AILERONS

FOLD PAPER LENGTHWISE 6 CM. FROM ONE EDGE AND ROLL LONGER PART ROUND A PENCIL TO MAKE THIS SHAPE. TAPE LONG EDGES TOGETHER

▲ You will need a drinking straw, glue, sticky tape, scissors and some stiff paper. A sheet 22.5 cm by 11 cm for the wings.

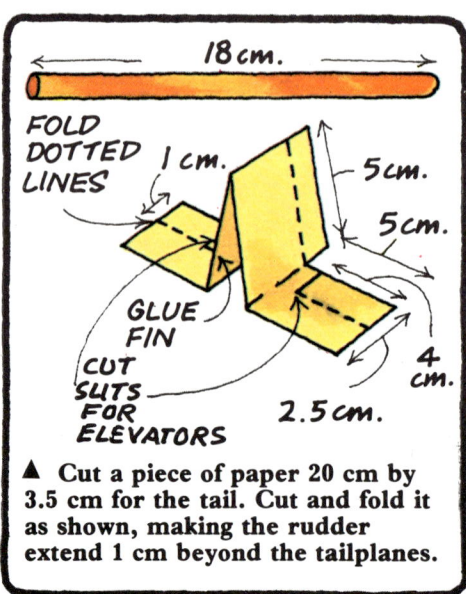

18 cm. FOLD DOTTED LINES 1 cm. 5 cm. 5 cm. GLUE FIN CUT SLITS FOR ELEVATORS 2.5 cm. 4 cm.

▲ Cut a piece of paper 20 cm by 3.5 cm for the tail. Cut and fold it as shown, making the rudder extend 1 cm beyond the tailplanes.

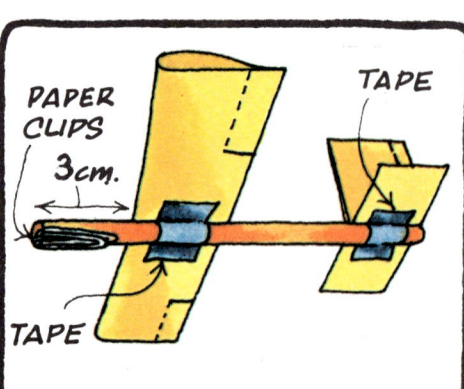

PAPER CLIPS 3 cm. TAPE TAPE

▲ Tape the wings and tail to the straw. Attach a paper-clip to the straw and test the glider. Go on attaching clips until the glider flies smoothly.

— Elevon

— Elevon

Anti-glare panel painted in front of cockpit

Wings shaped like triangles are called deltas after the Greek letter △ or delta. They are used on many high-speed planes. There is usually no tailplane on delta-winged planes, and the elevators and ailerons are combined to form elevons. The elevons move together to pitch the plane up or down, and in opposite directions for banking and rolling.

The jet on the left is a British Aerospace (BAC) Strikemaster ground attack plane of the Saudi Arabian Air Force. The plane above is a Mirage fighter-bomber with French markings.

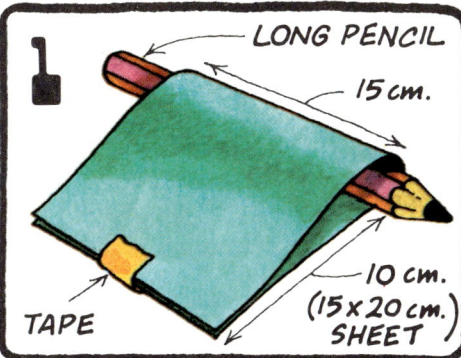

1 LONG PENCIL · 15 cm. · 10 cm. (15 x 20 cm. SHEET) · TAPE

▲ To find out how lift works, take a thin sheet of paper, about 20 cm. by 15 cm., and fold it into a wing shape as shown. Tape the two loose edges together. Find a pencil more than 15 cm. long and slide it into the loop of paper.

2 BLOW HARD · PAPER WING MOVES UPWARDS

▲ Hold the pencil so that the top edge of the 'wing' almost touches your lower lip. Now blow down over the outer surface. The wing will rise and remain level as long as you keep blowing. Your breath is acting like air over a plane wing.

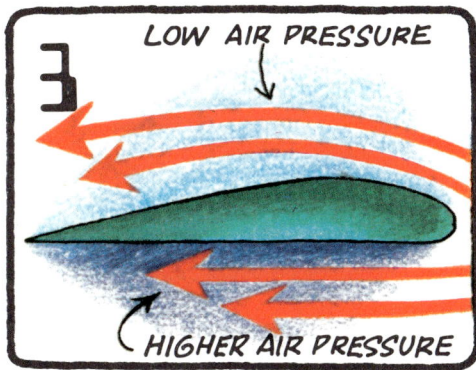

3 LOW AIR PRESSURE · HIGHER AIR PRESSURE

▲ The upper surface of an aircraft wing is more curved than the lower surface, and air has to accelerate over the top to catch up with that flowing underneath. This 'stretches' the air on top, creating an area of low pressure that sucks the wing up.

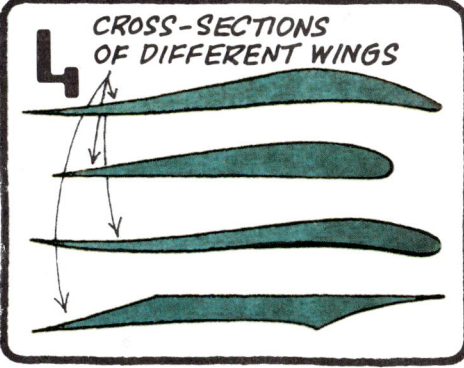

4 CROSS-SECTIONS OF DIFFERENT WINGS

▲ Wings, also known as aerofoils, have various shapes according to the sort of job they are designed for. They are usually thin on very fast planes, and may be flattened or wedge-shaped to increase lift under different conditions.

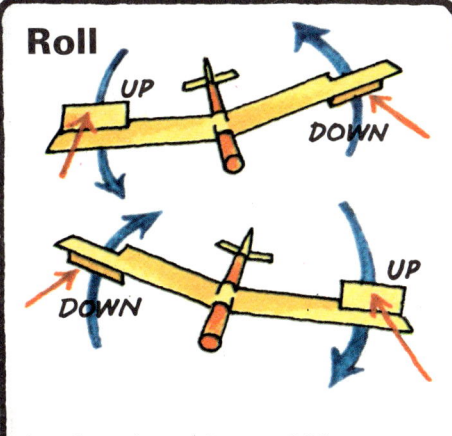

Roll · UP · DOWN · DOWN · UP

▲ The wings give stability across the plane. You can disturb the balance and make the plane roll by moving the ailerons as shown.

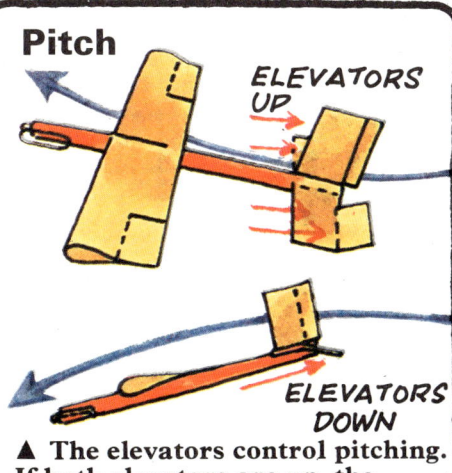

Pitch · ELEVATORS UP · ELEVATORS DOWN

▲ The elevators control pitching. If both elevators are up, the plane's nose will rise, while putting both down causes a dive.

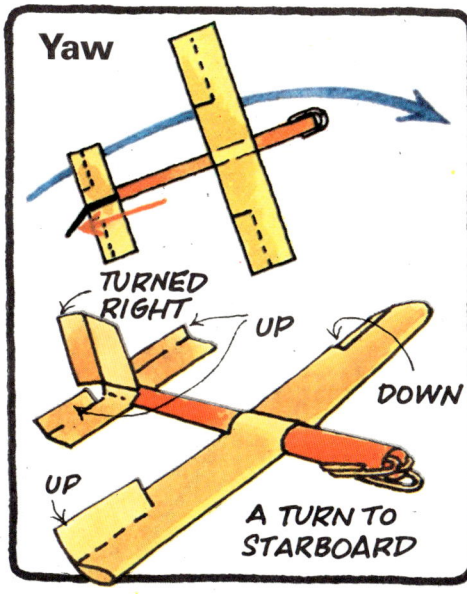

Yaw · TURNED RIGHT · UP · DOWN · UP · A TURN TO STARBOARD

JET-AGE AIRLINERS

The age of the pure-jet airliner dawned on May 2, 1952, when a Comet 1 owned by the British Overseas Airways Corporation made its first scheduled flight, from London to Johannesburg. Jet services halved flying times on long-distance trips. In 1959 Pan American World Airways started round-the-world flights with Boeing 707s. Nowadays almost all airliners are jet-powered.

The A300 Airbus, shown here in the old Air France livery, has been in service since 1974. A slightly smaller version – the A310 – will soon be in service alongside it.

1 Fuel tanks, two to each wing. Fuel can also be stored in the wing centre section.

2 Ram-air turbine drops down from the starboard wing root in case of emergency. A small propellor on the front rotates in the airflow and generates electrical power.

3 Wide-body cabin can seat more than 300 passengers. It is 5.65 m. across.

4 Fuselage is made of aluminium alloy – as are the tail and wings.

5 Flight deck for pilot, co-pilot and flight engineer.

6 Radome protects radar equipment, which detects clouds and rain.

7 General Electric CF6 engine, one under each wing. The CF6 is a turbofan giving 23,133 kg. of thrust.

8 Underfloor freight holds can carry pallets, containers or loose cargo.

9 Main undercarriage has four wheels on each leg.

10 Auxiliary power unit in the tail is a miniature jet engine providing electrical power, and compressed air for starting the engines and for air-conditioning.

The Comet crashes

▲ The de Havilland Comet 1 was a great success when it went into service in 1952. It halved journey times, carrying 36 passengers in comfort at nearly 800 k.p.h. well above the worst weather. For two years things went well.

▲ In January 1954, disaster struck. A Comet crashed into the sea after taking off from Rome, and all 35 people on board were killed. Flights were suspended for a time. When they resumed, a second Comet went down in flames, killing 17 people.

▲ All Comets were grounded. Royal Navy salvage vessels were sent to the scene of the first crash – the second plane had gone down in very deep water – and with the help of divers they recovered nearly two-thirds of the sunken plane.

Make a wing section

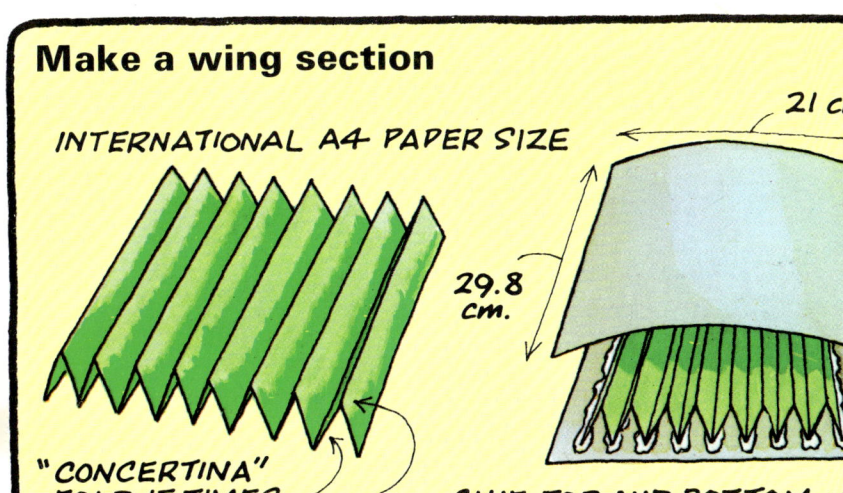

INTERNATIONAL A4 PAPER SIZE

"CONCERTINA" FOLD 15 TIMES

21 cm.

29.8 cm.

GLUE TOP AND BOTTOM

WEIGH EACH ITEM

▲ Aeroplane wings are not solid, but the honeycomb of metal struts that holds them together gives them great strength as well as low weight. You can make a surprisingly strong model wing simply by folding a sheet of paper.

▲ Do your best to make all the folds the same size, so that the load will be evenly distributed. Glue the folded sheet between two other sheets of the same size, placing it near one edge to give your wing the correct shape.

▲ Now test the wing to find out the weight that it can carry. You will find that it will take an unexpectedly heavy load without buckling. The model wing above could carry more than four-and-a-half kg.

The most complex wing ever?

The Airbus wing is designed to provide more lift over its rear section than normal wings, allowing a thicker but lighter wing to be used.

Flaps on the wing's trailing edge improve lift at low speeds, while there are twin ailerons for low- and high-speed flying. The spoilers, air-brakes and lift-dumpers can all be used to slow the plane down in flight and to allow low-speed approaches for landing.

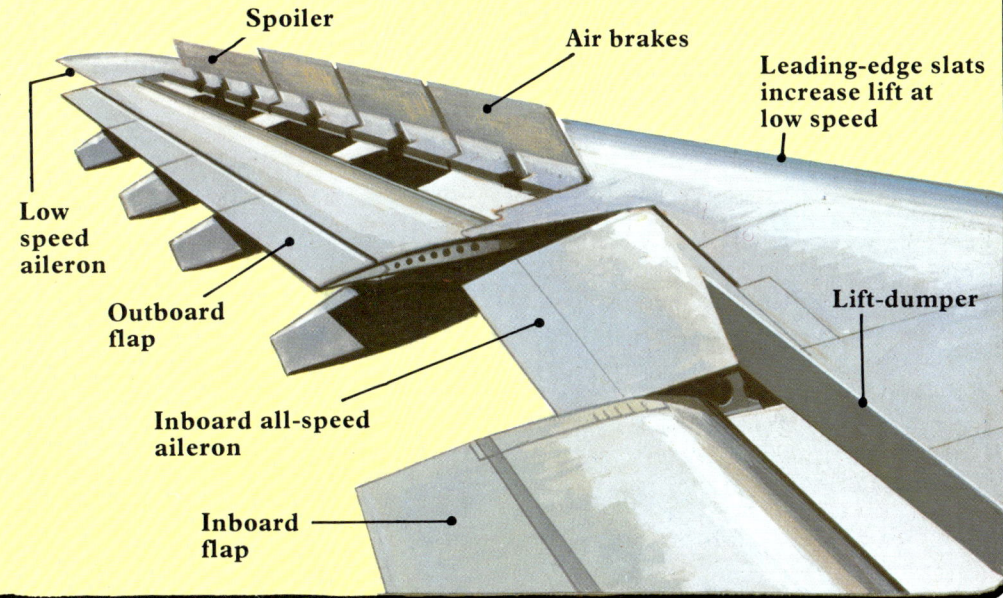

Spoiler

Air brakes

Leading-edge slats increase lift at low speed

Low speed aileron

Outboard flap

Inboard all-speed aileron

Inboard flap

Lift-dumper

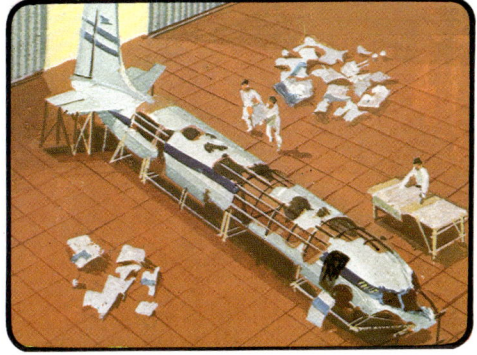

▲ The wreckage was sent back to Farnborough, England. It was reassembled on a frame the size and shape of a real Comet. Most of the fuselage, parts of the wings, and all four engines were found and wired into place.

▲ Another Comet was put in a tank, with its wings sticking out. Jacks bent the wings, while water was pumped into the fuselage to create strains equal to those of thousands of hours of flying. The fuselage eventually ripped apart.

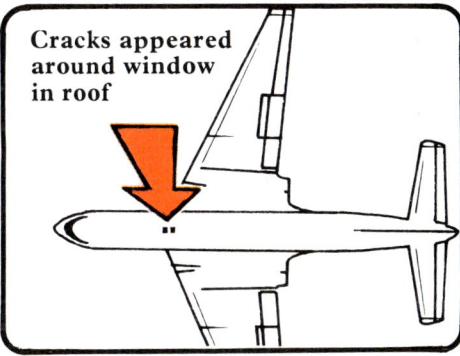

Cracks appeared around window in roof

▲ It was finally discovered that the crash had been caused by cracks spreading from a rivet hole, causing the pressurized cabin to explode. Jet design was altered as a result, and nowadays metal fatigue is kept under control.

INSIDE THE COCKPIT

The crew of a modern jet airliner must have all the information they need at their finger-tips, so a great deal of effort goes into designing the best flight-deck layout possible. The captain and the first officer each have controls for handling the plane, and there is an automatic pilot to do the routine flying.

Basic flight instruments are on the panel in front of them. On the console between them are the engine throttles and gauges, radio and navigation equipment, and such items as the parking brake.

The flight engineer has his own instrument panel behind theirs.

Order out of chaos

Flight controls. Each pilot has a control column and rudder pedals.

Basic instruments. Three of these are shown on the opposite page.

Engine controls include throttles for power and fuel and other gauges.

Flight engineer's panel. Dials record the working of all the plane's systems.

Radio transmitter and receiver, and weather radar equipment.

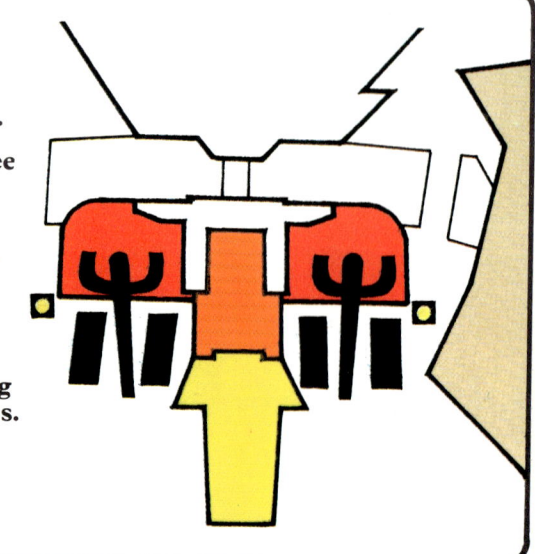

Altimeter

The altimeter shows how high the plane is. It works by measuring outside air pressure, which drops as the plane gains height. Most altimeters measure height in feet.

The figures on the dial only show the plane's height above sea level. In mountainous country the ground may be a lot closer than they suggest. Because of this, many airliners now carry radar safety devices to measure above-ground height.

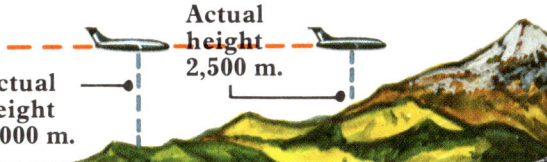

Actual height 5,000 m.

Actual height 4,000 m.

Actual height 2,500 m.

Airspeed indicator

The pilot uses this to find out the plane's speed, measured in knots as on ships. One knot equals 1.85 k.p.h. Aircraft that travel at or near supersonic speeds usually also carry a machmeter to measure speed in Mach numbers.

Airspeed indicators work by measuring the speed of the air rushing past the plane. To find this out, planes have hollow probes called pitot tubes that stick out into the airstream.

Pitot tube

Artificial horizon

This tells the pilot whether he is flying straight and level. The straight cross-bar represents the horizon. It is kept steady by a gyroscope. The T-bar represents the plane. The one shown here is banked to the right.

Make a model artificial horizon

BEND   BEND

CUT OUT TO THIS SHAPE

▲ You will need a small plastic pot with a lid (one with a circular depression in its base, as shown below, works best), a match, and a 5 cm.-by-8 cm. piece of card. Cut the card to the shape shown above.

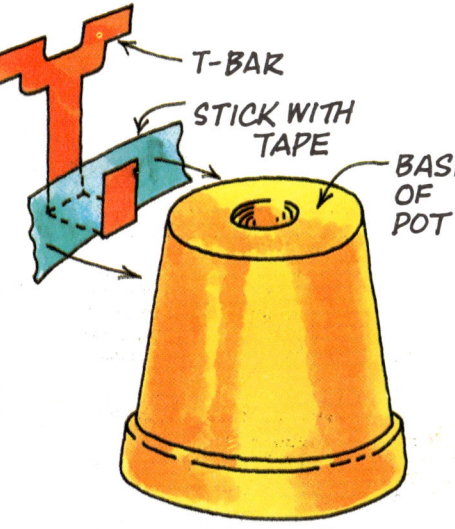

T-BAR

STICK WITH TAPE

BASE OF POT

SHARPEN MATCH

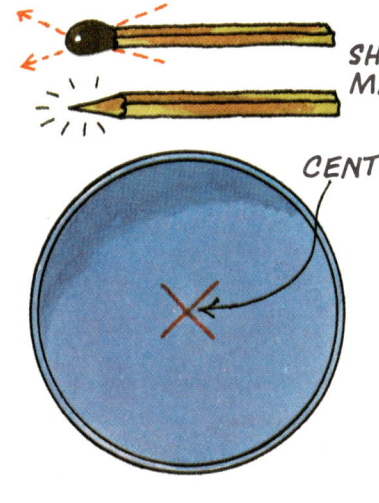

CENTRE

SPIN GENTLY

▲ Take the top off the pot. Turn the pot over, and tape the T-bar to it as shown, so it stands 1.5 cm. above the top. Make sure that it is level.

▲▶ Make a small hole in the exact centre of the lid. Push a sharpened matchstick through it, making sure it is a tight fit. This top serves as your gyro. Spin it, and you will find it stays level even if you tilt the pot.

STAND BY FOR TAKE-OFF

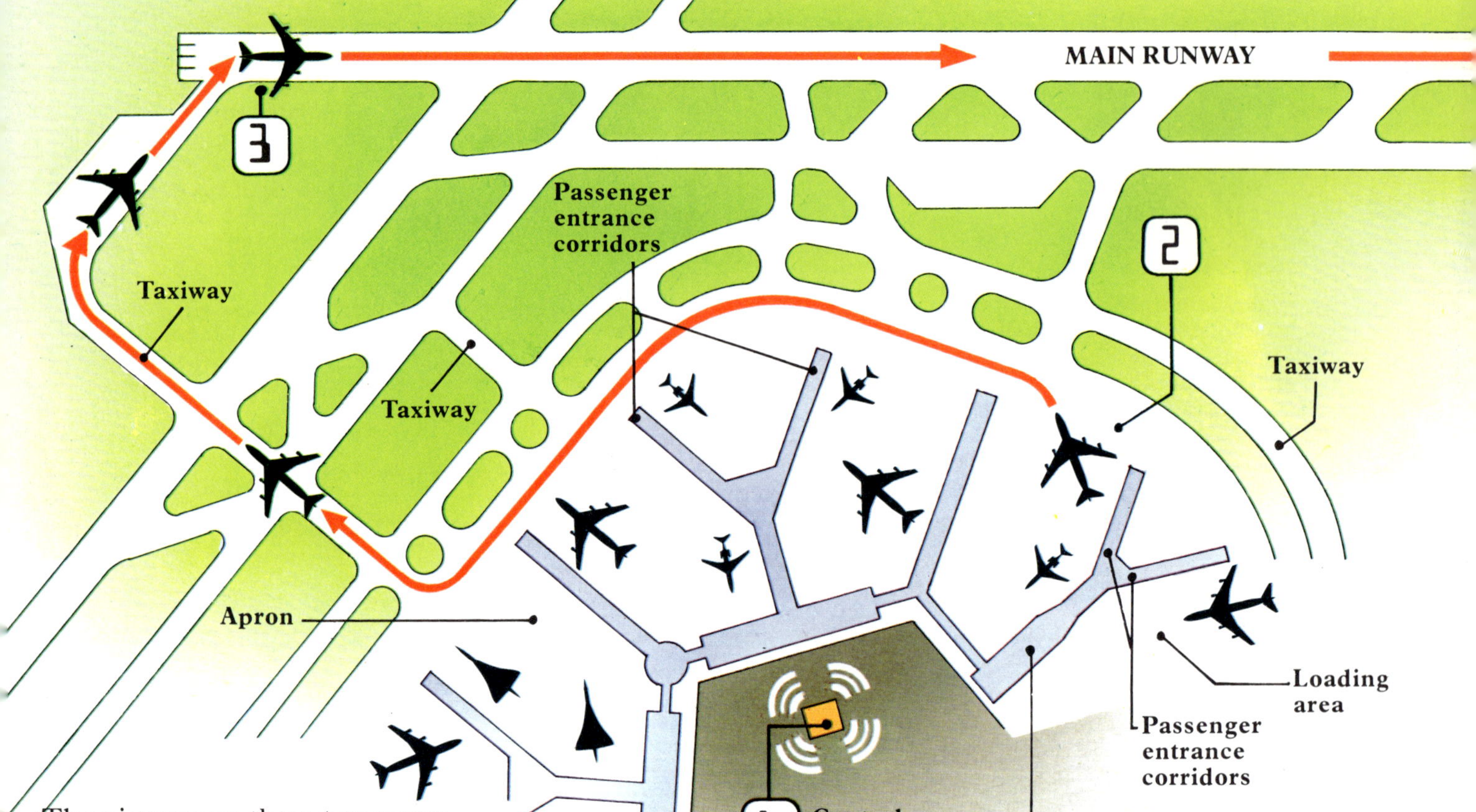

MAIN RUNWAY

3

Taxiway

Taxiway

**Passenger
entrance
corridors**

2

Taxiway

Apron

**Loading
area**

**Passenger
entrance
corridors**

**Control
tower**

Passenger terminal

Passenger terminal

The pictures on these two pages tell the story of one flight departure from a modern international airport. The numbers in the boxes refer to the figures on the illustration above.

1

▲ The most important building at any airport is the control tower. Behind windows with a clear view of all the runways, controllers pass instructions on taxiing and parking to pilots. Others control air traffic from radar screens.

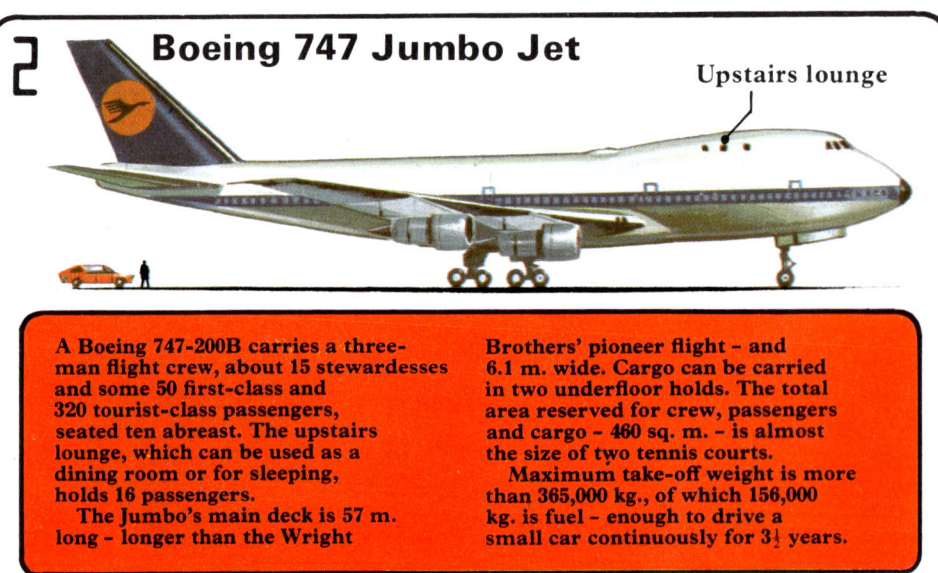

2 **Boeing 747 Jumbo Jet**

Upstairs lounge

A Boeing 747-200B carries a three-man flight crew, about 15 stewardesses and some 50 first-class and 320 tourist-class passengers, seated ten abreast. The upstairs lounge, which can be used as a dining room or for sleeping, holds 16 passengers.

The Jumbo's main deck is 57 m. long – longer than the Wright Brothers' pioneer flight – and 6.1 m. wide. Cargo can be carried in two underfloor holds. The total area reserved for crew, passengers and cargo – 460 sq. m. – is almost the size of two tennis courts.

Maximum take-off weight is more than 365,000 kg., of which 156,000 kg. is fuel – enough to drive a small car continuously for $3\frac{1}{2}$ years.

▲ Before an aircraft can take off, the pilot has to file a flight plan and work out take-off speeds, which vary according to the plane's weight, weather conditions, runway length and the height of the airport above sea level. The plane must be fuelled, food and drink put on board, and the cargo loaded.

The passengers get on board after clearing customs and passport control. Once they have fastened their seat-belts, the plane is ready to go.

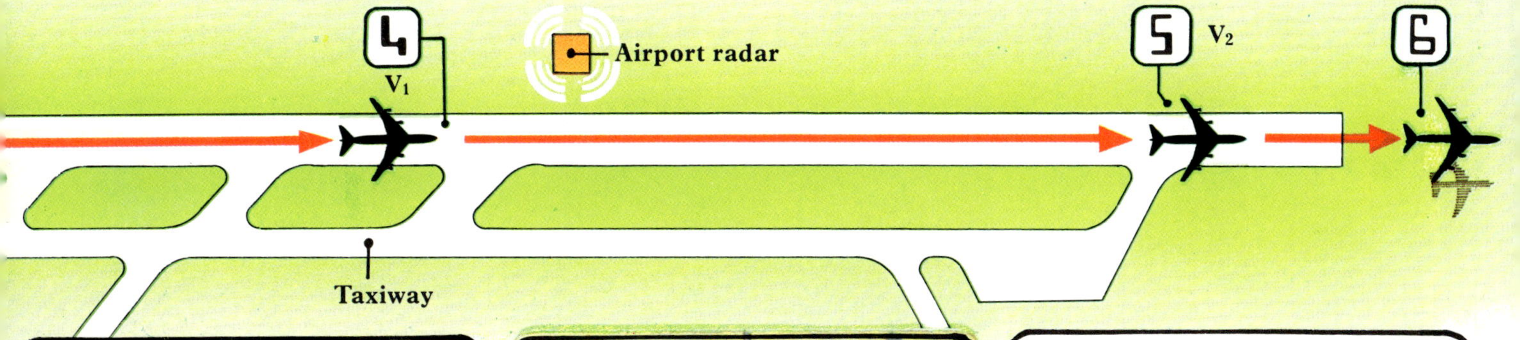

4 V₁

● Airport radar

5 V₂

6

Taxiway

3

4

5

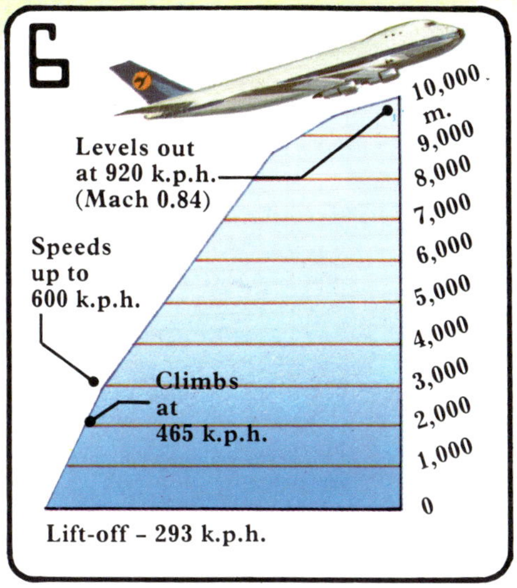

6
Levels out
at 920 k.p.h.
(Mach 0.84)

Speeds
up to
600 k.p.h.

Climbs
at
465 k.p.h.

10,000 m.
9,000
8,000
7,000
6,000
5,000
4,000
3,000
2,000
1,000
0

Lift-off – 293 k.p.h.

▲ The controllers give the pilot clearance to taxi to a holding point near the beginning of the runway. When checks have been completed, permission to take off is given. The aircraft taxis onto the runway and revs up its engines.

▲ The aircraft moves down the runway, gathering speed. Once V₁ is reached, the plane is going too fast to have room to stop. V₂ is safe flying speed. For a typical Jumbo take-off, these speeds are 265 and 293 k.p.h.

▲ As the plane climbs away from the runway it may have to throttle back to meet noise restrictions. Departure controllers guide the pilot onto the right course. On leaving the airport control area he set his course along an airway.

Keeping the engines supplied with fuel

A Jumbo Jet's four engines can gulp a total of more than 11,000 kg. of fuel every hour, but the plane is still one of the most economical forms of transport.

A separate tank is provided for each engine, but cross-feed valves allow all tanks to feed any engine.

Fuel-hungry jet liners

12,000
10,000
8,000
6,000
4,000
2,000
0

747 **707** **Air-bus** **DC10**

This chart shows how many kg. of fuel these aircraft use every hour of flight.

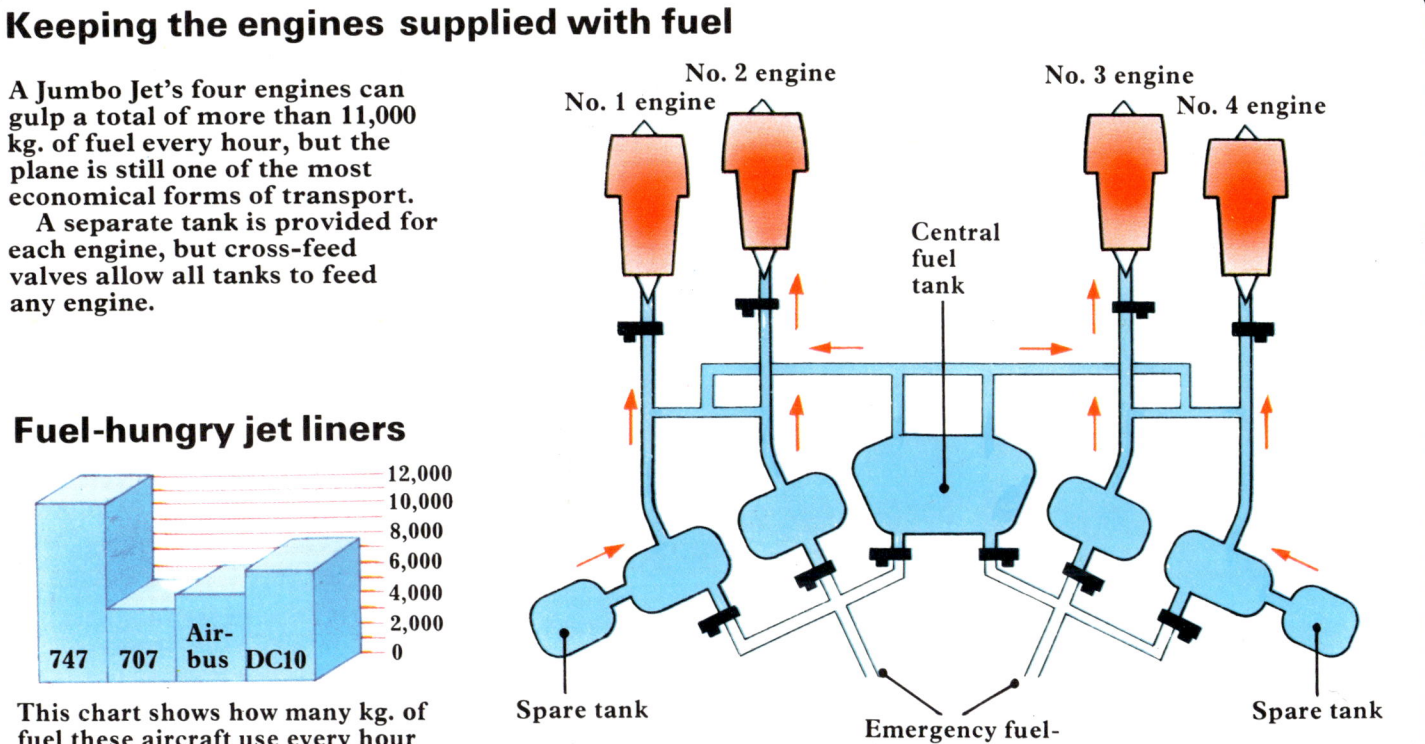

No. 1 engine
No. 2 engine
No. 3 engine
No. 4 engine

Central
fuel
tank

Spare tank

Emergency fuel-dumping pipes

Spare tank

15

FLIGHT 593 TO TOKYO

1

Local time 12.00 noon Body time 12.00 noon

▲ After a noon take-off from Heathrow Airport, Foxtrot Tango – the Boeing 747 of Flight 593 – gains height on its way to Tokyo. The clocks show local time (left) and body time – the real time since the flight began (right).

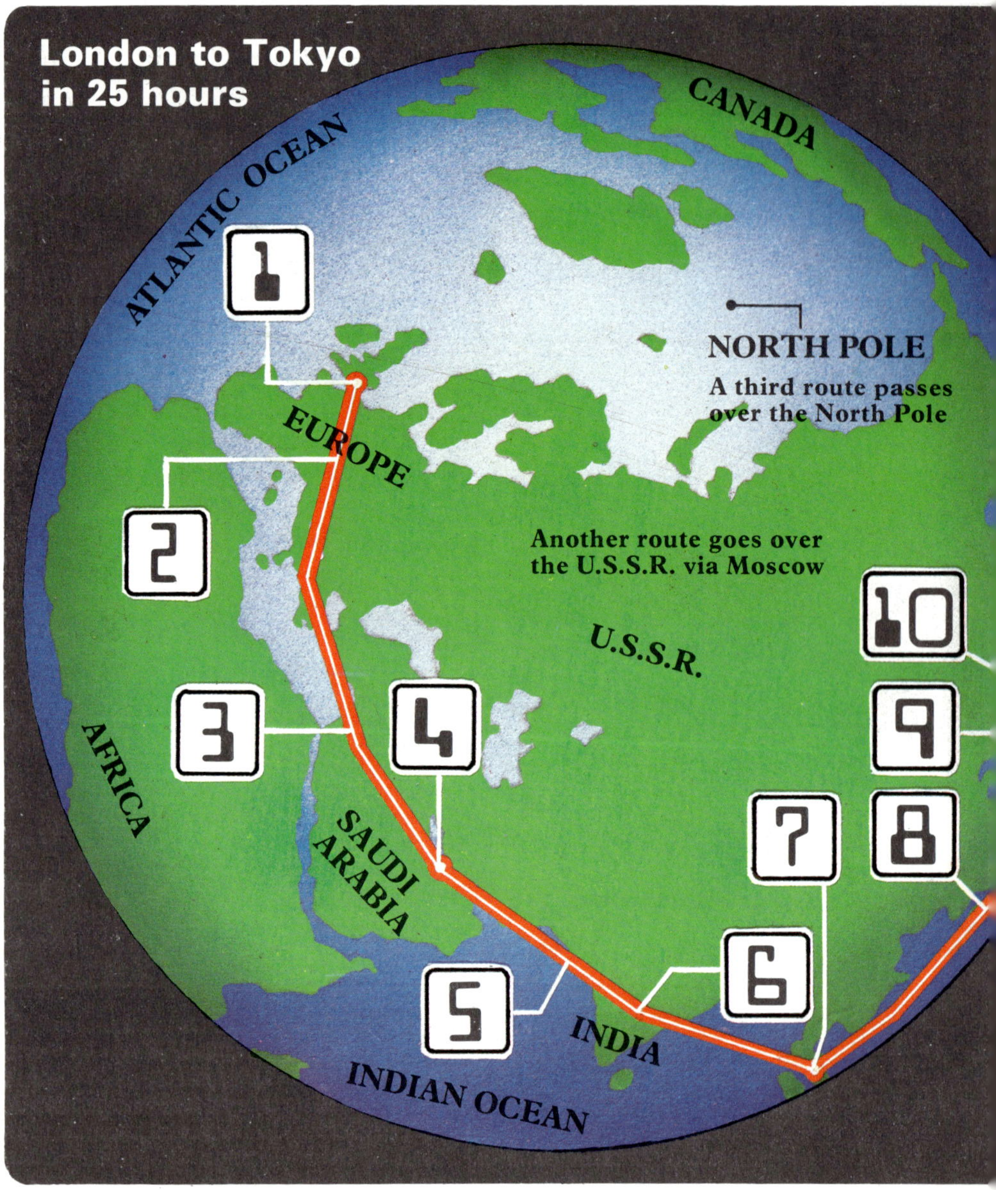

2

15.00 14.00

▲ Mealtime. The 15-strong cabin crew heat pre-packed frozen meals in fast-working microwave ovens in the Jumbo's three galleys. After the meal, passengers can watch a film or listen to a choice of taped entertainment on headphones.

London to Tokyo in 25 hours

ATLANTIC OCEAN

CANADA

NORTH POLE
A third route passes over the North Pole

EUROPE

Another route goes over the U.S.S.R. via Moscow

U.S.S.R.

AFRICA

SAUDI ARABIA

INDIA

INDIAN OCEAN

1 **2** **3** **4** **5** **6** **7** **8** **9** **10**

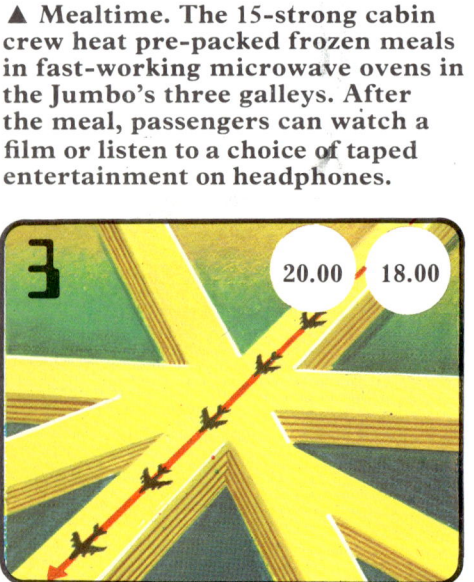

3

20.00 18.00

▲ The big jet flies down the airway chosen by ground control. Airways are corridors in the sky marked out by radio signal beacons. Pilots use these to check their position. Body time already lags two hours behind local time.

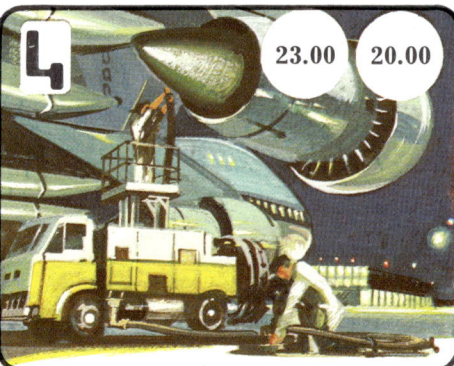

4

23.00 20.00

▲ After eight hours' flying, Foxtrot Tango makes its first stopover, at Bahrain in the Persian Gulf. The aircraft is refuelled, and a new flight crew take over. For safety reasons flight crews do not usually fly more than 11 hours at a time.

5

05.00 24.00 mid night

▲ The 747 flies 12,000 m. above the Indian Ocean on the second leg of its flight. The air temperature outside is −57°C. Water vapour from the jet exhausts freezes into tiny ice particles, forming condensation trails.

▲ As the chart shows, the hour of day at any one time differs around the world. One problem of long-distance jet flights is that they pass through several time zones too quickly for people to adapt.

Passengers like those on Flight 593, who land at 10 o'clock at night feeling as though it were one in the afternoon are said to be suffering from jet-lag.

▼ Radar equipment is used throughout the flight to check on weather conditions ahead of the plane. It can warn the pilot of thunderstorms 200 km. away, and can show him whether there is cloud cover over the airport he is heading for.

The radar weather picture is displayed on a yellow screen in the cockpit.

▲ Radar pulse is sent out from a dish in the plane's nose.

▲ Hitting a cloud, it bounces back towards the plane.

▲ Incoming pulses are transmitted from receiver to screen.

10 — 22.00 — 13.00

▲ A gentle touchdown, and Flight 593 is over. The passengers disembark after 25 hours with 9 hours of jet-lag. What seems to them to be lunchtime is nighttime in Tokyo. If they flew the other way, the time difference would be reversed.

9 — 21.45 — 12.45

▲ The pilot uses the plane's Instrument Landing System (ILS) as the Jumbo comes down. Radio signals from the airport move two needles on an instrument in the cockpit. When these form a cross the plane is on the right glidepath.

6 — 08.00 — 02.00

▲ The routine work of keeping the plane in straight and steady flight is done by a control mechanism called the automatic pilot. An electronic navigator constantly checks the plane's exact position, feeding the data to the autopilot.

7 — 11.00 — 03.30

▲ Foxtrot Tango lands for a second refuelling, at Singapore. The passengers' own sense of time is already very different from local time. Flight 593 has lasted over 15 hours so far, and it still has more than 5,000 km. to go.

8 — 21.30 — 12.30

▲ On the flight's last leg, the 747 starts to descend while more than 100 km. from its destination. So many craft are waiting to land at Tokyo that the plane is 'stacked', circling a radio beacon, while it waits for clearance to land.

THE SOUND BARRIER

MiG-25 36 km. height record

30km.

Temperature constant at −56.3°C in the stratosphere

25

SR-71

Mach 1 constant at 1,062.36 k.p.h. in stratosphere

STRATOSPHERE

20

Concorde

15

747

1,062

10

1,078

Mount Everest

1,094

1,109

DC-9

1,124

TROPOSPHERE

1,139

1,154

5

1,169

Mont Blanc

1,183

Speed of Mach 1 in k.p.h.

1,197

1

1,211

1,225

Sound travels at different speeds at different levels. At sea level its speed is about 1,225 k.p.h., but it slows down in the cold air higher up.

An Austrian scientist called Ernst Mach worked out a way of comparing speed through the air directly to the speed of sound which is called Mach 1 after him. Mach 2 is exactly twice the speed of sound, and so on.

Aircraft that travel faster than sound must pass through shock waves (see below) that slow them down. These waves are what is popularly known as the sound barrier.

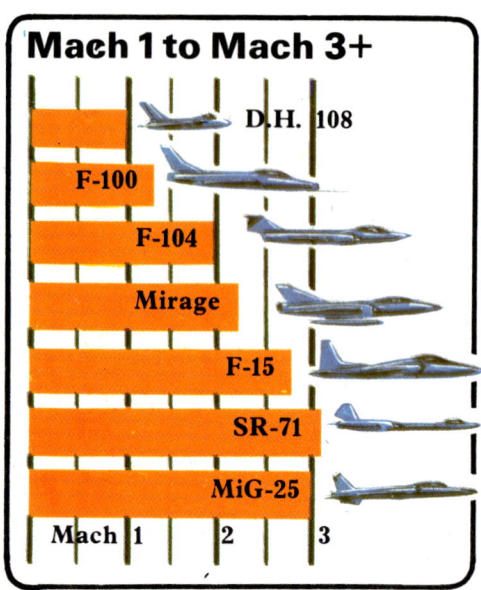

Mach 1 to Mach 3+

D.H. 108

F-100

F-104

Mirage

F-15

SR-71

MiG-25

Mach 1   2   3

Booming along on the shock cone

The illustration below shows three moments in the flight of a single jet, as it accelerates up to and beyond the speed of sound.

The nearly circular lines surrounding the aircraft (1) are the air disturbances its flight causes. They are known as pressure waves. As they move away from the plane they gradually get weaker, as

the ripples die away after a stone has been thrown into a pond. These pressure waves travel at exactly the speed of sound.

As the aircraft goes faster (2), it catches up on the pressure waves moving ahead of it. At Mach 1 it is travelling as fast as they are. It pushes all the air ripples that would previously have had

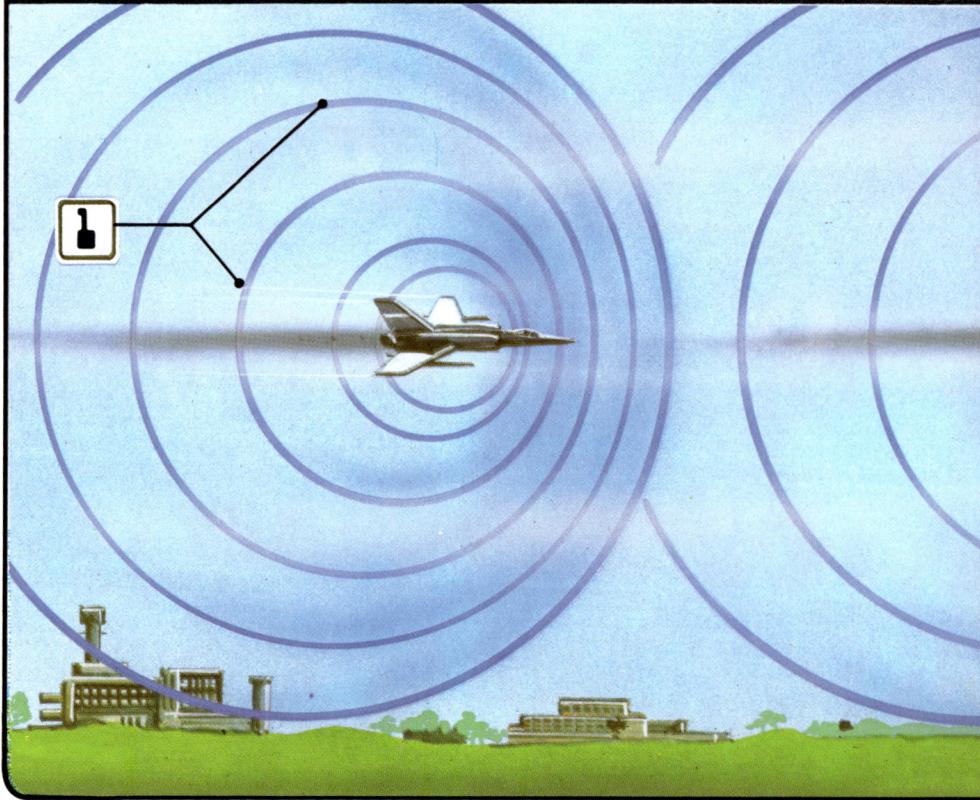

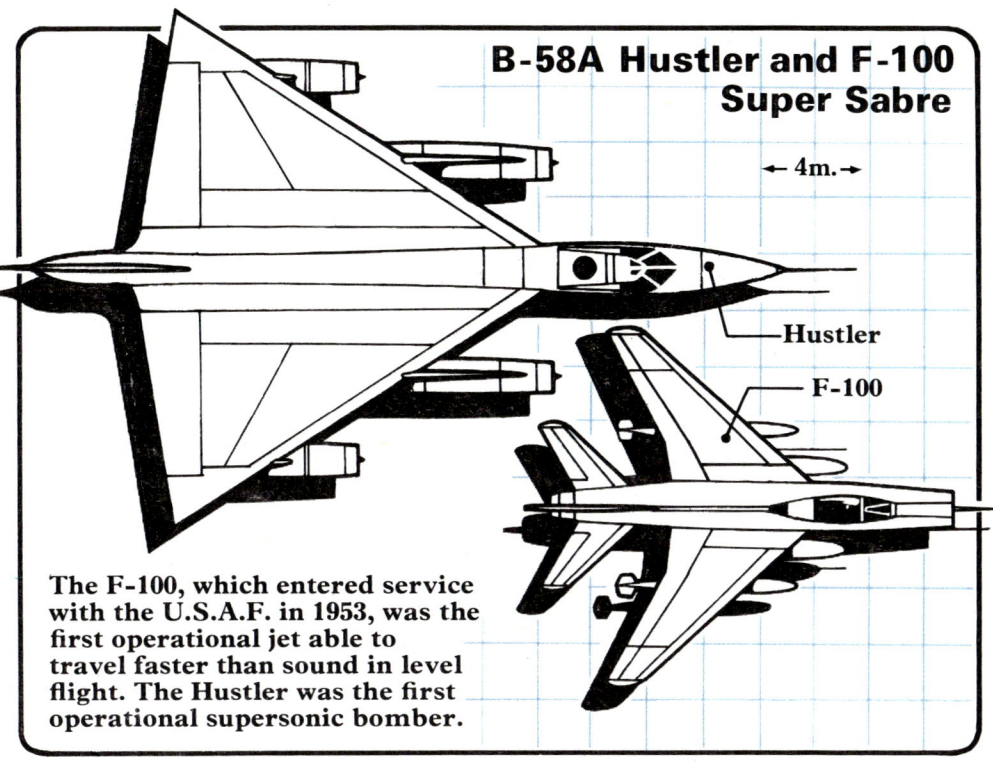

B-58A Hustler and F-100 Super Sabre

← 4m. →

Hustler

F-100

The F-100, which entered service with the U.S.A.F. in 1953, was the first operational jet able to travel faster than sound in level flight. The Hustler was the first operational supersonic bomber.

Sound power

The sonic boom is a spectacular example of sound power. Here is a small-scale sound experiment.

SUGAR

PIECE OF POLYTHENE

RUBBER BAND

▲ You will need a tin tray, an empty jar, some polythene and a little sugar. Put the polythene over the top of the jar, and fasten it with a rubber band. Smooth it down so that it is perfectly flat, and put a few grains of sugar on it.

time to spread out ahead of it into one vertical Mach wave (3).

When the plane is travelling faster than sound (4), it pushes the tip of the Mach wave with it, bending the wave into a cone shape. Where the lower edge of the cone reaches the ground, there is a sudden increase in air pressure that you can hear as a

double boom, or if the shock waves are very close together as one bang.

Supersonic planes trail the sonic boom in their wake over the entire region they pass over while travelling faster than sound. The area over which it can be heard is called the plane's 'carpet'. The carpet of Concorde, for example, is nearly 90 km. wide.

▲ Hold the tin tray about 10 cm. away from the jar, and hit it with something hard. The pressure wave that you hear as a bang will have the power to make the sugar jump. In the same way the sonic boom can damage windows and buildings.

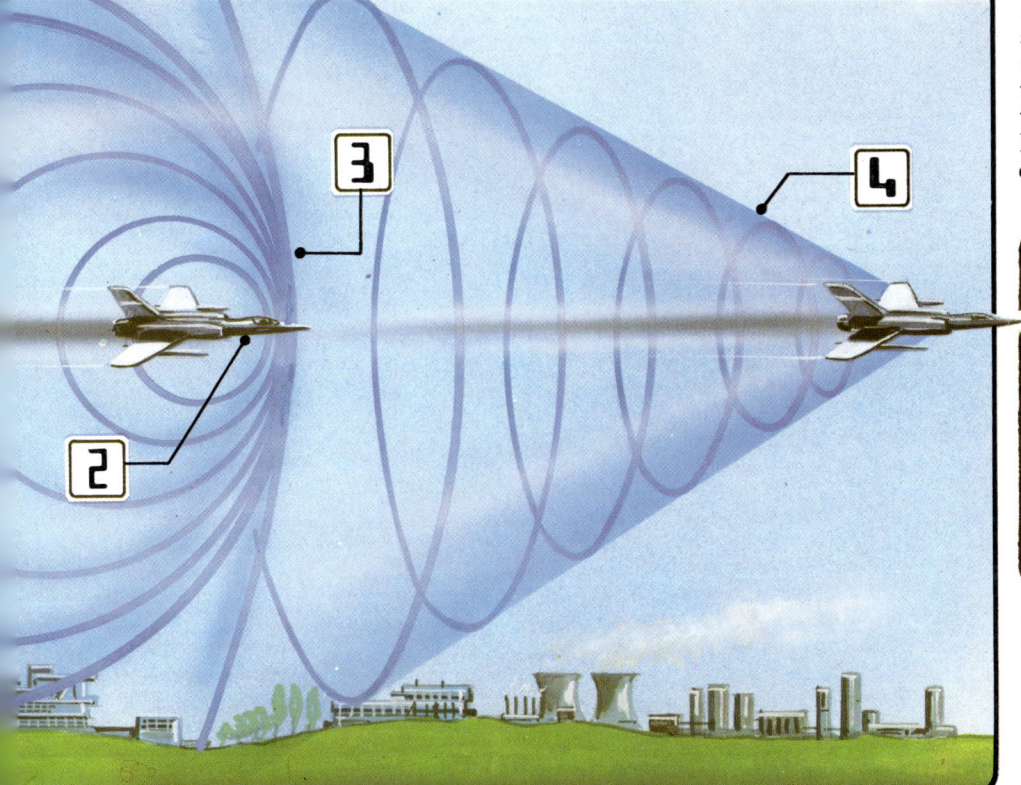

1 SECOND DELAY = 1/3 km. DISTANT

▲ Remembering the speed of sound can also be useful, for instance in a thunderstorm. To work out how many kilometres away it is, count the number of seconds between the lightning flash and the thunderclap and divide by 3.

SUPERSONIC AIRLINERS

Supersonic military planes have been in service since 1953, but civilian supersonic transports (SSTs) took longer to develop.

The first SST to fly was the Russian Tupolev Tu-144, in 1968. Concorde, developed jointly by British and French designers, made its maiden flight two months later. The Tupolev also went into service first, in December 1975.

The United States also laid plans for an SST in the 1960s. The project was eventually given up because of its cost, and as a result of public opposition based on fear of high noise levels and possible harm to the atmosphere.

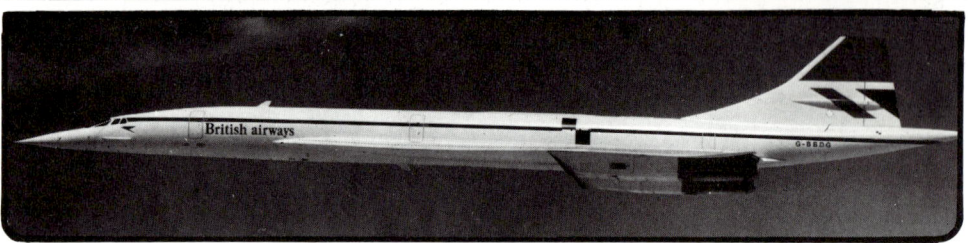

▲ The Tu-144 (top) and Concorde are very like one another in shape and purpose. Both have 'droop-snoot' noses that are lowered during landings to give the pilot a better view of the runway.

Concorde on the apron

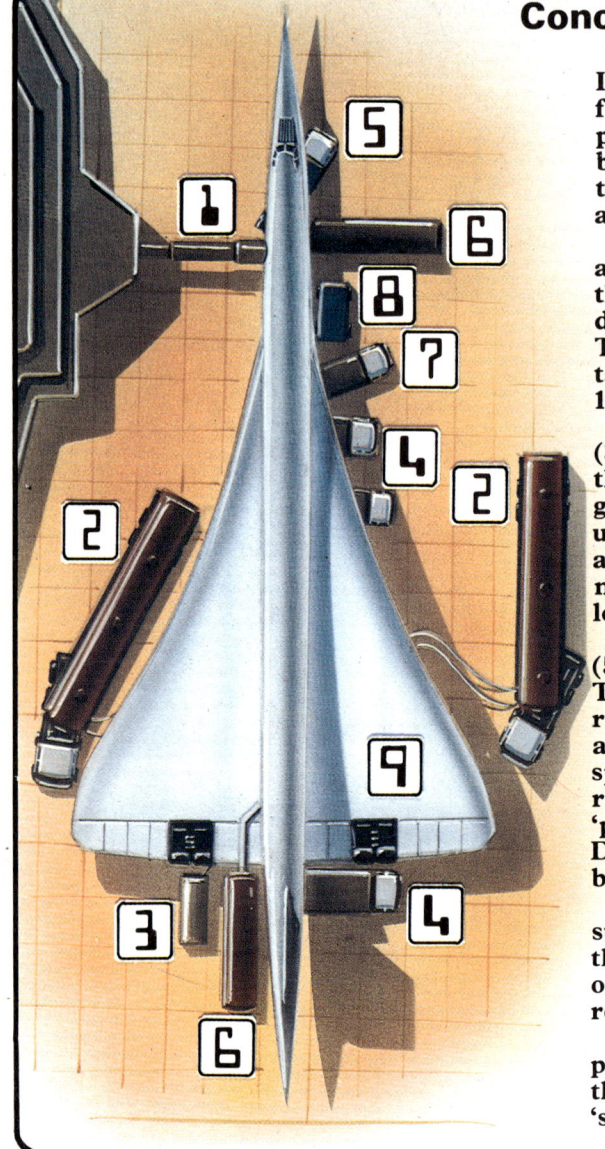

It only takes 30 minutes for Concorde to unload its passengers and their baggage, to refuel, and to take on new provisions and a new load of passengers.

As soon as the jet stops, a jetway (1) noses up to the exit. All passengers disembark in five minutes. Two giant refuellers (2) take 18 minutes to pump in 120,000 litres of kerosene.

The air-conditioning cart (3) pumps fresh air into the passenger cabin. Baggage vehicles (4) unload the underfloor compartments at a rate of 135 kg. a minute, and then put a new load aboard almost as fast.

The toilets are cleaned (5) and the drains checked. The plane's galleys are restocked with food, drinks and duty-free goods by special vehicles (6) which rise up to cabin level and 'plug in' to the doors. Drinking water is supplied by a bowser (7).

A ground power unit (8) supplies electricity while the jet's engines are shut off, and a similar truck restarts the engines (9).

By this time the new passengers are aboard with their baggage, and it's 'stand by for take off' again.

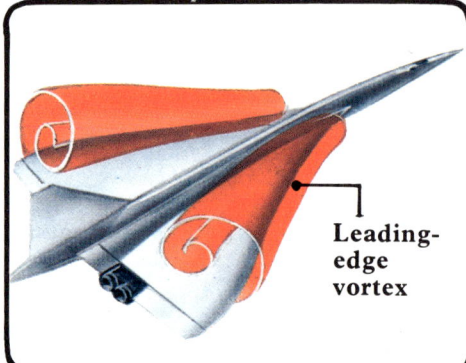

▲ The wings of the SSTs are ogival – shaped like a delta with the edges rounded off. A spiral current of air called the leading-edge vortex forms over them in flight. It stays there even at slow speeds, increasing lift.

Leading-edge vortex

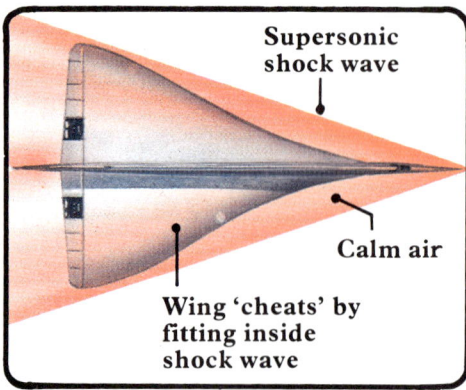

Supersonic shock wave

Calm air

Wing 'cheats' by fitting inside shock wave

▲ As Concorde rushes through the air at Mach 2, a supersonic shock wave streams back from the nose. Its wings fit inside the cone of undisturbed air behind the shock wave, giving the plane and its passengers a smooth ride.

AIRCRAFT AND NOISE

All aircraft are noisy, and jets are noisier than most. Noise levels, particularly around airports, have mounted as more and bigger jets have come into service. Public criticism of jet noise has also grown, and designers now spend a lot of thought on finding ways of making jets quieter.

The roar of a jet engine is produced mainly by the violent mixing of its exhaust gases with the outside air. How loud it is depends on the speed at which the gases meet the air. It is greatest when the engines are run up to full power just before the plane takes off.

One way of reducing noise is to use turbofan engines in which much of the air taken in bypasses the combustion chamber, thus reducing the exhaust speeds. Turbofans are now used in most modern jet transports.

Jet noise is usually measured in effective perceived noise decibels (EPNdB), which take into account the tone of a noise and how long it lasts as well as its loudness. The figures below are all given in EPNdB.

An increase of ten EPNdB means twice the amount of noise – so a sound that measures 60 EPNdB seems twice as noisy to the listener as one of 50 EPNdB, and so on.

Inside the ear

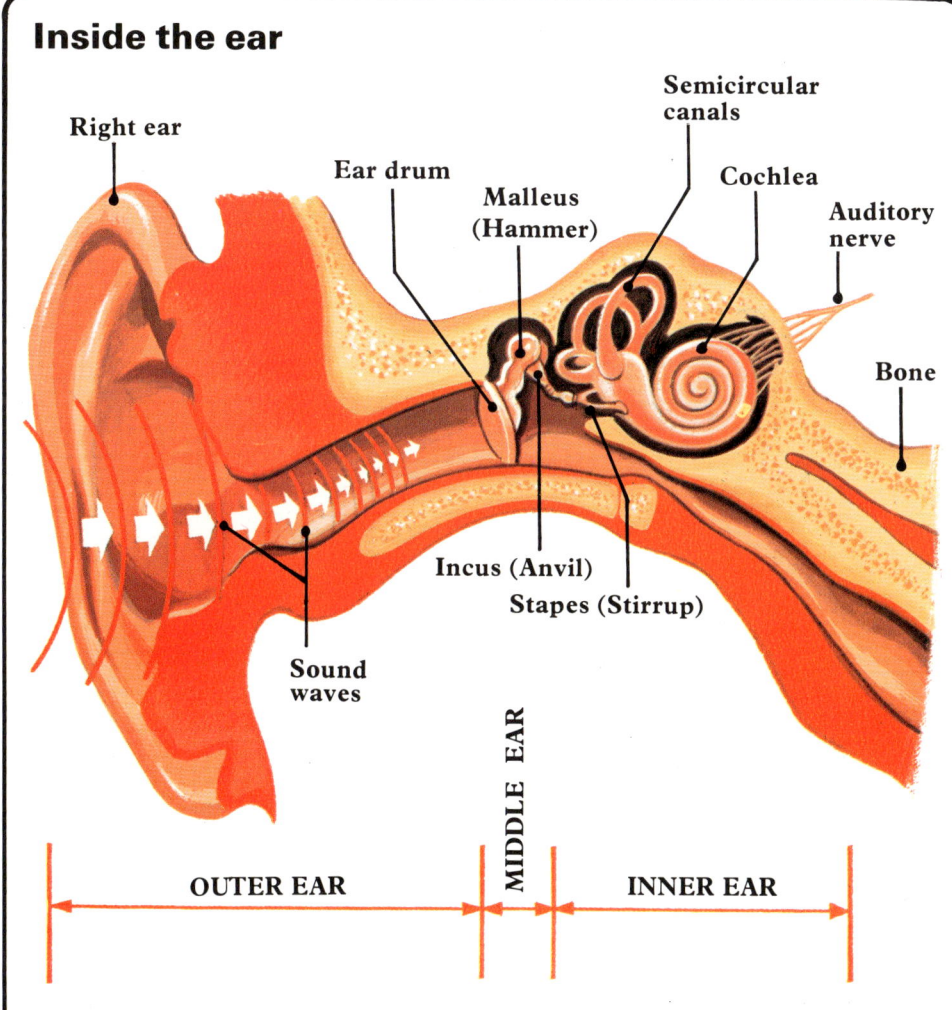

Right ear · Ear drum · Malleus (Hammer) · Semicircular canals · Cochlea · Auditory nerve · Bone · Incus (Anvil) · Stapes (Stirrup) · Sound waves · OUTER EAR · MIDDLE EAR · INNER EAR

▲ As a jet flies above you, it sends out sound waves in the form of variations in pressure in the air. The waves cause vibrations in your ear drum, which transmits them through three small bones – the hammer, anvil and stirrup – in the air-filled middle ear.

The vibrations next move into the fluid-filled inner ear, passing through the semi-circular canals (which control your balance) and the cochlea. The auditory nerve detects movements of fluid in the cochlea, and turns them into coded impulses. These pass to the brain, where the impulses are decoded and the sound is 'heard'.

Sound	EPNdB
The rustling of leaves in a gentle breeze.	33
Soft whispering between 1 and 2 m. away.	47
Normal speech, or the noise in a busy shop.	73
The background hum in a crowded restaurant.	78
Loud music on a record-player in a large room.	95
The roar of city traffic. A diesel lorry 8 m. away.	105
A Boeing 747 taking off overhead.	107
A motor-mower cutting a lawn, or an air compressor.	112
A Boeing 707 coming in to land at an airport.	118
Concorde taking off overhead.	120

JET FIGHTERS

Jet fighters have come a long way since Me 262s and Meteors flew in World War 2. Subsonic Sabres and MiG-15s met in the first jet combats in 1950, during the Korean War, and now air forces throughout the world are equipped with advanced supersonic fighters.

The aircraft shown here date from the Korean War to the present day. Other classic fighters include the Mirage F.1C (see p. 3) and the MRCA (p. 27). All but the Sabre and the MiG-15 use afterburning jet engines and carry target-detecting radar equipment.

The dates give the year of each plane's entry into service.

North American F-86 Sabre 1949

◀ The North American F-86 Sabre was the second American plane to break the sound barrier, and at one time held the world air speed record at 1,073 k.p.h. It really made its mark in the Korean War, in which a total of 792 MiG-15s fell victim to its six 12.7 mm. machine-guns and rockets.

◀ Russia's MiG-15, flown by Chinese pilots, was more than a match for early American jet fighters over Korea, being 100 k.p.h. faster than the U.S.A.F.'s F-80C Shooting Star and the U.S. Navy's F9F Panther. But it did not always win, and in its first week of use one was shot down to become the first victim of an all-jet combat.

Mikoyan MiG-15 1948

Mikoyan MiG-21 1959

▶ The single-seat, delta-winged MiG-21 'Fishbed' is a short-range interceptor that is in widespread use in the Middle East, India and elsewhere. It has an air intake in the nose, like the Lightning, and carries missiles almost identical to the American Sidewinders.

Lockheed F-104 Starfighter 1958

▶ The Starfighter has been nick-named 'the missile with a man in it' because of its slim, needle-nosed shape and small wings. The wings are so sharp that the leading edges have to be covered to protect ground workers from cutting themselves.

Saab JA-37 1978

▲ The Swedish Viggen (Thunderbolt) fighter was developed from the AJ-37 attack version. Now in service, the JA-37 will be in production until the mid 1980s. Like the earlier versions it can operate from ordinary roads as well as airfields.

General Dynamics F-16 1979

▲ Intended as the U.S.A.F.'s latest air combat fighter, the Fighting Falcon has also been selected by several European countries as a replacement for their Starfighters. It is one of the most manoeuvrable fighters ever built. A slightly lower-powered version known as the F-16/79 will be available from 1983.

B.A.C. Lightning 1960

Detachable fuel tank.

▲ The Lightning was the first supersonic plane to enter service with the R.A.F. It can accelerate from Mach 1 to Mach 2 in 3½ minutes.

The Lightning is outstanding as a high-level interceptor, being able to climb almost vertically straight after take-off. At least one unsuspecting U-2 spy plane flying at 25,000 m. has been pounced on by a Lightning.

McDonnell Douglas F-4 Phantom II 1960

▲ The Phantom is one of the world's most widely used advanced warplanes. It was developed because the U.S. Navy needed a twin-engined fighter to operate from aircraft carriers. Although no longer produced, well over 2,000 are still in service and are constantly updated.

The Phantom has a large radar for air combat and is armed with air-to-air missiles and a built-in six-barrelled cannon. It can also be used for ground attack with bombs, missiles and the cannon.

Dassault Mirage III 1961

▶ France's delta-winged Mirage is a Mach 2 interceptor and fighter-bomber that is in use throughout the world. The most recent models can operate close to the ground in all weathers.

Mikoyan MiG-23 1972

▶ Russia's swing-winged MiG-23 fighter-bomber flies from bases in East Germany, and has also been supplied to Middle-East countries. The all-weather fighter version has a large nose to house radar equipment. There are also ground-attack and two-seat trainer versions.

Grumman F-14 Tomcat 1974

▶ The Tomcat is in service on the U.S. Navy's aircraft carriers. Its main purpose is fleet defence and tactical air support. An additional role is photographic reconnaissance. Its radar can detect targets 250 km away and can track up to 24 objects at the same time.

23

SPIES IN THE SKY

The plane is built almost entirely of heat-resistant titanium.

Shock cones in the engine inlets deflect the supersonic shock wave through the engine cowl. On rare occasions the wave gets out of place, making the plane yaw and shudder.

Mid-air re-fuelling hatch. The plane carries enough fuel to fly 4,800 km. at a height of 24,000 m.

Friction caused by air rushing past raises the skin temperature to over 550°C.

Air reconnaissance started in the days of man-carrying balloons, but it first became really important in World War 2.

Today it plays a basic part in keeping the balance of power between nations. Political leaders rely on information received from sky-spies in making their most important decisions. The information comes in the form of photographs, radar soundings or high-frequency radio recordings.

A lot of routine reconnaissance work is now done by unmanned satellites. But manned spy planes are still needed for special tasks.

Map-making from 24 kilometres up

The spy plane's long-focus camera scans a 200-km. strip of land beneath the flight path. Back at base, the developed photographs are fitted together into a map.

With its cloud-piercing infra-red cameras, the SR-71 can map more than 150,000 sq. km. – half the area of Italy – in an hour. It also carries heat detectors and sideways-looking airborne radar (SLAR).

1 Why is the Blackbird painted black?

The SR-71 is black because dark objects give off heat faster than light-coloured ones. The plane's skin is heated up by friction, in places to 550°C as air rushes past at Mach 3 speeds. But the fuel and electronic equipment must be kept cool. Black paint can reduce the skin temperature by up to 28°C.

You can check the fact that heat escapes faster from black objects with this simple experiment that uses the principle that water contracts as it cools.

America's Lockheed SR-71A Blackbird is the most advanced reconnaissance plane in the world. It also holds the world speed and sustained height records (3,331 k.p.h. and 24,462 m. respectively).

The SR-71's two-man crew consists of a pilot and a reconnaissance systems operator (RSO). They get into the plane through two cockpit canopy hatches off a mobile platform. Both wear spaceman-like suits and helmets to protect them in case they have to eject.

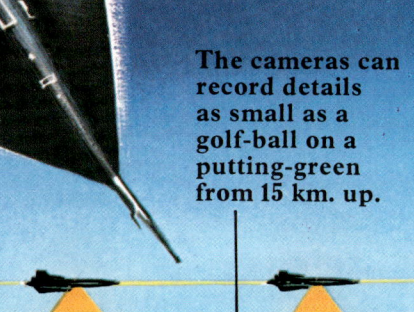

The cameras can record details as small as a golf-ball on a putting-green from 15 km. up.

▲ Find two identical narrow-necked bottles (the bigger the better), two straws, some modelling clay, and black and white paints – enamel or acrylic are ideal. Paint one bottle black and the other white. Put the bottles aside to dry thoroughly.

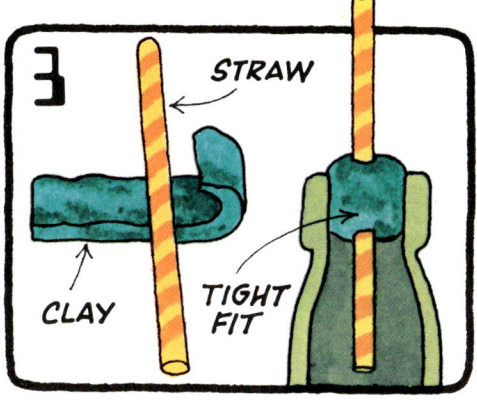

▲ Flatten out two strips of modelling clay. Wrap the strips around drinking straws, then fit the straws into the tops of the two bottles. Check that there is enough clay around each to fill the neck. Squeeze the clay over the neck to make an airtight fit.

▲ Take the corks out again, and fill each bottle with hot water from the same tap or kettle. Tint the water with ink, then replace the corks. Press the clay down till water rises to the same level in each straw. Mark the levels.

▲ Now watch the water levels. You have constructed two working thermometers, and as heat escapes the levels in both straws will sink. But because the black bottle radiates heat more quickly, its level will go down faster.

Two more sky spies . . .

The Foxbat flies at about the same height and speed as the SR-71 and was the first Russian plane fast enough to be out of reach of fighter interception. It carries SLAR, and has five cameras in its nose.

The U-2 has a cruising speed of only 740 k.p.h. But its long wings give a lot of lift in the thin atmosphere at high altitudes, and it can glide for long distances to save fuel.

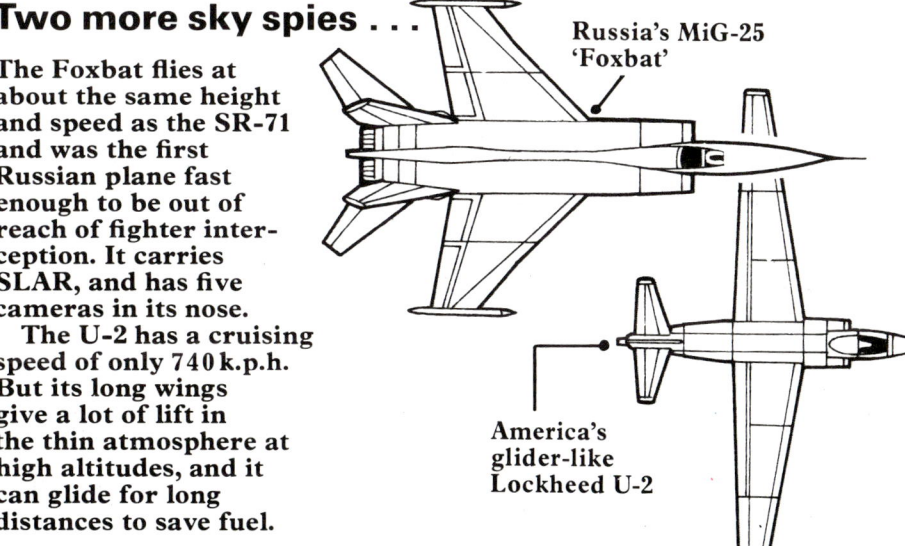

Russia's MiG-25 'Foxbat'

America's glider-like Lockheed U-2

25

JUMP-JETS AND SWING-WINGS

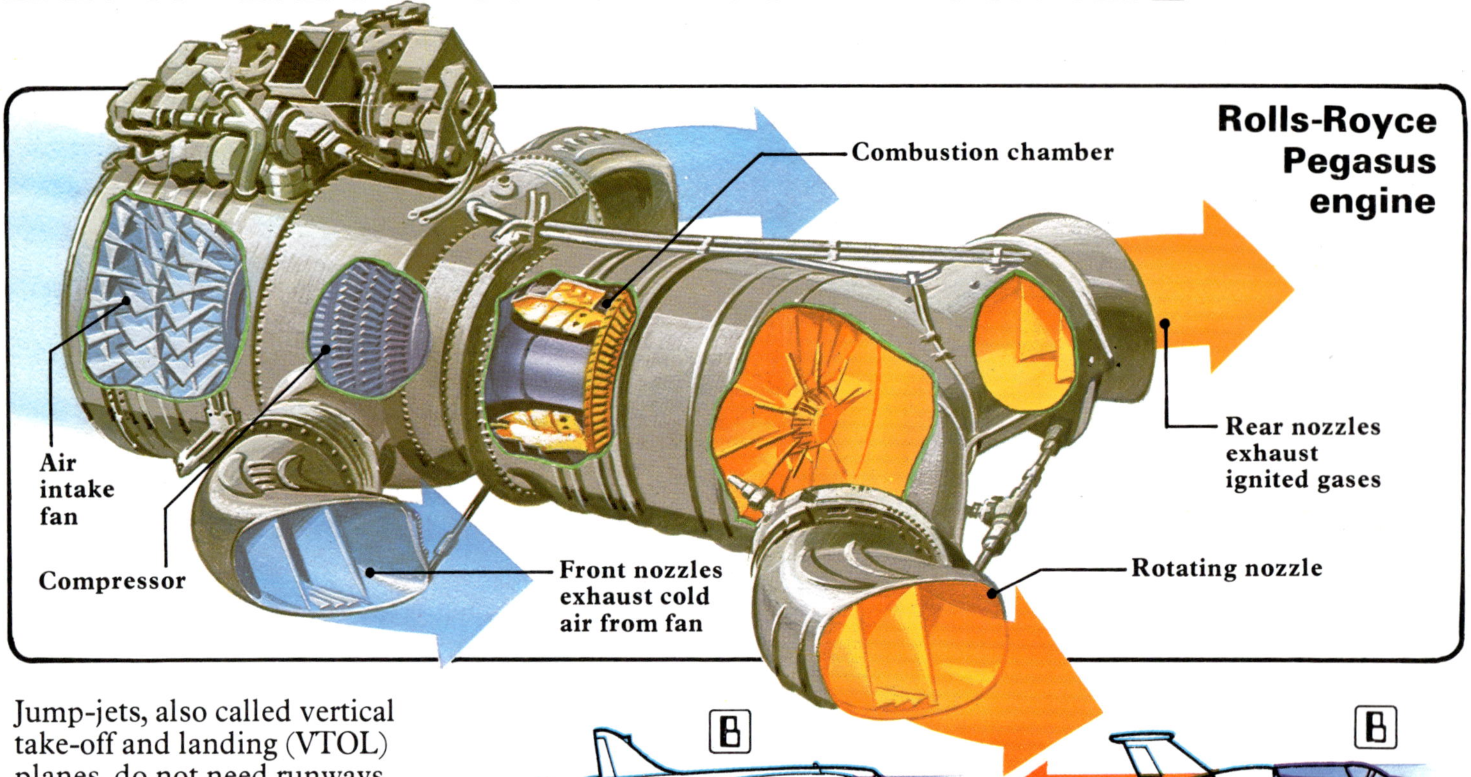

Rolls-Royce Pegasus engine

Combustion chamber

Rear nozzles exhaust ignited gases

Rotating nozzle

Air intake fan

Compressor

Front nozzles exhaust cold air from fan

Jump-jets, also called vertical take-off and landing (VTOL) planes, do not need runways. This means that military jump-jets are not put out of action if their airfield is bombed. They can also operate from decks of small ships without using catapults and arrester wires.

Early work on VTOL was done with the 'Flying Bedstead' (see page 30), and experimental VTOL craft have been built in America, Russia, France and Germany. The Hawker Siddeley Harrier, powered by the Pegasus engine shown above, was the first jump-jet to enter service, in 1969.

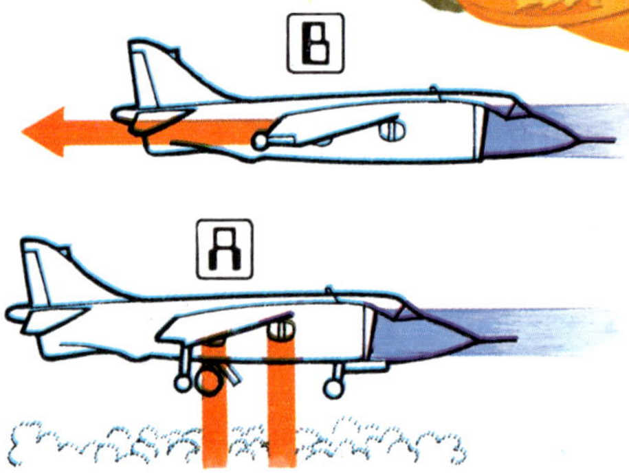

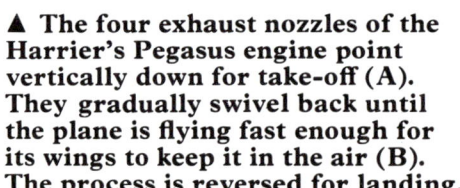

▲ The four exhaust nozzles of the Harrier's Pegasus engine point vertically down for take-off (A). They gradually swivel back until the plane is flying fast enough for its wings to keep it in the air (B). The process is reversed for landing.

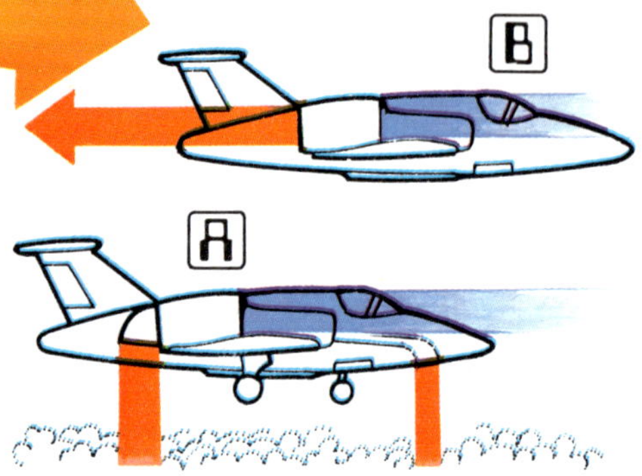

▲ The projected McDonnell Douglas 260 had three fans, one in the nose and the other two above the wings. The company has since concentrated on an advanced version of the Harrier for the U.S. Marine Corps.

▲ VTO works just like normal jet flight, except that the jet is deflected downwards and so forces the aircraft up. Try holding a hand-shower over the bath, and turning it on fast. The force of the water gushing out will push your hand up.

1

Faster enemy jet closing in to attack

Harrier pilot turns his jet nozzles to forward position

▲ The jump-jet is at an advantage in air-to-air combat. If a Harrier is being chased by another fighter it can escape by a technique called V.I.F.F. (Vectoring In Forward Flight). The pilot swivels the nozzles from the fully back position

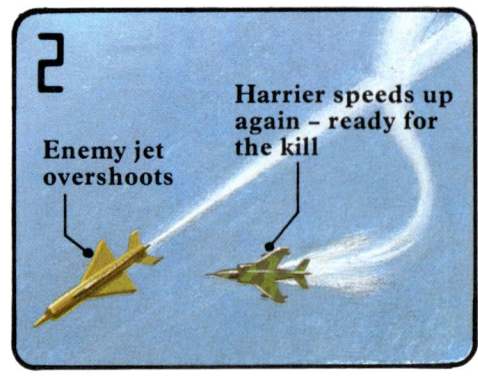

2

Enemy jet overshoots

Harrier speeds up again – ready for the kill

to as far forward as they will go. Its jets now slow the Harrier down much faster than air brakes can, so the pursuing fighter flies past. The Harrier pilot can then turn the nozzles back and get on the tail of the other plane.

Tri-national swing-wing – the Panavia Tornado

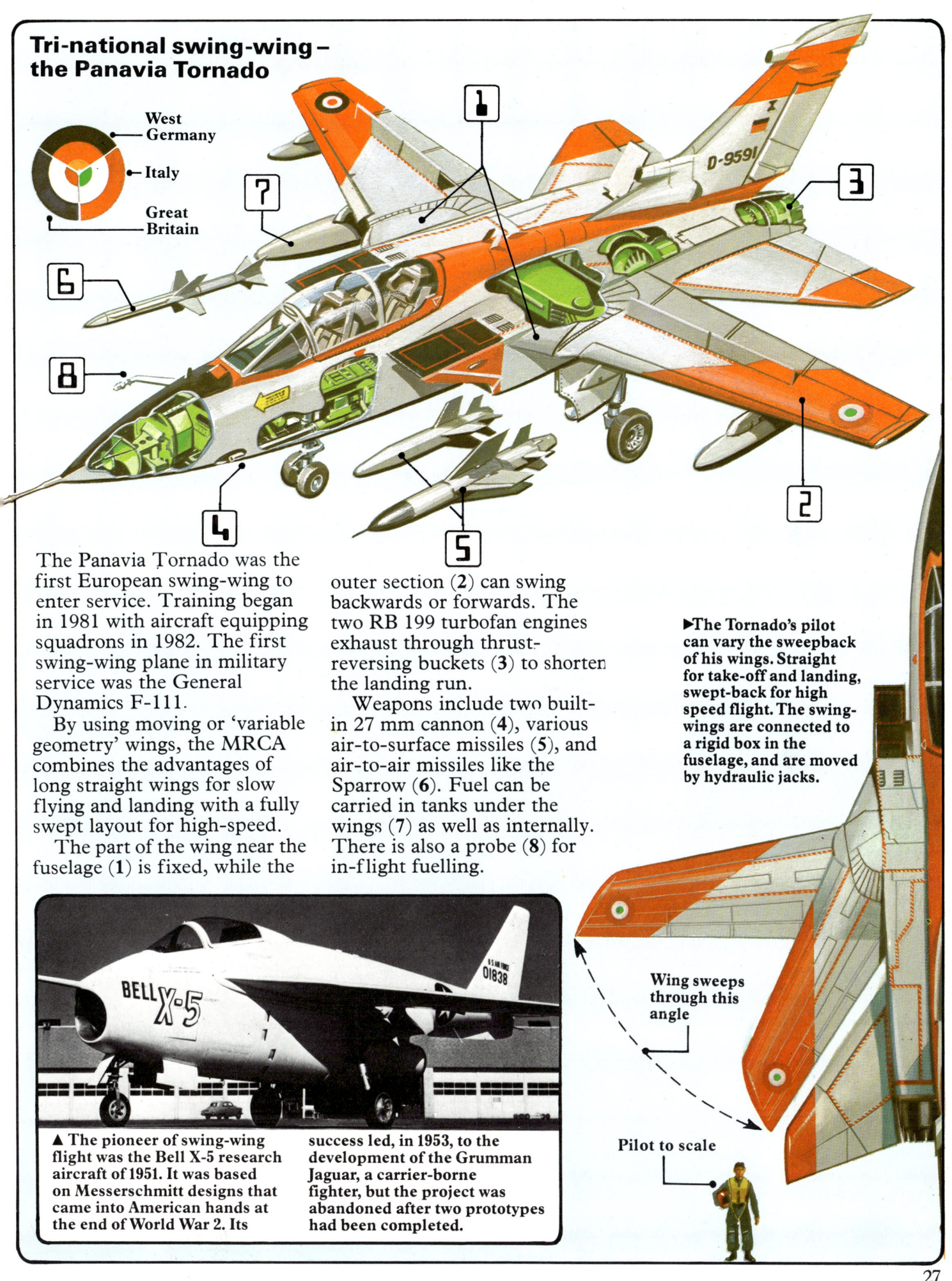

West Germany

Italy

Great Britain

1

3

7

6

8

4

5

2

D-9591

The Panavia Tornado was the first European swing-wing to enter service. Training began in 1981 with aircraft equipping squadrons in 1982. The first swing-wing plane in military service was the General Dynamics F-111.

By using moving or 'variable geometry' wings, the MRCA combines the advantages of long straight wings for slow flying and landing with a fully swept layout for high-speed.

The part of the wing near the fuselage (**1**) is fixed, while the outer section (**2**) can swing backwards or forwards. The two RB 199 turbofan engines exhaust through thrust-reversing buckets (**3**) to shorten the landing run.

Weapons include two built-in 27 mm cannon (**4**), various air-to-surface missiles (**5**), and air-to-air missiles like the Sparrow (**6**). Fuel can be carried in tanks under the wings (**7**) as well as internally. There is also a probe (**8**) for in-flight fuelling.

▶The Tornado's pilot can vary the sweepback of his wings. Straight for take-off and landing, swept-back for high speed flight. The swing-wings are connected to a rigid box in the fuselage, and are moved by hydraulic jacks.

Wing sweeps through this angle

Pilot to scale

BELL X-5

01838

▲ The pioneer of swing-wing flight was the Bell X-5 research aircraft of 1951. It was based on Messerschmitt designs that came into American hands at the end of World War 2. Its success led, in 1953, to the development of the Grumman Jaguar, a carrier-borne fighter, but the project was abandoned after two prototypes had been completed.

JETS OF THE FUTURE

In the future jets will continue to get bigger, faster and quieter. There are plans for a double-decker Boeing 747 that would carry nearly a thousand passengers. Mach 3 supersonic airliners will one day cross the Atlantic in two hours.

Jet engines already make less noise than they used to, and this trend will continue. Engineers are looking for other strong new materials like the titanium used for building the SR-71, and air-data computers are being developed and improved to make in-flight calculations faster than the human brain can.

▲ One design with a future is the supercritical wing. Its flattened top and downward-curving rear section slow down the formation of shock waves. A passenger jet equipped with wings like this would be able to fly at Mach 0.95 on the amount of power now needed for flying at Mach 0.8.

The aircraft shown above is a modified U.S. Navy Crusader fighter developed by the National Aeronautics and Space Administration (NASA).

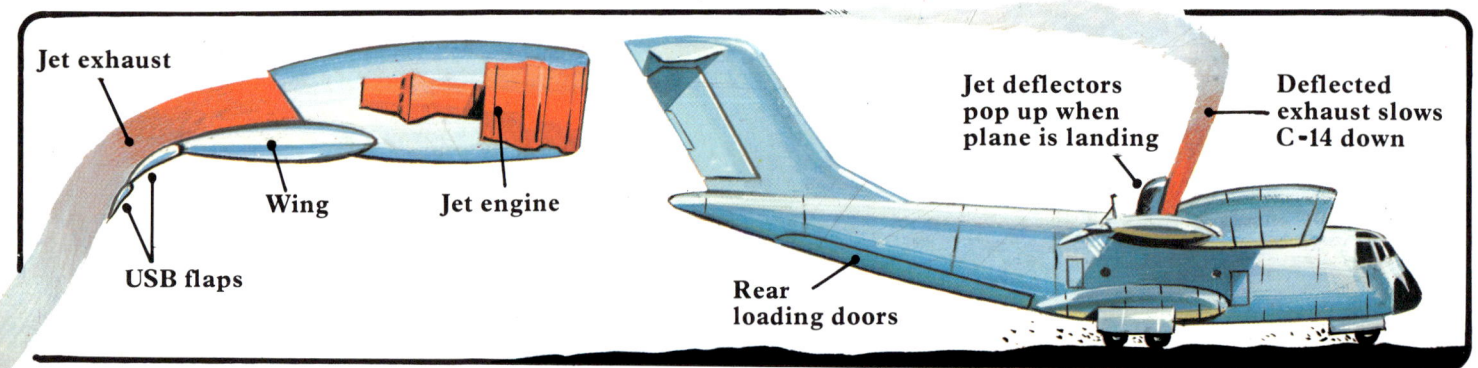

▲ The Boeing C-14 STOL transport plane has its engines mounted over the wings. It uses a system called U.S.B. (Upper Surface Blowing) to make short take-offs and landings.

U.S.B. works like this: Jet exhaust gases blow over the wing's upper surface. U.S.B. flaps curve down behind the wing's trailing edge, pointing towards the ground. The exhaust gases stick to the flaps and are deflected almost straight downwards, creating lift.

You can see what happens by holding the back of a spoon against the water from a tap. The gases stick to the flaps just as the water curves around the spoon. This is known as the Coanda effect, after the Rumanian scientist who first noticed it in the 1930s.

Hypersonic ramjets

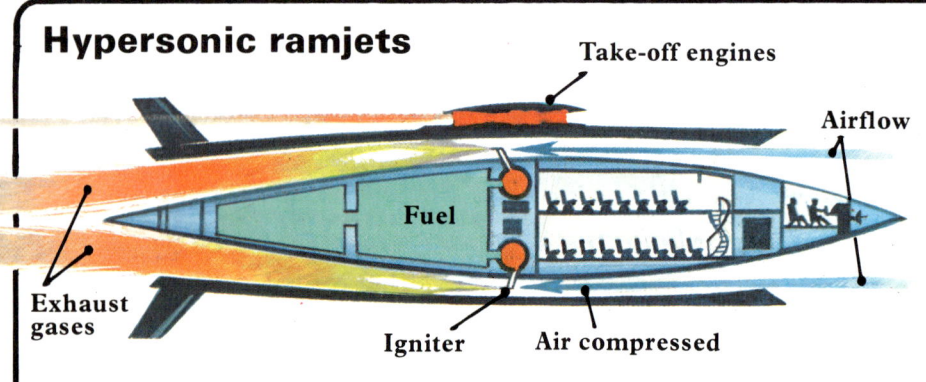

Ramjet engines are very simple, but they only work at high speeds. Air is 'rammed' into the engine as the craft rushes forward, and it compresses itself as it flows through a narrow throat. Fuel is injected and ignited as in a normal jet engine. Plans for the airliner shown here have not yet got off the drawing-board.

▲ The German/Dutch Fokker-VFW 614 short-range jetliner has its two turbofan engines mounted on top of the wings. This is one way of reducing the noise the aircraft makes as it lands and takes off. The wings act as a sound deflector.

The roar of the engines is bounced off them and diverted upwards, making the 614 quieter than normal jets when heard from the ground.

The diagram on the right (2) shows the way in which the wings bounce the jet roar upwards.

Sound is bounced off the wing, protecting the ground beneath from most of the jet roar.

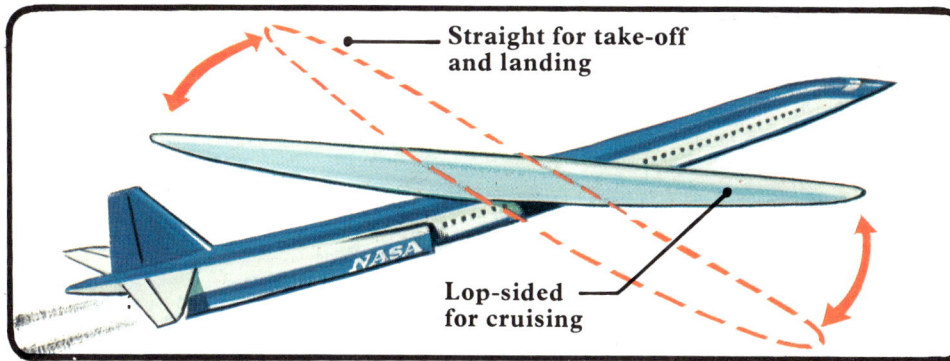

Straight for take-off and landing

Lop-sided for cruising

▲ This McDonnell Douglas design for the 1990s would carry 273 passengers at around Mach 2.2. It has unusual arrow-shaped wings that are planned to cause less drag than ogival wings of the type used on Concorde.

▲ The weird, scissor-like swing-wing aircraft above is a design study by NASA. It would be an easy and lightweight way to give jet airliners swing-wings, because the design only calls for one swivel point – the heaviest part

of any swing-wing aircraft. The four turbofan engines are mounted in long ducts on the tail.

The idea is not new. German designers drew up similar plans in World War 2, for a fighter to be called the Blohm und Voss P 202.

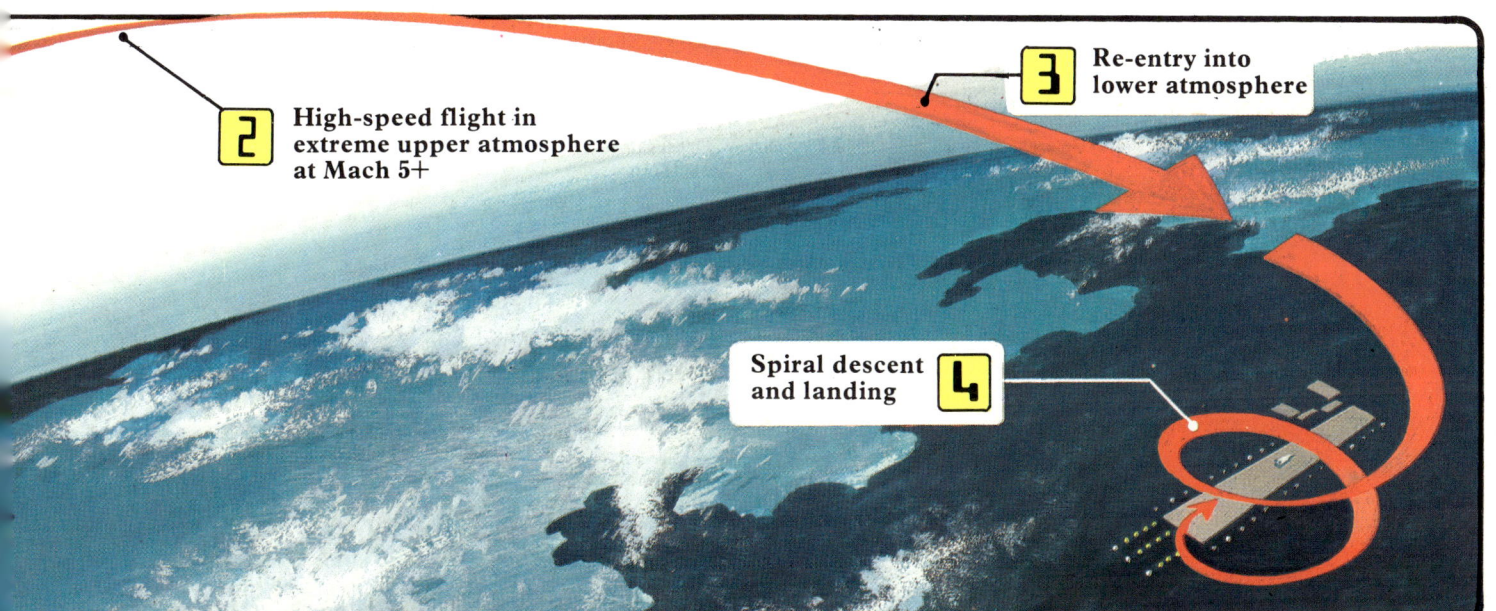

2 High-speed flight in extreme upper atmosphere at Mach 5+

3 Re-entry into lower atmosphere

4 Spiral descent and landing

JET FIRSTS

The first man to suggest jet air travel was the French balloonist Joseph Montgolfier. In 1783 he proposed (but did not succeed in) using the hot air that kept his balloons up to drive them forward. Here are some later pioneers from jet flight's short but crowded history.

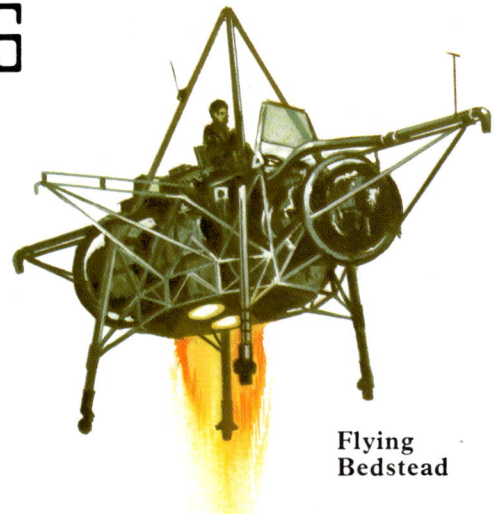

Flying Bedstead

1865
First real design for a jet-propelled plane drawn up by de Louvrié, a French engineer.

1865's jet

August 27, 1939
Capt. Erich Warsitz made the first jet flight, in a Heinkel He 178 test plane.

November 30, 1941
First cross-country jet flight, made in the Italian Caproni-Campini N-1 from Milan to Rome.

July 27, 1944
Gloster Meteors of the RAF made first jet combat flight, against V-1 flying bombs.

September 18, 1948
The Convair XF-92A research aircraft was the first delta-wing jet to fly.

July 27, 1949
The de Havilland Comet was the first pure-jet airliner to fly. It went into service in 1952.

November 8, 1950
First jet-vs.-jet air victory won by a Lockheed F-80 over a Chinese MiG-15 in Korean War.

August 3, 1954
First VTO jet flight, made by Rolls-Royce test pilot R.T. Shepherd in the 'Flying Bedstead'.

May 27, 1955
The Caravelle, the first airliner with rear-mounted engines, made its maiden flight.

October 1959
First round-the-world jet passenger service started by Pan American, using Boeing 707s.

March 29, 1967
The Marut jet fighter became India's first home-designed warplane to fly.

December 31, 1968
Russia's Tupolev Tu-144 made its maiden flight, becoming the first SST to fly.

April 1, 1969
Hawker Siddeley Harriers of the RAF became the first operational VTOL aircraft.

January 22, 1970
First Boeing 747 'Jumbo Jet' entered service on Pan Am's New York – London route.

January 21, 1976
Concorde made the first SST passenger flights. The Tu-144 had made mail flights earlier.

ABBREVIATIONS

BAC	British Aircraft Corporation	RAF	(British) Royal Air Force
BAe	British Aerospace	SLAR	Sideways-Looking Airborne Radar
EPNdB	Effective Perceived Noise Decibels	SST	Supersonic Transport
Flt. Lt.	Flight Lieutenant	STOL	Short Take-Off and Landing
MRCA	Multi-Role Combat Aircraft	USAF	United States Air Force
NASA	National Aeronautics and Space Administration	VTOL	Vertical Take-Off and Landing

JET FACTS

Did you know that jet fighters can fly faster than the shells they fire, and that at least one jet has shot itself down? These are some other odd facts about jets and the men who fly them.

The world's most expensive plane is America's E-3A AWACS (Airborne Warning and Control System), used for detecting attacks and controlling fighters. It has been developed from the Boeing 707 airliner, and each one costs $178 million (£89 million).

The longest scheduled non-stop flight is from Brussels to Hawaii, a distance of 11,791 km., which takes 14 hours in a Boeing 747.

A modified MiG-25 Foxbat fighter has reached a height of 36.24 km., the world absolute altitude record. It can reach a height of 35 km. in 4 mins. 11.3 secs, at a climbing speed of 400 m. a second (well over Mach 1).

On December 20, 1968, United Air Lines carried 118,519 passengers in one day in its all-jet fleet of airliners.

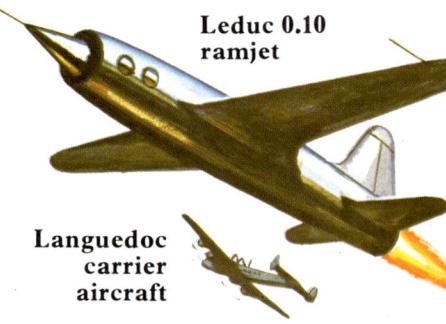

Leduc 0.10 ramjet

Languedoc carrier aircraft

Three prototype ramjets called Leduc 0.10s were built and successfully tested in France, making their first powered flight in 1949. They were air-launched from larger planes, and reached speeds of up to 800 k.p.h. on half-power. A later French research plane, the Nord Griffon, used a turbo-jet engine in the centre of a huge ramjet to provide power for take-off and climbing. The ramjet took over when the plane was flying high and fast.

Dornier Do31

One of the most interesting VTOL experimental aircraft was the Dornier Do31E military transport. It was powered by ten engines, with a Pegasus turbofan on each side of its fuselage and four lift-jets in removable pods on each wing-tip, and had a cruising speed of 650 k.p.h. The project was finally abandoned because of its cost and complexity.

The B-58 Hustler carried a giant-sized streamlined pod underneath its fuselage. This had two parts. The lower one was a fuel tank that could be dropped in flight once the fuel was used up. The upper part carried both fuel and a bomb or missile. This was dropped over the target zone, so that the Hustler could fly home faster and lighter.

The highest point from which airmen have made an emergency escape is 17,000 m. – nearly twice as high as Mt. Everest. On April 9, 1958, two crew members of an English Electric Canberra bomber that exploded at this height escaped unharmed. They fell 14,000 m. before their parachutes opened automatically.

The fastest jet flying-boat ever built was the Martin Seamaster, which could fly at nearly 1,000 k.p.h. Its four engines were mounted in pairs above the swept-back wings.

On December 29, 1974, a record 674 people were squeezed into a QANTAS airlines jumbo. They were being evacuated from disaster in Darwin, Australia after the town had been hit by a hurricane.

JET WORDS

The glossary only includes words that are not fully explained anywhere else in the book. You will find other engine words explained on pages 6 and 7, and flight words on pages 8 and 9.

Afterburning
A boosting system (also called reheat) in which fuel is injected and ignited in the jet exhaust to give extra thrust.

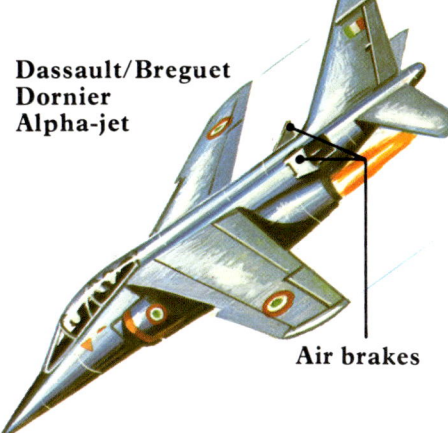

Dassault/Breguet Dornier Alpha-jet

Air brakes

Air brakes
Controls that increase drag, and so slow aircraft down.

Apron
Open space at an airport on which aircraft are parked for loading, refuelling etc.

Bowser
A tanker truck used for refuelling aircraft.

Console
An aircraft instrument panel.

Flight deck
An airliner's crew compartment.

Galley
Space for cooking food on board an airliner.

Glidepath
The path an aircraft follows as it comes in to land.

Interceptor
A fast, light warplane designed for cutting attacking aircraft or missiles off.

Jet core
The central part of the jet engine, made up of the compressor and fuel injection and ignition systems.

Leading edge
The front edge of the wing.

Operational
In service – the opposite of experimental.

Pallet
A platform for carrying cargo, with openings to fit the prongs of a fork-lift truck.

Prototype
The first model (or models) of a new make of aeroplane.

Radome
A protective covering for radar equipment.

Sensor
Any reconnaissance instrument that gathers information.

Skin temperature
The temperature on the outside of a plane.

Spoilers
Long metal plates that can be raised to disturb the airflow over wings, reducing lift.

Stacking
An air traffic control system by which aircraft approaching a busy airport are left circling a radio beacon at gradually descending levels until they are cleared to land.

Subsonic
Slower than Mach 1. Speeds between Mach 1 and Mach 5 are supersonic. Hypersonic means faster than Mach 5.

Forward flight – buckets open

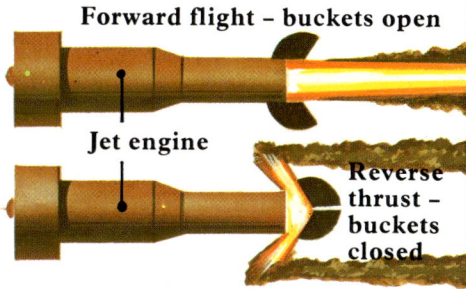

Jet engine

Reverse thrust – buckets closed

Thrust-reversing buckets
Controls in the rear of a jet engine. They deflect the jet exhaust forwards, slowing the plane down.

Trailing edge
The rear edge of a wing.

Turbine
In jet engines, a wheel with curved blades that is turned by exhaust gases and itself turns the compressor.

AEROLOG

Here are some aircraft you can see at many of the world's airports. Record the place, date and time when you saw them on the dotted lines printed next to each plane.

Aerospatiale SE210 Caravelle Super B

British Aerospace (BAC) One-Eleven

Boeing 707

Boeing 727

Dassault Falcon 20

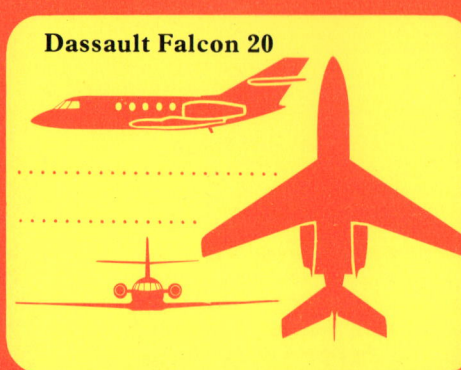

A300 Airbus

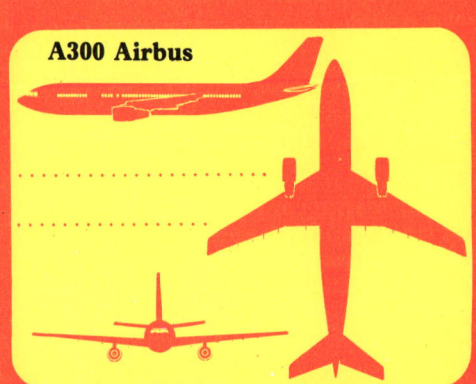

Fokker F.28 Fellowship

Gates Learjet

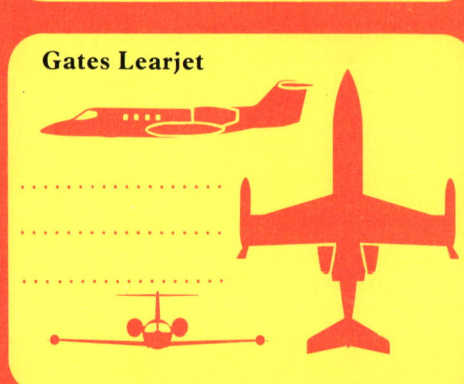

British Aerospace 125

Hawker Siddeley Trident 3

McDonnell Douglas DC-9

McDonnell Douglas DC-10

Boeing 737

Tupolev Tu-154

PART 2: SPACEFLIGHT

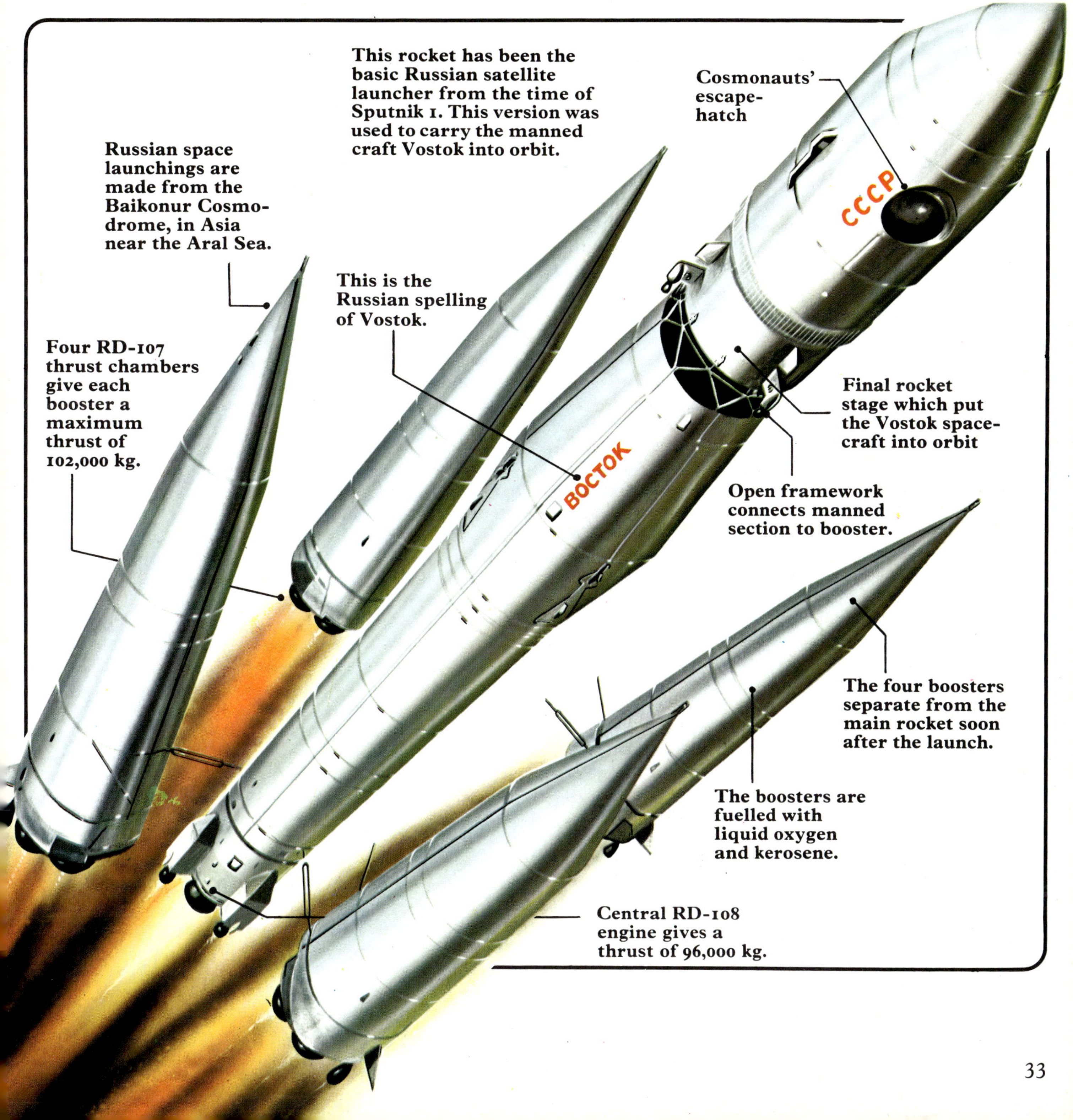

This rocket has been the basic Russian satellite launcher from the time of Sputnik 1. This version was used to carry the manned craft Vostok into orbit.

Cosmonauts' escape-hatch

Russian space launchings are made from the Baikonur Cosmodrome, in Asia near the Aral Sea.

This is the Russian spelling of Vostok.

Four RD-107 thrust chambers give each booster a maximum thrust of 102,000 kg.

CCCP

ВОСТОК

Final rocket stage which put the Vostok spacecraft into orbit

Open framework connects manned section to booster.

The four boosters separate from the main rocket soon after the launch.

The boosters are fuelled with liquid oxygen and kerosene.

Central RD-108 engine gives a thrust of 96,000 kg.

CREDITS

Written by
Kenneth Gatland
Art and editorial direction
David Jefferis
Text editor
Tony Allan
Educational advisor
Frank Blackwell
Scientific advisor
Ian Ridpath

Illustrators
Sydney Cornford, Gordon Davies,
Malcolm English, Brian Lewis,
John Marshall, Michael Roffe,
David Slinn, Craig Warwick

The picture on this page shows the
Pioneer 10 spaceprobe passing
Jupiter, biggest planet in the
Solar System. The fly-by took
place in 1973.

THE EXPERIMENTS

Here is a checklist of the equipment you will need for the
experiments and things to do included in Part 2.

General equipment

Notebook and pencil
Rule or tape-measure
Sticky tape
Glue
Scissors
Watch
Rubber bands
Paper-clips, used matchsticks
Sheet of thin card

Special experiments

Action and reaction (p.36):
Sausage-shaped balloons
Thin wire (fuse-wire is ideal)
Nylon fishing-line or thread

Air expansion (p.38):
Some small balloons
Narrow-necked glass bottle
Bucket and cloth

Satellite orbits (p.43):
Ballpoint pen case
Plasticine
Fishing-line or thread

Heat insulation (p.45):
Polystyrene ceiling tile
Two ice-cubes

Space Shuttle glider (p.50):
Balsa wood, craft knife and
balsa cement OR stiff paper,
scissors and tape

Mars Roving Vehicle (p.56):
Two plastic bottles (washing-
up liquid bottles are ideal)
Polystyrene foam
Stiff wire
Ballpoint pen case
Four necklace-beads

Rotating space station (p.58):
Three plastic bottles
Thick wire
Glass or plastic necklace-beads
Two small balsawood blocks
54 cm. length of thick card
Model astronaut

WEIGHTS AND MEASURES

All the weights and measures in Part 2 are metric.
Here are some imperial equivalents.

cm. = centimetres
(1 inch = 2.54 cm.)

m. = metres
(1 yard = 0.91 m.)

km. = kilometres
(1 mile = 1.6 km.)

k.p.h. = kilometres per hour
(1,000 m.p.h. = 1,609 k.p.h.)

sq. km. = square kilometres
(1 square mile = 2.59 sq. km.)

kg. = kilograms
(1 stone = 6.35 kg.)

A tonne is 1,000 kg.
(1 ton = 1.02 tonnes)

kg./sq. cm. = kilograms per
square centimetre
(1 pound per square inch =
0.07 kg./sq. cm.)

1 litre is 1.76 pints

C = degrees Centigrade

PART 2: SPACEFLIGHT

ABOUT SPACEFLIGHT

Spaceflight is about the exploration of mankind's new frontier. In simple language and with more than a hundred full-colour illustrations, it tells the story of the Space Age from the V-2 rocket to the present day and beyond.

It explains how rockets work and why satellites stay in orbit. You will find out about the dangers of travelling through space and what astronauts can do to overcome them. There are detailed descriptions of America's re-usable Space Shuttle, and of how an industrial base may look when men finally settle on the Moon.

Spaceflight also includes lots of projects and things to do. There are safe and easy experiments involving such principles as heat insulation and the expansion and contraction of air, and you will learn how to make working models of a revolving space station and a Mars Roving Vehicle.

CONTENTS

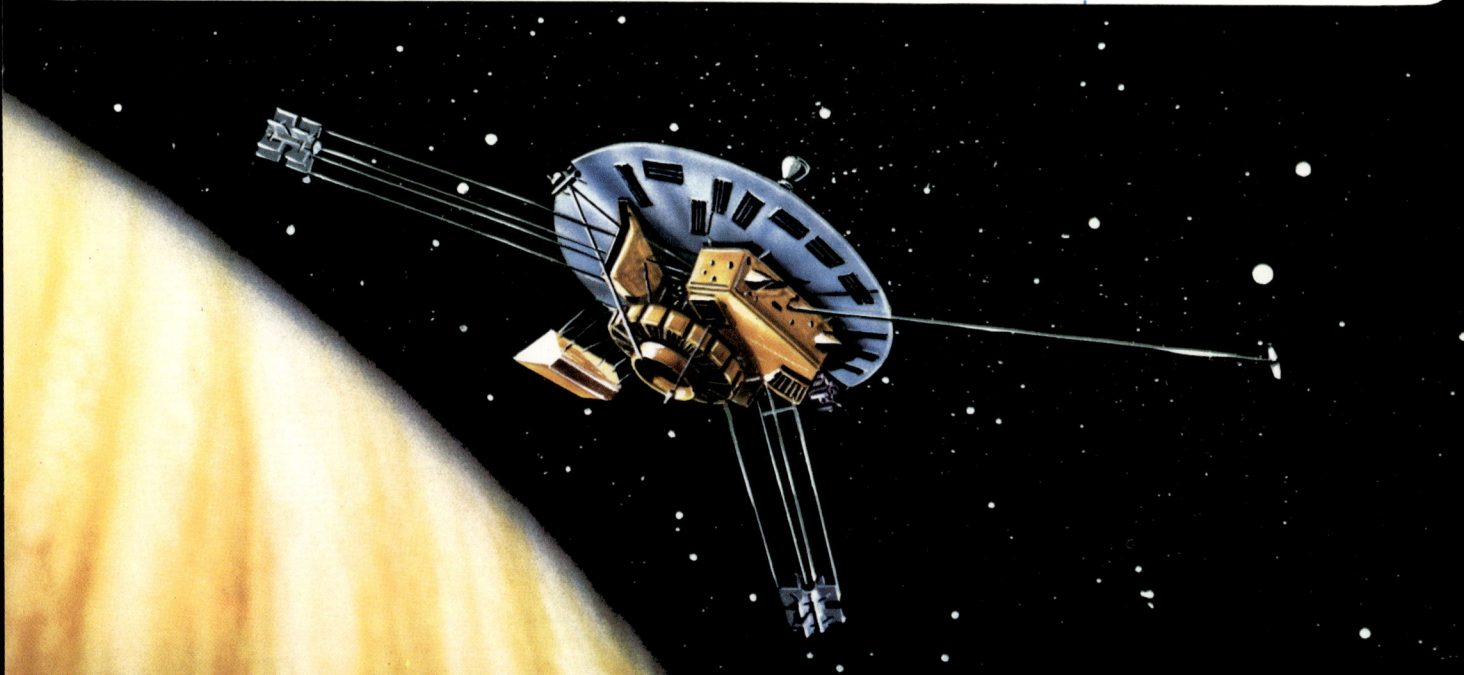

THE ROCKET ENGINE

No-one knows who invented the rocket. Perhaps the Chinese have the best claim. They are said to have shot 'fire-arrows' at invading Mongols in AD 1232 at the Battle of K'ai-Fung-Fu.

For the next five centuries, rockets were used chiefly as fireworks but sometimes also as weapons.

An Englishman called William Congreve made improved solid-fuel rockets around 1800, but the big step did not come until the start of the 20th century when the Russian Konstantin Tsiolkovsky suggested the use of liquid propellants.

▲Dr. Robert H. Goddard (1882–1945) did extensive research with solid and liquid fuels. In 1920 he proposed sending a rocket loaded with flash powder to the Moon, and observing the flash through a telescope when it hit the Moon.

▲It was Goddard who launched the world's first liquid-propellant rocket, in March 1926. Fuelled with liquid oxygen and gasoline, it was in the air for just 2½ seconds, covering a distance of 56 m. at an average speed of 103 k.p.h.

Action, reaction and rocket racers

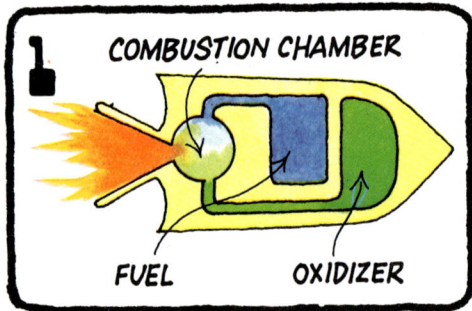

1. COMBUSTION CHAMBER
FUEL   OXIDIZER

▲A liquid fuel rocket has a fuel and an oxidizer, which are fed to the combustion chamber by gas pressure or, more often, by pumps. They ignite there. The oxidizer is needed to provide oxygen, without which nothing can burn.

2. NOZZLE
ACTION   REACTION

▲The burning liquids produce a powerful exhaust, which expands backwards through a nozzle. The action of the exhaust causes a reaction of equal pressure pushing in the opposite direction that drives the rocket forward.

3. BEND ENDS INTO HOOK SHAPES
2 cm.   2 cm.   THICK WIRE

▲This experiment is a quick and simple way of demonstrating the principle of action and reaction. You will need a few sausage-shaped balloons, some thin wire, and a length of nylon fishing-line or thread. Bend the wire as shown.

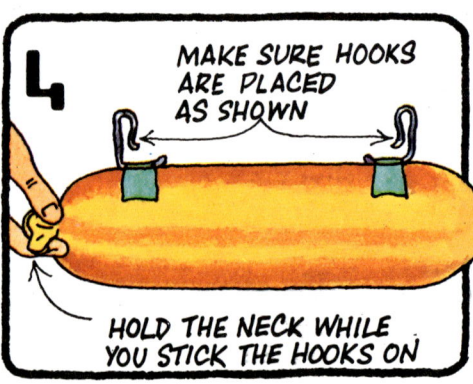

4. MAKE SURE HOOKS ARE PLACED AS SHOWN
HOLD THE NECK WHILE YOU STICK THE HOOKS ON

▲Blow up a balloon and seal the end with tape. Fix the two hooks carefully to it, making sure they are in a straight line with one another and with the balloon. Ease the tape off the neck and let the air out slowly.

5. TAPE
TAUT NYLON FISHING LINE

▲Attach one end of the fishing-line firmly to a wall or door. Stretch the line across the room, and tie or tape the other end to a chair-back or wall fitting. The line should be taut and should slope downwards a little.

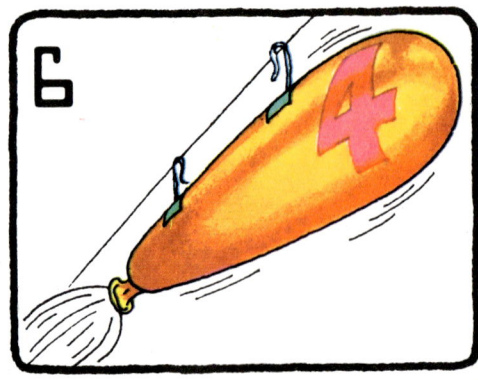

6.

▲Blow up the balloon again. Hold the neck firmly. Hook the balloon over the line, then let go and watch it speed forward. With several lines and a packet of balloons, you can have rocket-races with your friends.

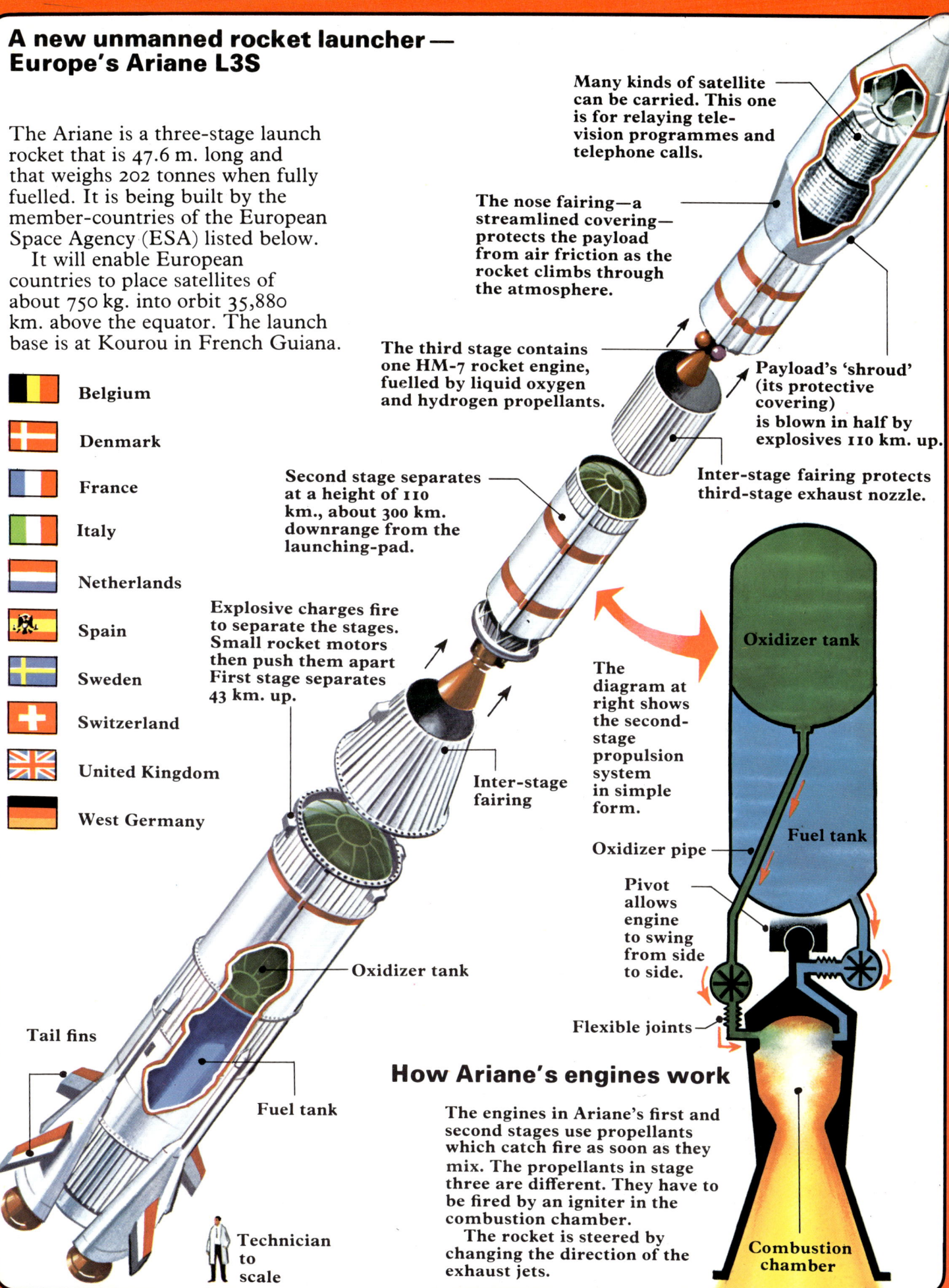

A new unmanned rocket launcher — Europe's Ariane L3S

The Ariane is a three-stage launch rocket that is 47.6 m. long and that weighs 202 tonnes when fully fuelled. It is being built by the member-countries of the European Space Agency (ESA) listed below.

It will enable European countries to place satellites of about 750 kg. into orbit 35,880 km. above the equator. The launch base is at Kourou in French Guiana.

Belgium

Denmark

France

Italy

Netherlands

Spain

Sweden

Switzerland

United Kingdom

West Germany

Many kinds of satellite can be carried. This one is for relaying television programmes and telephone calls.

The nose fairing—a streamlined covering—protects the payload from air friction as the rocket climbs through the atmosphere.

The third stage contains one HM-7 rocket engine, fuelled by liquid oxygen and hydrogen propellants.

Payload's 'shroud' (its protective covering) is blown in half by explosives 110 km. up.

Inter-stage fairing protects third-stage exhaust nozzle.

Second stage separates at a height of 110 km., about 300 km. downrange from the launching-pad.

Explosive charges fire to separate the stages. Small rocket motors then push them apart First stage separates 43 km. up.

Inter-stage fairing

The diagram at right shows the second-stage propulsion system in simple form.

Oxidizer tank

Fuel tank

Oxidizer pipe

Pivot allows engine to swing from side to side.

Flexible joints

Oxidizer tank

Tail fins

Fuel tank

Technician to scale

How Ariane's engines work

The engines in Ariane's first and second stages use propellants which catch fire as soon as they mix. The propellants in stage three are different. They have to be fired by an igniter in the combustion chamber.

The rocket is steered by changing the direction of the exhaust jets.

Combustion chamber

37

BALL OF LIFE

Planet Earth, our island home in space, takes $365\frac{1}{4}$ days to travel around the Sun, and rotates once every 23 hours 56 minutes. These are our years and days. Oceans cover seven-tenths of its surface, and its poles are always covered by ice.

The air we breathe is mainly nitrogen (78%) and oxygen (21%). It is warmed by the Sun during the day and cools off at night. Temperature alterations cause movements of air, as the experiments below show. The constant interchange of air between sea and land is the main cause of changes in the weather.

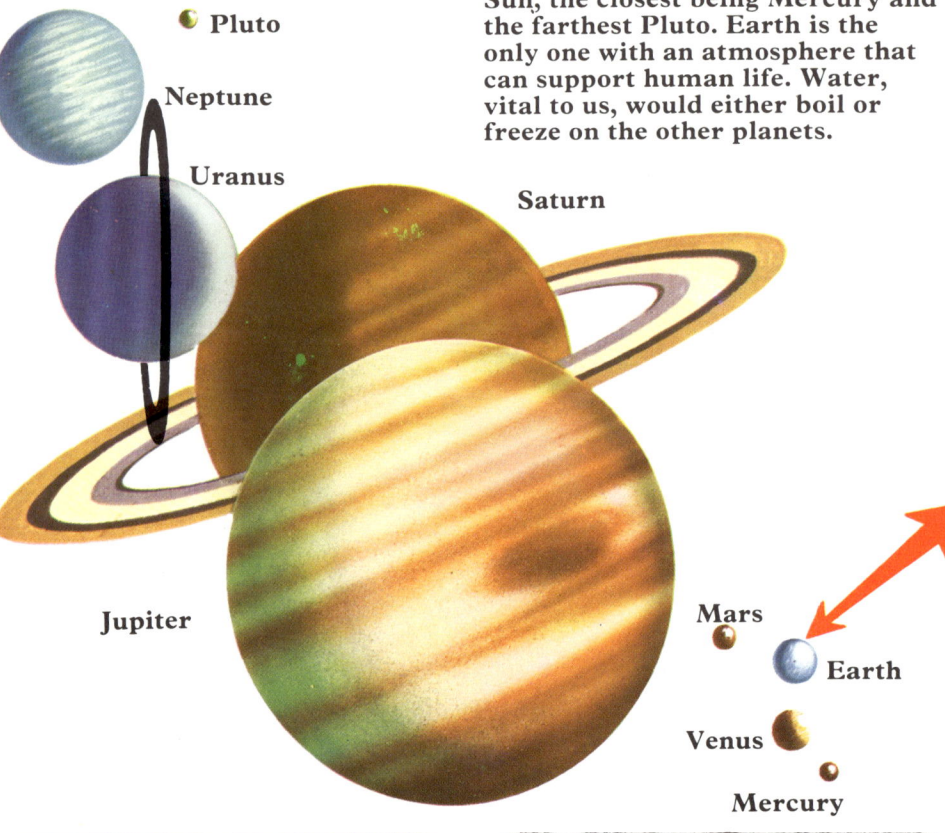

◀ Nine planets revolve around our Sun, the closest being Mercury and the farthest Pluto. Earth is the only one with an atmosphere that can support human life. Water, vital to us, would either boil or freeze on the other planets.

Pluto

Neptune

Uranus

Saturn

Jupiter

Mars

Earth

Venus

Mercury

The Earth's life-giving layer of air

North Pole

Mount Everest 8,848 m.

---

1 Expanding and contracting air

The Earth's layer of air is thin. Just 10 km. from the surface there is already too little of it for men to survive. Manned spaceflight is only possible because man has learned how to take air into space with him.

Our air is a mixture of gases, and like all gases it expands when heated and contracts when cooled.

Movements of air in the atmosphere create our weather. Nowadays satellites are used to keep watch on this (see p.48).

STRETCH SMALL BALLOON OVER NECK

COLD BOTTLE

▲This experiment with a bottle and a balloon shows how air expands when heated. Cool the bottle by running cold water over it, then stretch the balloon tightly over its neck. It will dangle loosely, empty of air.

HOT WATER

▲Now fill a sink or bucket with hot water, and stand the bottle in it. As the air in the bottle heats up, it will expand upward into the balloon, blowing it up. Take the bottle out of the bucket, and the balloon will slowly go limp again.

Earth's air layer is very thin—relatively thinner than the peel of an orange. At sea level it exerts a pressure of 1.03 kg. per sq. cm., but it gets less higher up, where it gradually fades away into airless space. Three-quarters of the mass of air lies below the level of Mt. Everest's summit.

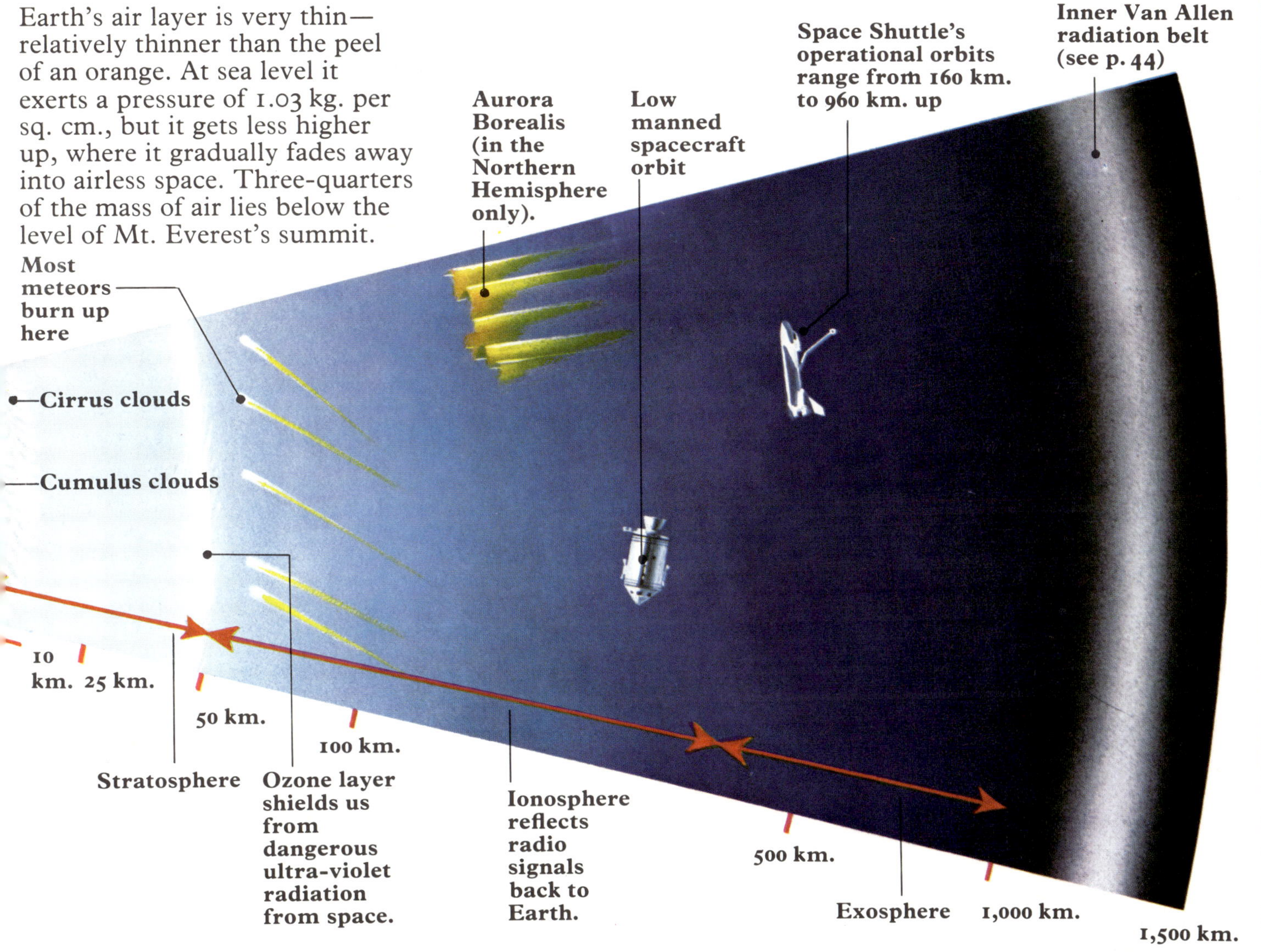

Aurora Borealis (in the Northern Hemisphere only).

Low manned spacecraft orbit

Space Shuttle's operational orbits range from 160 km. to 960 km. up

Inner Van Allen radiation belt (see p. 44)

Most meteors burn up here

Cirrus clouds

Cumulus clouds

10 km. 25 km.

50 km.

100 km.

500 km.

1,000 km.

1,500 km.

Stratosphere

Ozone layer shields us from dangerous ultra-violet radiation from space.

Ionosphere reflects radio signals back to Earth.

Exosphere

4

HOT WATER

FILL TO OVER-FLOWING

▲You can reverse the experiment by first pouring hot (NOT boiling) water into the bottle. Leave it to stand for a minute while the air inside warms up, then empty it. Stretch the balloon by blowing it up a couple of times.

5

STRETCH BALLOON OVER NECK

LOW AIR PRESSURE INSIDE

▲Fasten the balloon over the bottle's neck. As the hot air in the bottle cools down, it will contract, causing low pressure inside the bottle. There is now higher pressure outside the bottle than inside.

6

AIR TURNS BALLOON INSIDE-OUT

POP!

▲The higher pressure outside pushes the balloon down into the bottle. In pressurized spacecraft, the higher pressure *inside* presses out against the crafts' sides towards airless space. So they need strong hulls to keep the pressure in.

DAWN OF THE SPACE AGE

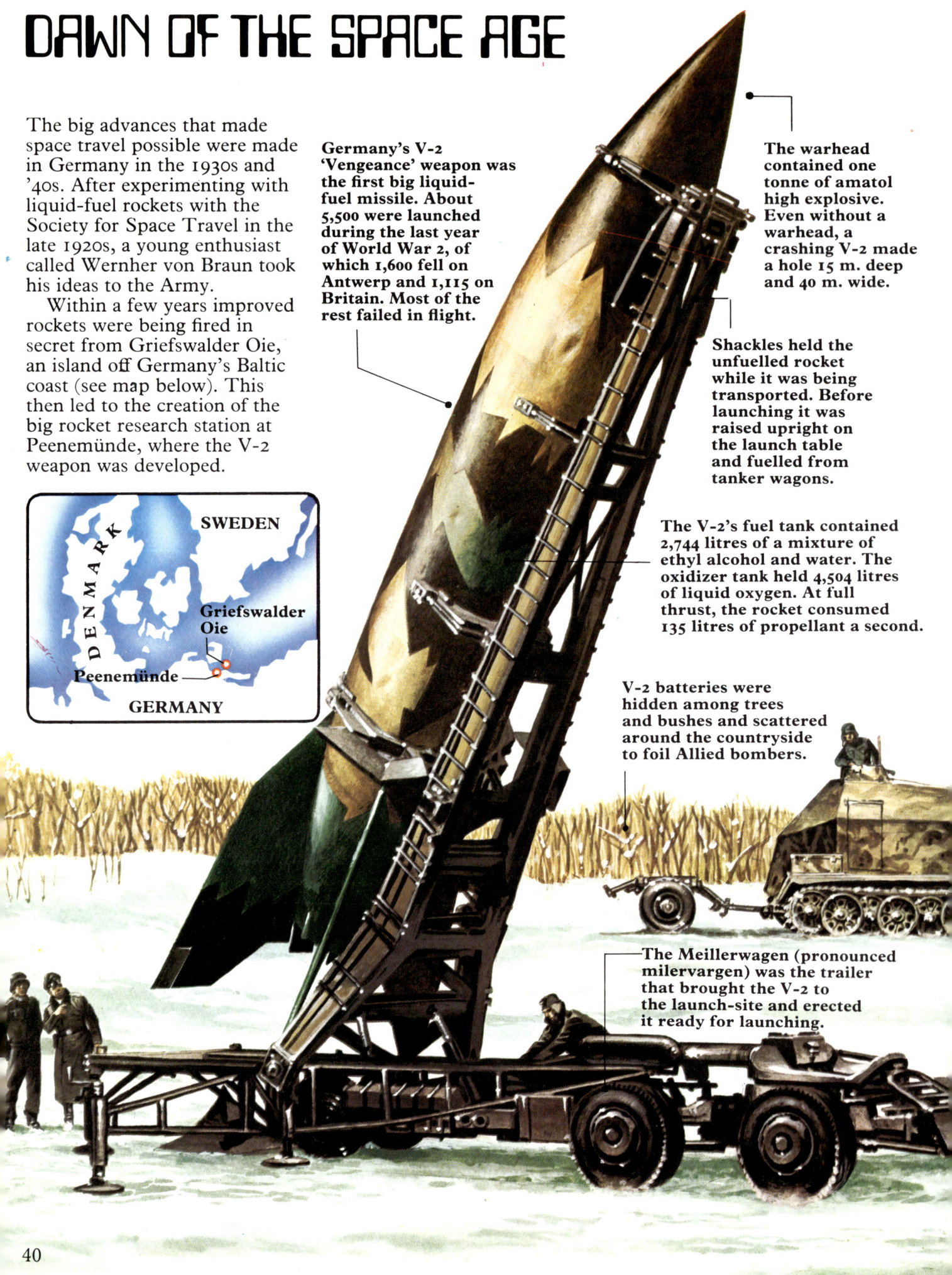

The big advances that made space travel possible were made in Germany in the 1930s and '40s. After experimenting with liquid-fuel rockets with the Society for Space Travel in the late 1920s, a young enthusiast called Wernher von Braun took his ideas to the Army.

Within a few years improved rockets were being fired in secret from Griefswalder Oie, an island off Germany's Baltic coast (see map below). This then led to the creation of the big rocket research station at Peenemünde, where the V-2 weapon was developed.

Germany's V-2 'Vengeance' weapon was the first big liquid-fuel missile. About 5,500 were launched during the last year of World War 2, of which 1,600 fell on Antwerp and 1,115 on Britain. Most of the rest failed in flight.

The warhead contained one tonne of amatol high explosive. Even without a warhead, a crashing V-2 made a hole 15 m. deep and 40 m. wide.

Shackles held the unfuelled rocket while it was being transported. Before launching it was raised upright on the launch table and fuelled from tanker wagons.

The V-2's fuel tank contained 2,744 litres of a mixture of ethyl alcohol and water. The oxidizer tank held 4,504 litres of liquid oxygen. At full thrust, the rocket consumed 135 litres of propellant a second.

V-2 batteries were hidden among trees and bushes and scattered around the countryside to foil Allied bombers.

The Meillerwagen (pronounced milervargen) was the trailer that brought the V-2 to the launch-site and erected it ready for launching.

SWEDEN

DENMARK

Griefswalder Oie

Peenemünde

GERMANY

▲A Russian schoolteacher called Konstantin Tsiolkovsky worked out that rockets would travel in airless space. Although he never fired a rocket, he drew up designs in 1903 for a spaceship powered by liquid oxygen and liquid hydrogen.

▲Wernher von Braun went to the USA after World War 2. There he led the team that launched America's first successful artificial satellite, Explorer 1. He also developed the Saturn rockets that took astronauts to the Moon.

▲A big step was taken as early as 1949, when a small WAC-Corporal rocket was launched from the nose of a V-2 high above White Sands Proving Ground, New Mexico. It reached a record height of 393 km. and a speed of 8,286 k.p.h.

A London-bound V-2 blasts off. About 500 of the missiles fell on the city.

The V-2's launching was controlled by the missile site commander from this armoured vehicle.

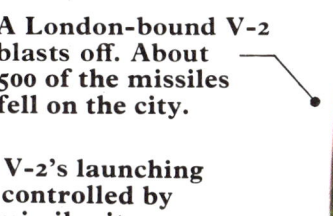

Launch table for V-2

▲ Sergei Korolev was a pioneer of Russian rocketry in the 1930s. He later developed the rockets which put Sputnik 1 and Yuri Gagarin, the world's first spaceman, into orbit.

▲ Russian scientists rocketed dogs into space in the 1950s to find out more about space travel. Laika, shown in the picture above, was sent into orbit in 1957.

Tow truck for Meillerwagen

A V-2 with wings

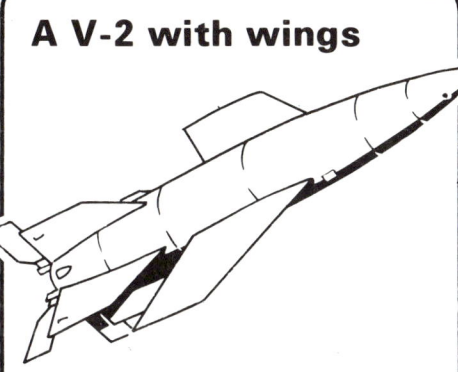

Von Braun's team also built two experimental missiles called A4bs, designed to glide for up to 750 km. The A4b was shelved in 1944, to make way for the V-2.

INTO ORBIT

On October 4, 1957, Russia shook the world by launching the first artificial satellite, Sputnik 1.

American scientists had already made plans to launch their own satellite during the International Geophysical Year (1957–58). But their first attempt failed when the Vanguard rocket toppled over on the launching-pad and burst into flames.

Von Braun's Army team was called in. Its four-stage Juno 1 rocket put Explorer 1 into orbit on February 1, 1958. The 'space race' had begun.

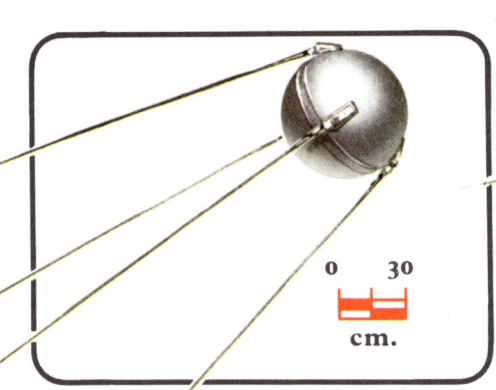

0   30
cm.

▲ Sputnik 1, a sphere 58 cm. in diameter, weighed 83.6 kg.—the weight of a large man. It was little more than an orbiting radio transmitter, with long 'whip' aerials. It circled the Earth for 92 days, then burned up.

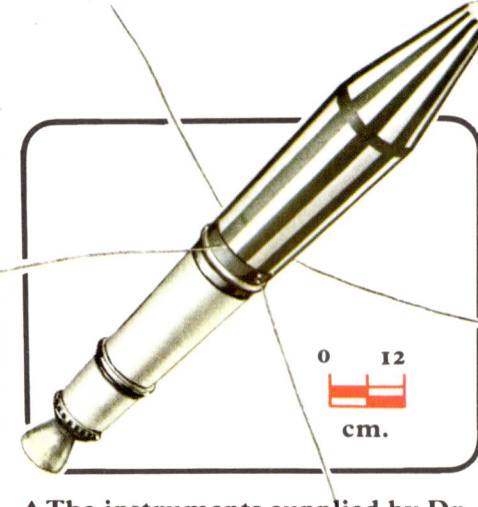

0   12
cm.

▲ The instruments supplied by Dr. James Van Allen of Iowa University for Explorer 1 included a geiger counter which led to the discovery of the Earth's radiation belts (see p. 44). The satellite stayed in orbit for 12 years.

Stage rockets

The manned spacecraft shown below all needed multi-stage rockets to send them into space. Each one had two or more propulsion units, which dropped off to make the craft lighter and more efficient as soon as the propellants they were fuelled with were used up.

The illustration (right) shows the launching of the three-stage Saturn 5.

The stages speed the payload up into orbit or into deep space.

Third stage carries the payload into space.

Second stage burns out, and drops away.

First stage burns out, and drops away.

Take-off. First stage at full power.

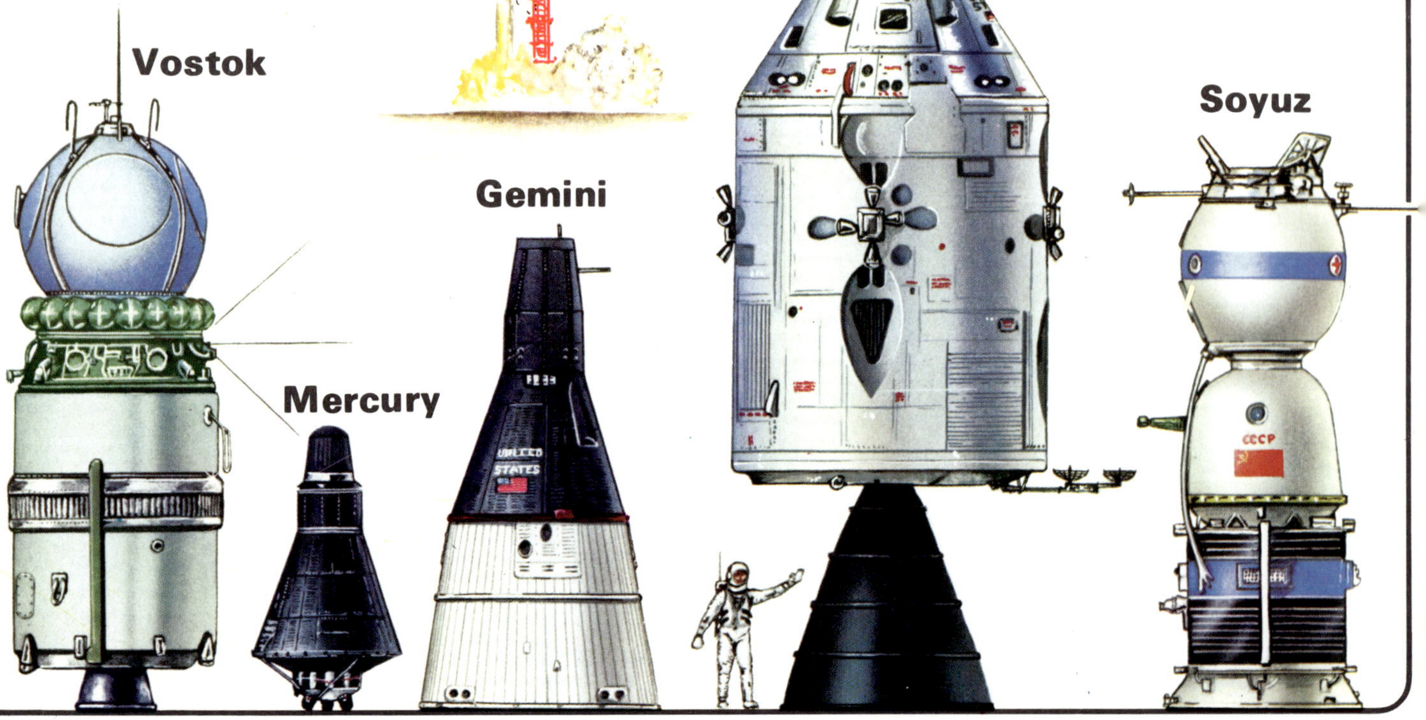

Vostok

Gemini

Mercury

Apollo

Soyuz

▲To understand how a satellite goes into orbit, imagine a gun firing shells from the peak of a high mountain. The speed at which the shells are fired carries them a short way, then the force of gravity pulls them to the ground.

▲Suppose the gun is powerful enough to fire a shell halfway round the world. Gravity still acts on the shell, stopping it from flying off into space. It finally falls back to Earth once it begins to slow down.

▲To go into orbit, the shell would have to travel very fast indeed—at about 29,000 k.p.h. if it were 100 km. up. Gravity would still try to pull it down. But at that speed the outward pull of centrifugal force balances gravity exactly.

Centrifugal force

A satellite in orbit is exactly balanced between two forces pulling in opposite directions. One is the Earth's gravity, which pulls it downwards. The other, which pulls it outwards towards deep space, is called centrifugal force. The size of this depends on the speed at which the satellite is moving.

Because the forces are equally balanced, a change in either one will swing the satellite out of orbit—unless the other force changes too.

The pull of gravity is stronger the closer the satellite is to the Earth. This means that satellites near the Earth have to orbit faster than those farther out for their centrifugal force to balance the stronger pull of gravity.

Satellite speeds

Distance from Earth (in km.)	Orbital speed (in k.p.h.)
160	27,950
800	26,650
16,000	15,050
35,880	11,070
(At this distance and speed, a satellite seems to stand still over a fixed point on Earth. It is called synchronous orbit.)	
382,000	3,620
(This is the Moon's orbit.)	

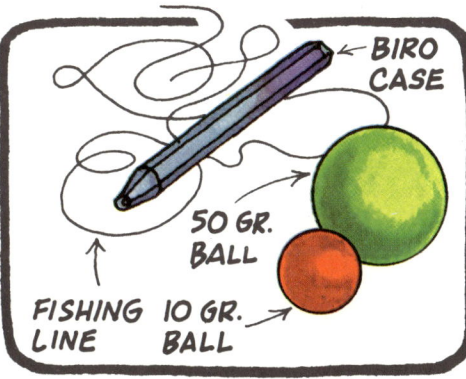

▲You can make a model satellite with some plasticine, a ballpoint pen case, some fishing-line or thread, and two paper-clips. Split the plasticine into two lumps, one five times heavier than the other.

▲Thread the line through the pen case. Tie paper-clips to each end, and push one clip into each ball of plasticine. Holding the pen case upright with the small ball on top, swing the case fast in a circle.

▲The small ball will swing out, pulling the big ball up. The outward pull of the small ball is its centrifugal force. For a satellite, this must exactly balance gravity if it is to stay in orbit.

▲Hold the case steady. As the small ball slows down, its centrifugal force lessens and it moves back towards the case—like a used-up satellite spiralling back to Earth out of orbit.

DANGERS OF SPACE

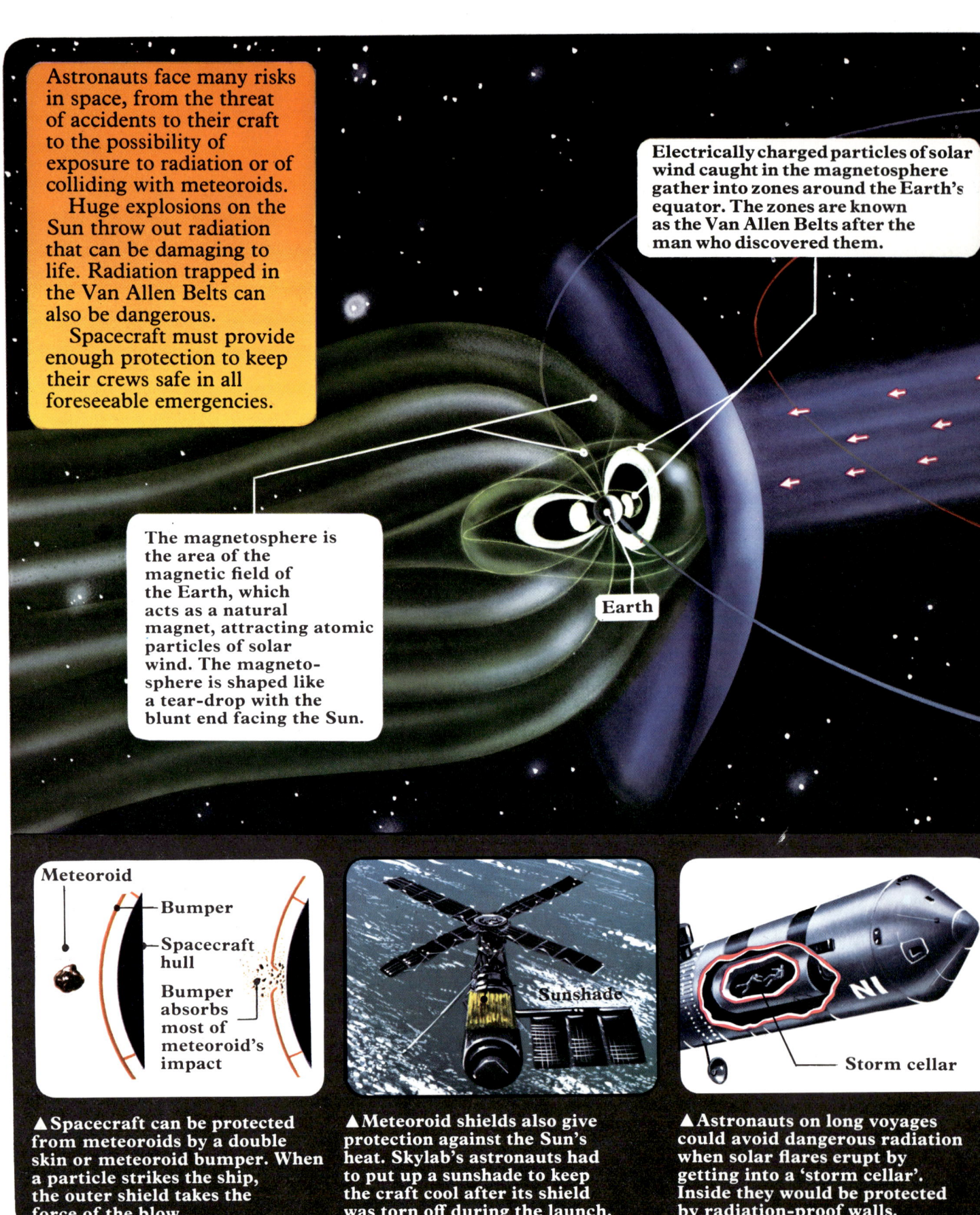

Astronauts face many risks in space, from the threat of accidents to their craft to the possibility of exposure to radiation or of colliding with meteoroids.

Huge explosions on the Sun throw out radiation that can be damaging to life. Radiation trapped in the Van Allen Belts can also be dangerous.

Spacecraft must provide enough protection to keep their crews safe in all foreseeable emergencies.

Electrically charged particles of solar wind caught in the magnetosphere gather into zones around the Earth's equator. The zones are known as the Van Allen Belts after the man who discovered them.

The magnetosphere is the area of the magnetic field of the Earth, which acts as a natural magnet, attracting atomic particles of solar wind. The magnetosphere is shaped like a tear-drop with the blunt end facing the Sun.

Earth

Meteoroid
Bumper
Spacecraft hull
Bumper absorbs most of meteoroid's impact

Sunshade

NI
Storm cellar

▲Spacecraft can be protected from meteoroids by a double skin or meteoroid bumper. When a particle strikes the ship, the outer shield takes the force of the blow.

▲Meteoroid shields also give protection against the Sun's heat. Skylab's astronauts had to put up a sunshade to keep the craft cool after its shield was torn off during the launch.

▲Astronauts on long voyages could avoid dangerous radiation when solar flares erupt by getting into a 'storm cellar'. Inside they would be protected by radiation-proof walls.

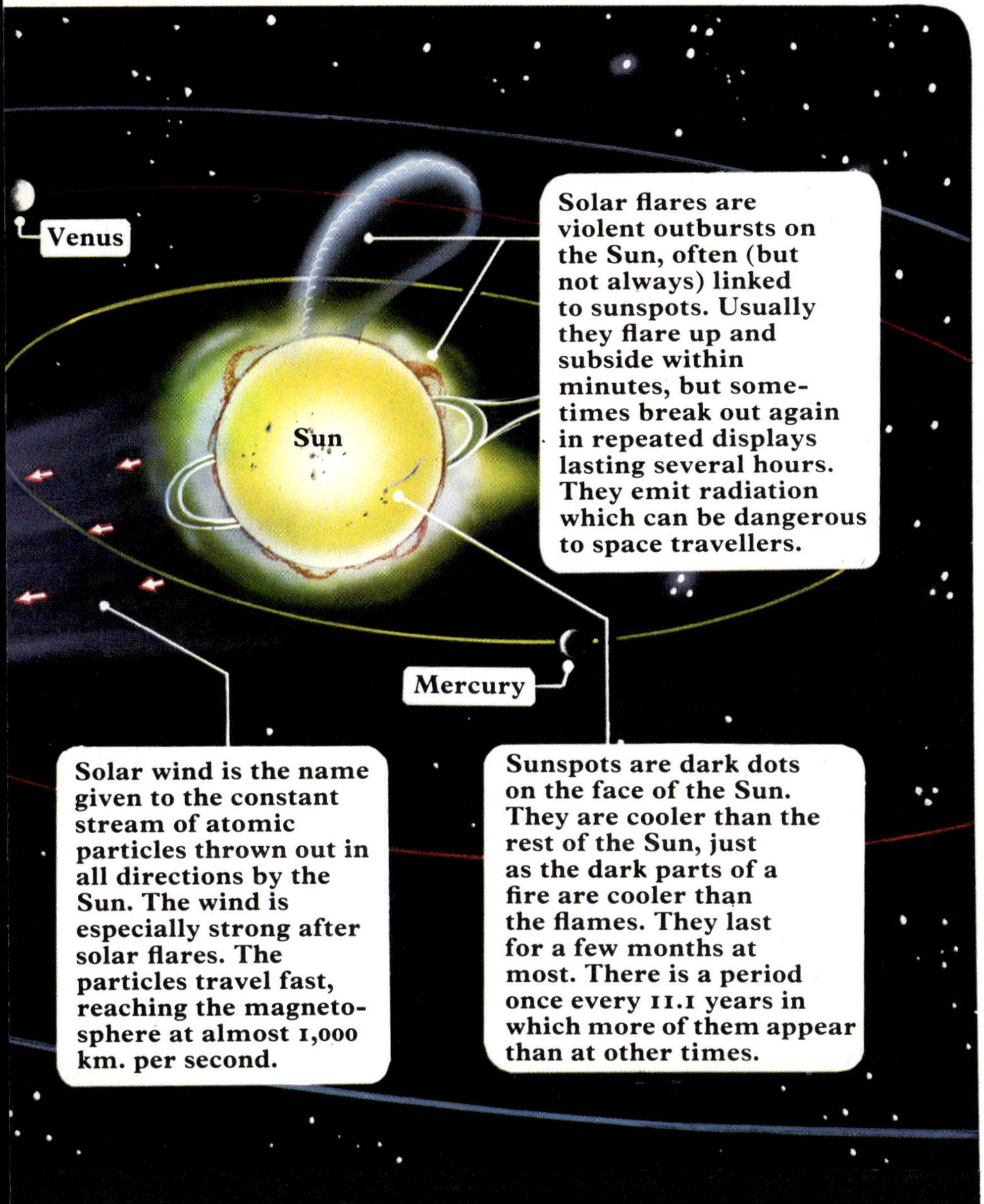

Solar flares are violent outbursts on the Sun, often (but not always) linked to sunspots. Usually they flare up and subside within minutes, but sometimes break out again in repeated displays lasting several hours. They emit radiation which can be dangerous to space travellers.

Venus

Sun

Mercury

Solar wind is the name given to the constant stream of atomic particles thrown out in all directions by the Sun. The wind is especially strong after solar flares. The particles travel fast, reaching the magnetosphere at almost 1,000 km. per second.

Sunspots are dark dots on the face of the Sun. They are cooler than the rest of the Sun, just as the dark parts of a fire are cooler than the flames. They last for a few months at most. There is a period once every 11.1 years in which more of them appear than at other times.

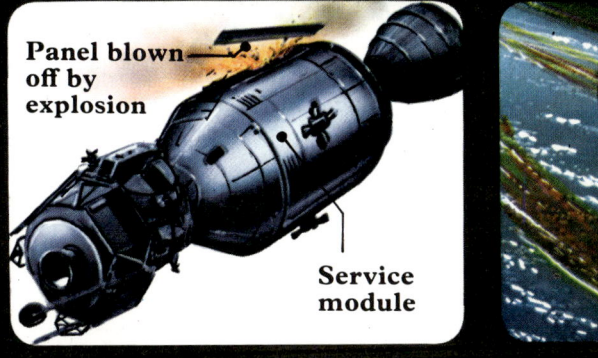

Panel blown off by explosion

Service module

▲An explosion partly crippled Apollo 13 when she was 330,000 km. from Earth. Mission control worked out a return path and sent instructions by radio. The astronauts got back safely.

▲Spacecraft unprotected from air friction would burn up as they re-entered the Earth's atmosphere at speeds of up to 40,000 k.p.h. Thick heatshields are needed to prevent this.

Keeping cool in space

SHADOW TEMPERATURE -160°C.

TEMPERATURE IN THE SUN 83°C.

▲It is lethally hot in space in the glare of the Sun's rays, and unbearably cold in the shadows. To prevent astronauts from freezing or burning, spacecraft must be protected by insulating materials. Polystyrene is one that is used.

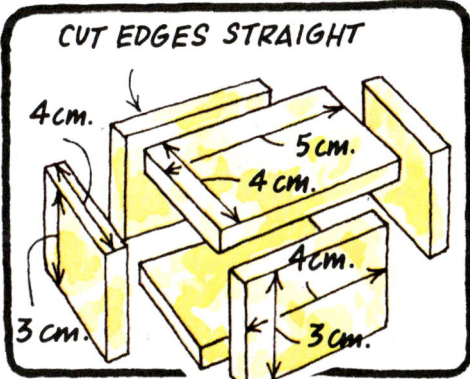

CUT EDGES STRAIGHT

4cm. 5cm. 4cm. 4cm. 3cm. 3cm.

▲Test polystyrene for yourself like this. Make a box as shown above from a ceiling-tile (you can buy these at do-it-yourself shops). Glue the base and sides together with polystyrene cement. You will also need two ice-cubes.

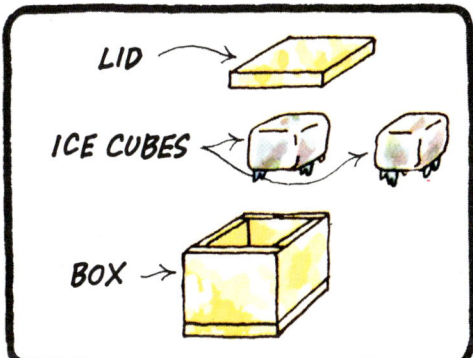

LID

ICE CUBES

BOX

▲Put one cube in the box and put the lid on. Leave the other in the open. Now wait for them to melt. You will find that the insulated cube will melt much the more slowly, as it is shielded by the polystyrene from outside heat.

WHAT ASTRONAUTS WEAR

Man cannot step into airless space without the protection of a spacesuit. It wraps him in his own protective atmosphere, gives him oxygen to breathe, and keeps his body under pressure. Without these he would die.

The Apollo moonsuit (right) held oxygen in a backpack that kept the suit's pressure at 0.27 kg./sq.cm. Though it looked cumbersome, the suit was flexible enough for the wearer to walk, jump and bend. Beneath it, the astronaut wore a cooling garment in which water circulated in plastic tubes.

▲Wiley Post, who in 1933 became the first man to fly solo around the world, was also a pioneer of pressure-suit development. His experience helped his sponsors, Lockheed Aircraft, to develop an experimental pressure-cabin plane.

▲The first moonsuit was designed in 1948 by Harry Ross of the British Interplanetary Society. It had a backpack oxygen supply, flexible joints and thick-soled boots. A silvered cape was draped behind it for temperature control.

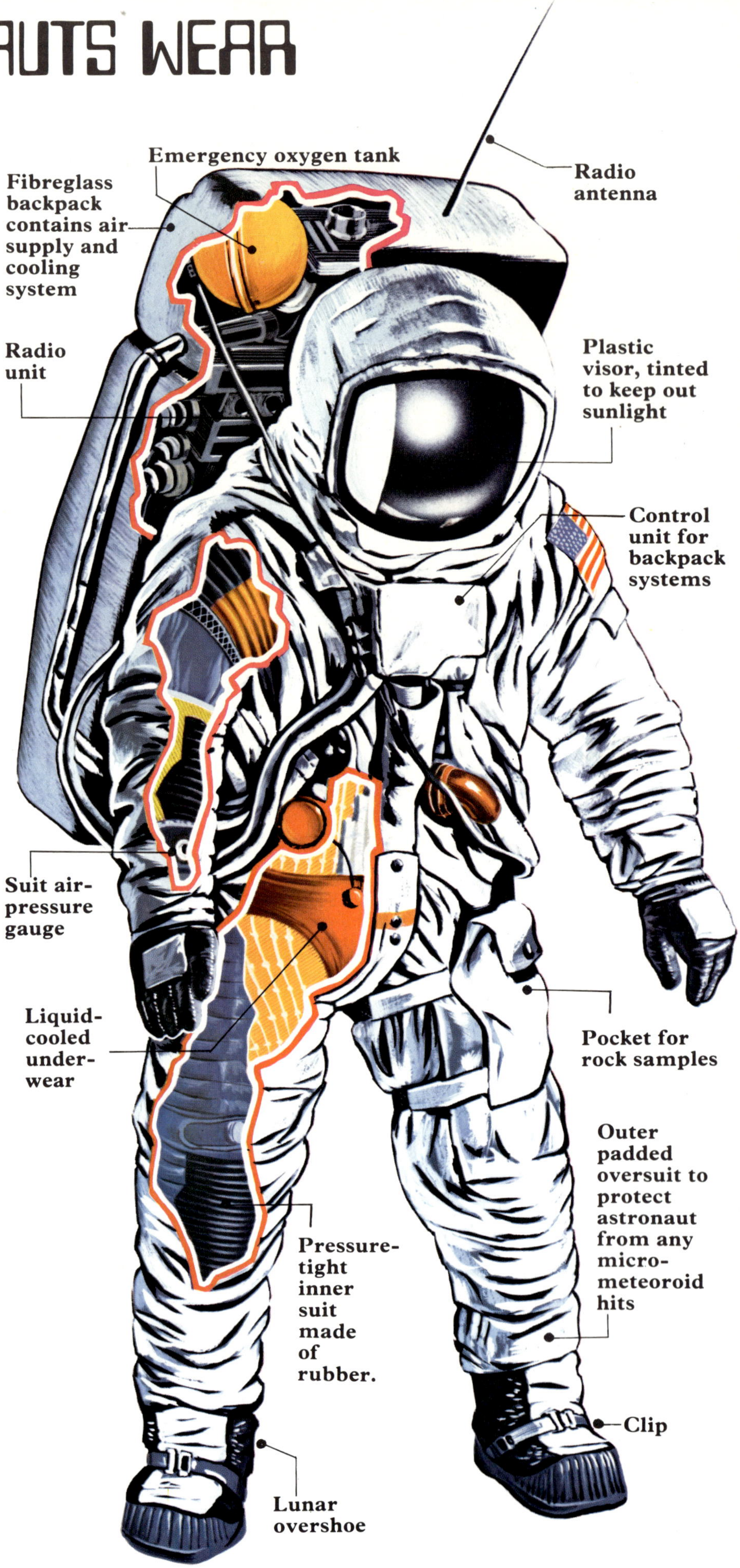

Emergency oxygen tank

Fibreglass backpack contains air supply and cooling system

Radio antenna

Radio unit

Plastic visor, tinted to keep out sunlight

Control unit for backpack systems

Suit air-pressure gauge

Liquid-cooled underwear

Pocket for rock samples

Outer padded oversuit to protect astronaut from any micro-meteoroid hits

Pressure-tight inner suit made of rubber.

Clip

Lunar overshoe

What next — heraldry in space?

In the future, many men and women will work together in space. There will be engineers, assemblers, electricians, pilots, payload specialists and scientists. If they all wear similar spacesuits how will they tell each other apart?

On the Moon the Apollo 17 astronaut Eugene Cernan (right) wore a coloured armband for easy recognition on television screens. The astronauts also had their names on their suits.

Future astronauts may wear symbols and numbers showing who they are and what they do. Like knights of old they may work out their own brand of heraldry. Here are a few ideas. You can invent some more.

Symbols for the job . . .

Pilot

Hand holding control    Spaceship    Fireball

Communications

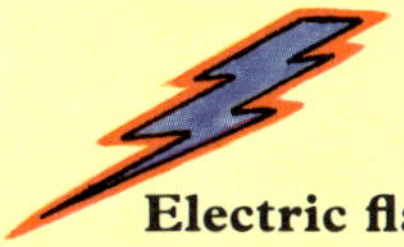

Electric flash    Radio mast    TV screen

Navigator

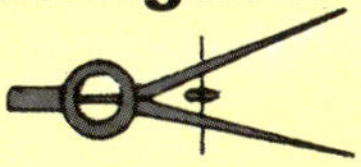

Compasses    Earth/Moon globes 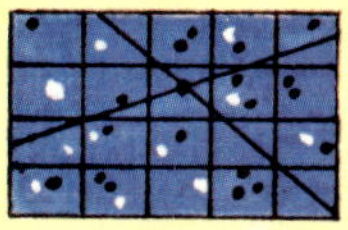   Star chart

Astronomer

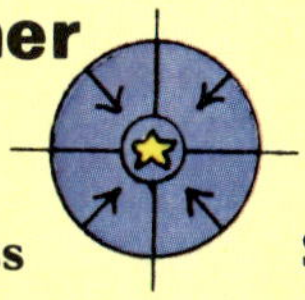

Sightglass    Star and planet    Telescope

Technician

Spanner    Meter gauge    Screwdriver

Moonminer

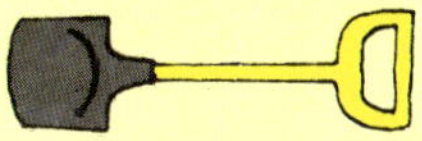

Spade 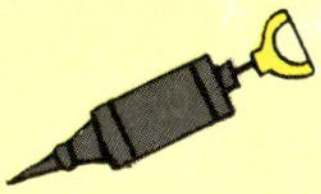   Rock drill    Explosion

. . . and how they might look on the backpack and helmet

Moonmine blasting engineer
3 0

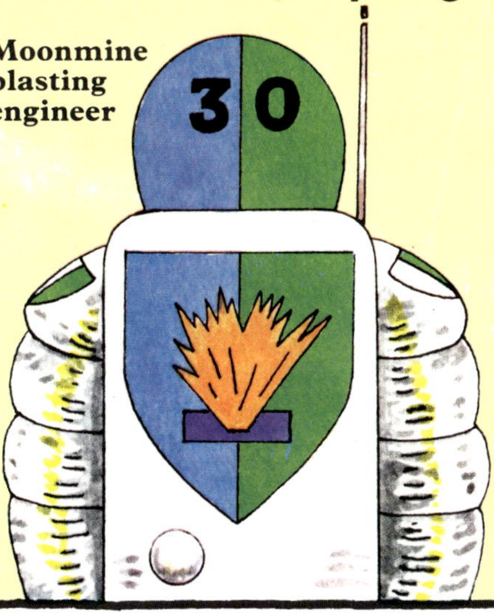

Technician Grade 1
1

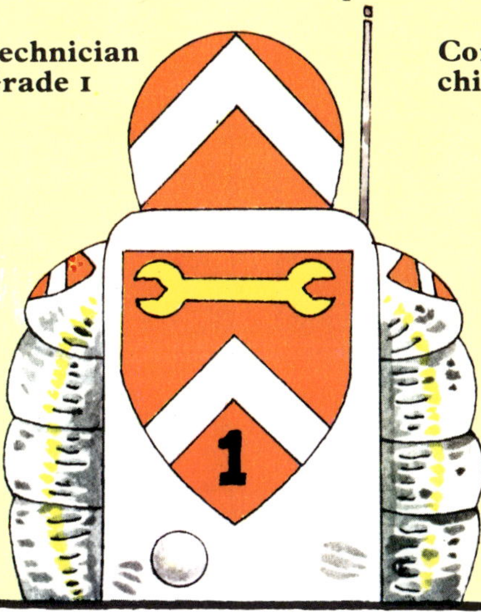

Communications chief
21

47

SERVANTS IN THE SKY

MAROTS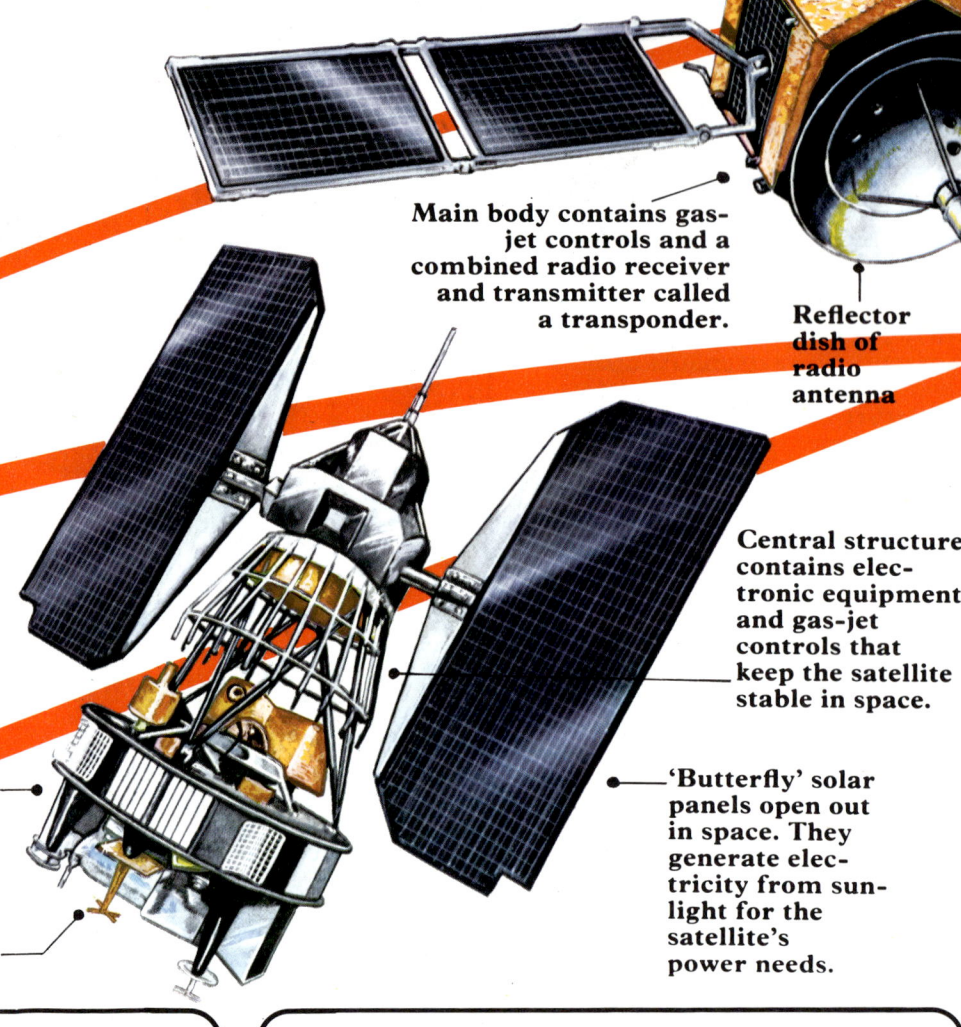

Every day artificial satellites are helping to improve living conditions on Earth. They help us keep watch on weather changes and storms. They enable men to locate deposits of minerals, oil and natural gas.

They form a global web of communications. Because of them the number of international telephone calls grew from three million in 1965 to more than 50 million in 1974. They also relay television programmes around the world.

LANDSAT

Main body contains gas-jet controls and a combined radio receiver and transmitter called a transponder.

Reflector dish of radio antenna

Central structure contains electronic equipment and gas-jet controls that keep the satellite stable in space.

Sensory ring holds cameras and other instruments for collecting data about the Earth's surface.

'Butterfly' solar panels open out in space. They generate electricity from sunlight for the satellite's power needs.

Landsat's systems can map more than 161 million sq. km. a week.

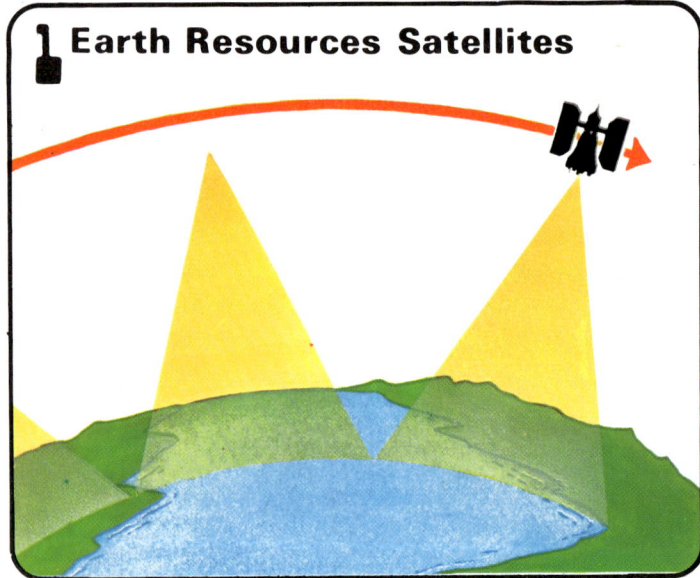

1 Earth Resources Satellites

2 Sea satellites

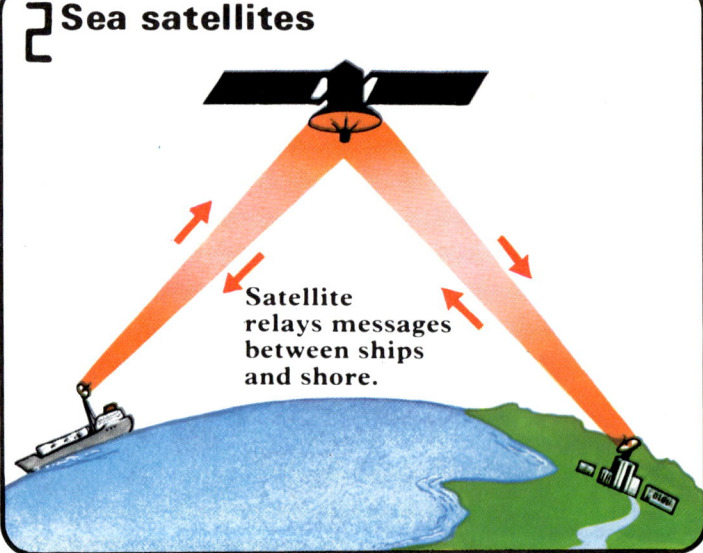

Satellite relays messages between ships and shore.

▲ Besides locating natural resources, these satellites keep track of pollution and give warning of drought, floods and forest fires. Photographs they take have many uses—for instance, they can show whether food crops are diseased or healthy. Blighted crops show up blue-black, healthy crops pink or red.

▲ MAROTS is short for Maritime Orbital Test Satellite. It is used to link ships to shore stations, and can also alert rescue services. Other sea satellites serve as 'radio stars' that allow ships to navigate accurately in all weathers, and help to control the movement of jet aircraft on long-distance flights.

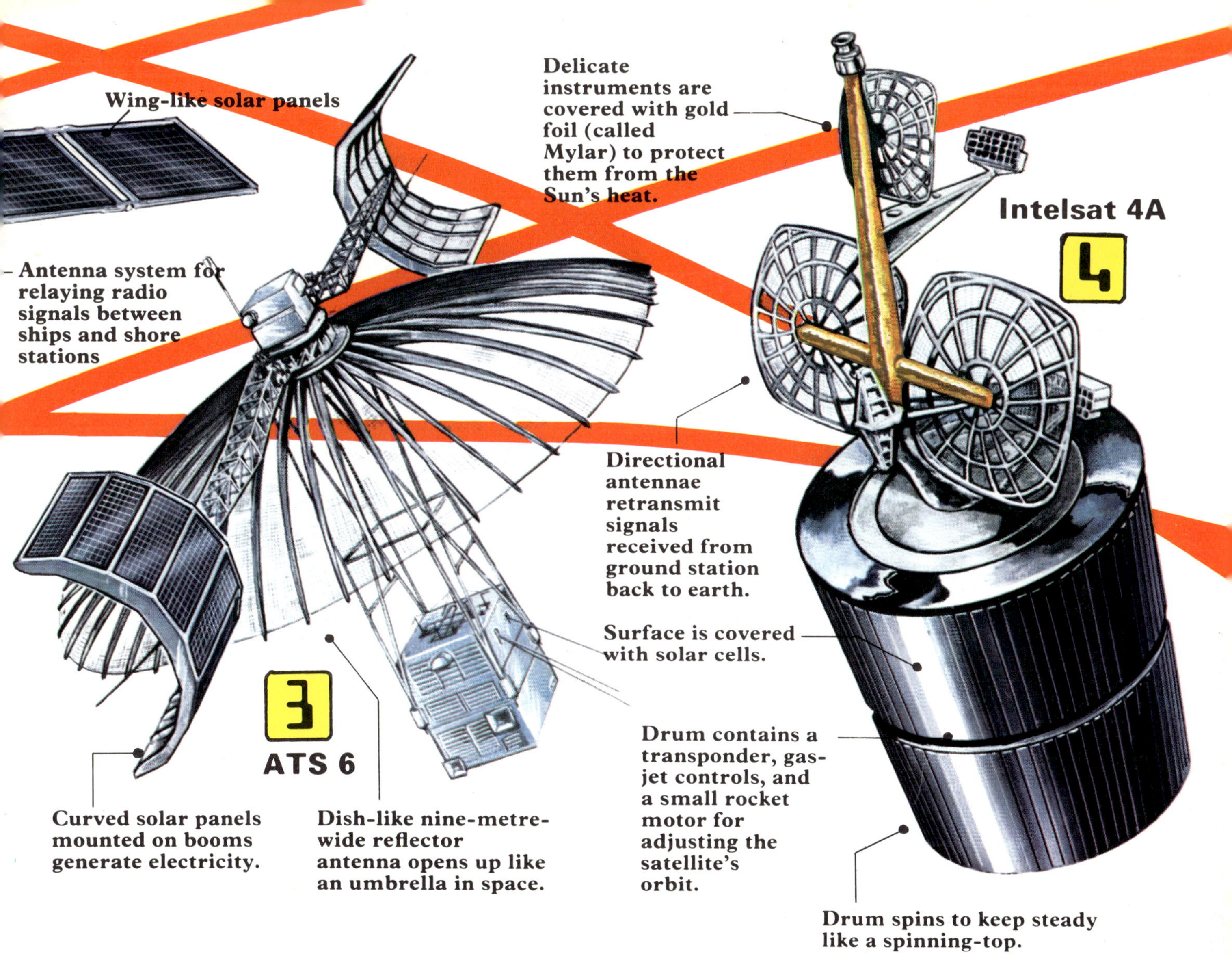

Wing-like solar panels

Delicate instruments are covered with gold foil (called Mylar) to protect them from the Sun's heat.

Intelsat 4A

4

Antenna system for relaying radio signals between ships and shore stations

Directional antennae retransmit signals received from ground station back to earth.

Surface is covered with solar cells.

3

ATS 6

Curved solar panels mounted on booms generate electricity.

Dish-like nine-metre-wide reflector antenna opens up like an umbrella in space.

Drum contains a transponder, gas-jet controls, and a small rocket motor for adjusting the satellite's orbit.

Drum spins to keep steady like a spinning-top.

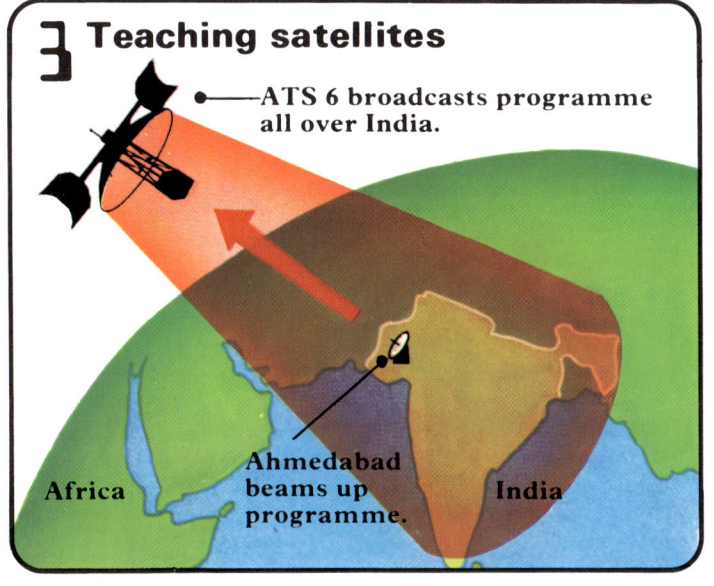

3 Teaching satellites

ATS 6 broadcasts programme all over India.

Africa

Ahmedabad beams up programme.

India

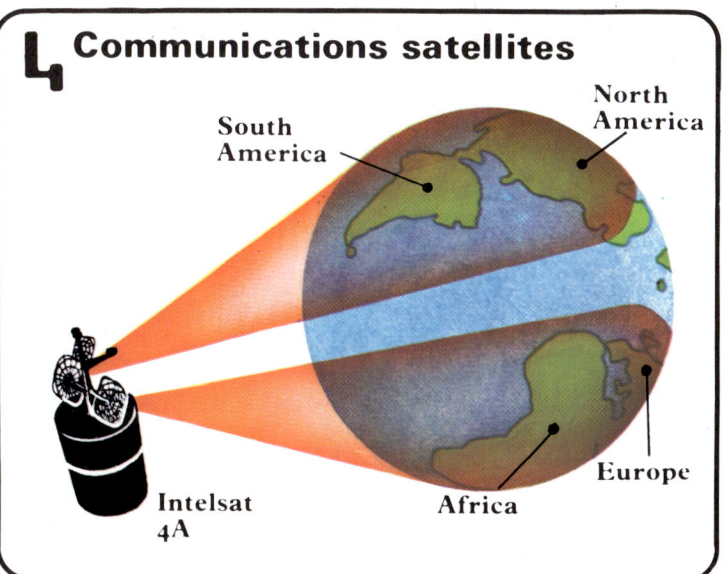

4 Communications satellites

North America

South America

Europe

Africa

Intelsat 4A

▲ Satellites can be used to educate people in out-of-the-way places.
A powerful satellite stationed 35,880 km. above East Africa has been used to broadcast educational programmes beamed up from a transmitter in Ahmedabad to 5,000 towns and villages in India. Each of them had its own dish aerial and TV set.

▲ Many parts of the world are now linked by telephone, telegraph and television by satellites that keep pace with the Earth's rotation 35,880 km. above the Atlantic, Pacific and Indian Oceans. One Intelsat 4A satellite can relay 12 colour television programmes or over 6,000 telephone calls.

THE SPACE SHUTTLE 1: HOW IT WORKS

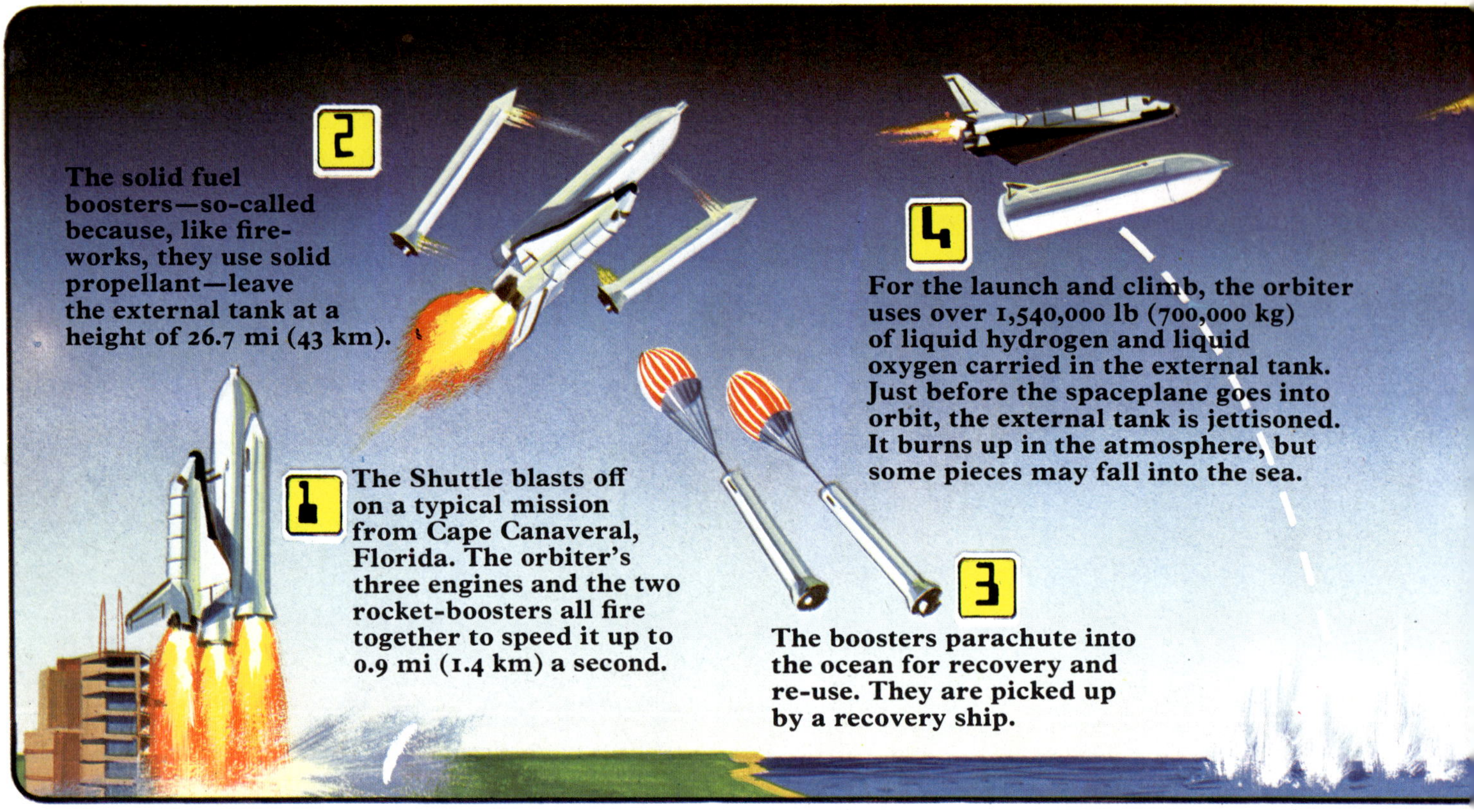

2 The solid fuel boosters—so-called because, like fire-works, they use solid propellant—leave the external tank at a height of 26.7 mi (43 km).

1 The Shuttle blasts off on a typical mission from Cape Canaveral, Florida. The orbiter's three engines and the two rocket-boosters all fire together to speed it up to 0.9 mi (1.4 km) a second.

4 For the launch and climb, the orbiter uses over 1,540,000 lb (700,000 kg) of liquid hydrogen and liquid oxygen carried in the external tank. Just before the spaceplane goes into orbit, the external tank is jettisoned. It burns up in the atmosphere, but some pieces may fall into the sea.

3 The boosters parachute into the ocean for recovery and re-use. They are picked up by a recovery ship.

The Space Shuttle is designed to cut the cost of space travel by making it more like normal aircraft flight. Unlike earlier launch rockets which fell to destruction, the major parts of the Shuttle—the orbiter, or spaceplane, and rocket boosters—can be recovered and re-used.

The crew consists of a pilot and co-pilot, and one or more mission specialists. When it carries the four-person European Spacelab (see p. 20), the orbiter becomes a miniature space station.

A300 Airbus

Space Shuttle

From the nose of the external tank to the tip of the orbiter's tail, the Shuttle is roughly the same length as an A300 jetliner.

1 Build your own Space Shuttle glider

▲ This model is a 1:200 scale replica of the aerospace plane of the 1980s. Trace it off the plan on p. 19. You can make it from stiff paper, using adhesive tape to stick the parts together, or from balsa wood, using balsa cement.

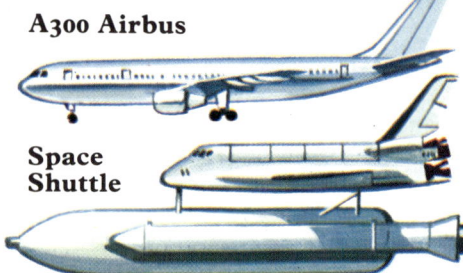

ASSEMBLE THE MODEL LIKE THIS

TAPE BOTH SIDES, ABOVE AND BELOW THE WING

TAPE THESE INTO PLACE

2

▲ Once you have fitted the four parts into place, weight the model with two or three paper-clips. Slide them onto the nose just over the wings.

3

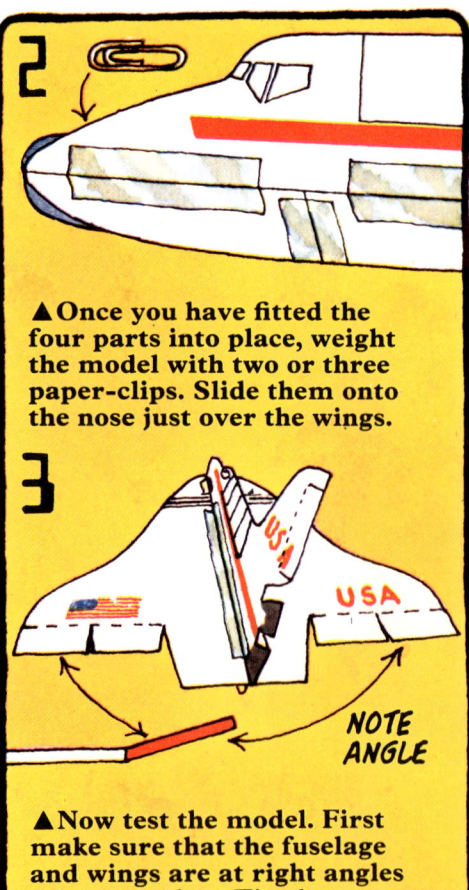

NOTE ANGLE

▲ Now test the model. First make sure that the fuselage and wings are at right angles to one another. Tip the outer elevons to the angle shown above.

5 The spaceplane arrives in orbit under thrust from small maneuver engines. It can orbit the Earth for between 7 and 30 days at a height of 115 mi (185 km) and a speed of 17,586 mph (28,300 kph).

Shuttle facts and figures

Length at launch: 185.1 ft (56.1 m)

Length of orbiter: 112.5 ft (34.1 m)

Orbiter's wing-span: 78.5 ft (23.8 m)

Maximum payload: 64,865 lb (29,484 kg)

Lift-off weight: 4,378,000 lb (1,990,000 kg)

6 The cargo bay doors open to release the orbiter's satellite payload and an attached propulsion unit. The orbiter can also carry the European Spacelab, which remains in the bay.

It lands on a 5,027 yd (4,570 m) runway at 215 mph (346 kph). After being serviced, it can be ready for another flight, with a new payload, within two weeks.

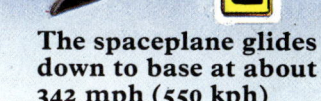

7 The orbiter fires retro rockets to brake itself out of orbit. Parts of the spaceplane glow red-hot from air friction. It is protected by strong surface insulation.

8 The spaceplane glides down to base at about 342 mph (550 kph).

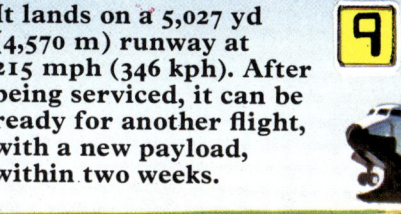

9

Scale plans for the Rockwell International Space Shuttle orbiter

Scale 1:200

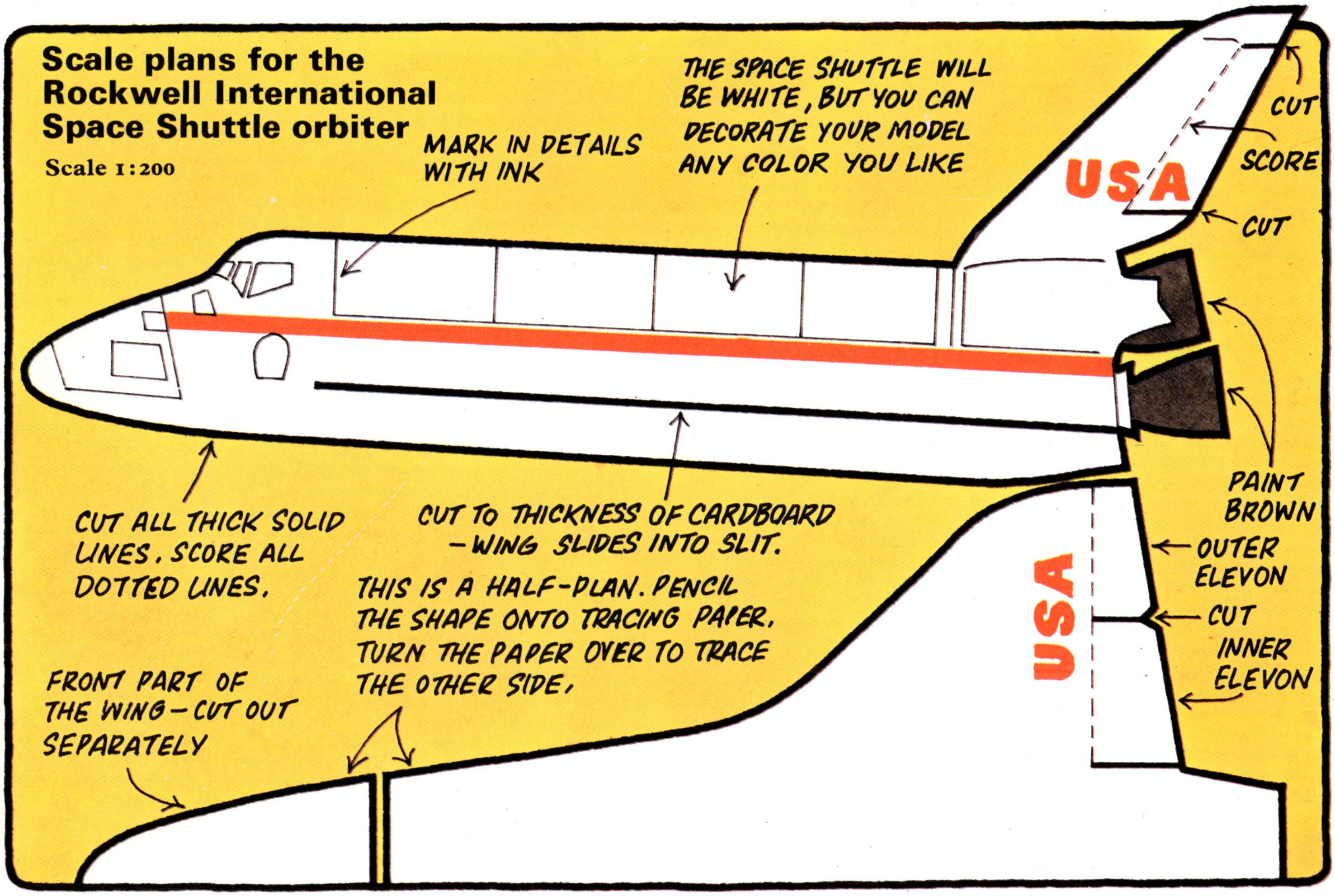

MARK IN DETAILS WITH INK

THE SPACE SHUTTLE WILL BE WHITE, BUT YOU CAN DECORATE YOUR MODEL ANY COLOR YOU LIKE

USA

CUT

SCORE

CUT

PAINT BROWN

OUTER ELEVON

CUT INNER ELEVON

USA

CUT ALL THICK SOLID LINES, SCORE ALL DOTTED LINES.

CUT TO THICKNESS OF CARDBOARD — WING SLIDES INTO SLIT.

THIS IS A HALF-PLAN. PENCIL THE SHAPE ONTO TRACING PAPER, TURN THE PAPER OVER TO TRACE THE OTHER SIDE.

FRONT PART OF THE WING — CUT OUT SEPARATELY

The Space Shuttle will have many commercial, scientific and military uses. It will deliver, service and retrieve satellites of all kinds, and will be able to handle several different jobs on a single mission.

Though most of its payloads will be unmanned, its cargo bay will be big enough to carry a fully equipped manned laboratory. The world's leading scientists will be able to go into orbit in the Spacelab now being developed by ten European countries.

Unlike earlier Russian and American space stations that were abandoned in space, the Spacelab will return to Earth each time it is used.

Space rescue

Ball with man inside

▲ Astronauts who have to abandon a crippled orbiter could be carried to safety in NASA's 85-cm. 'Personal Rescue Enclosure'.

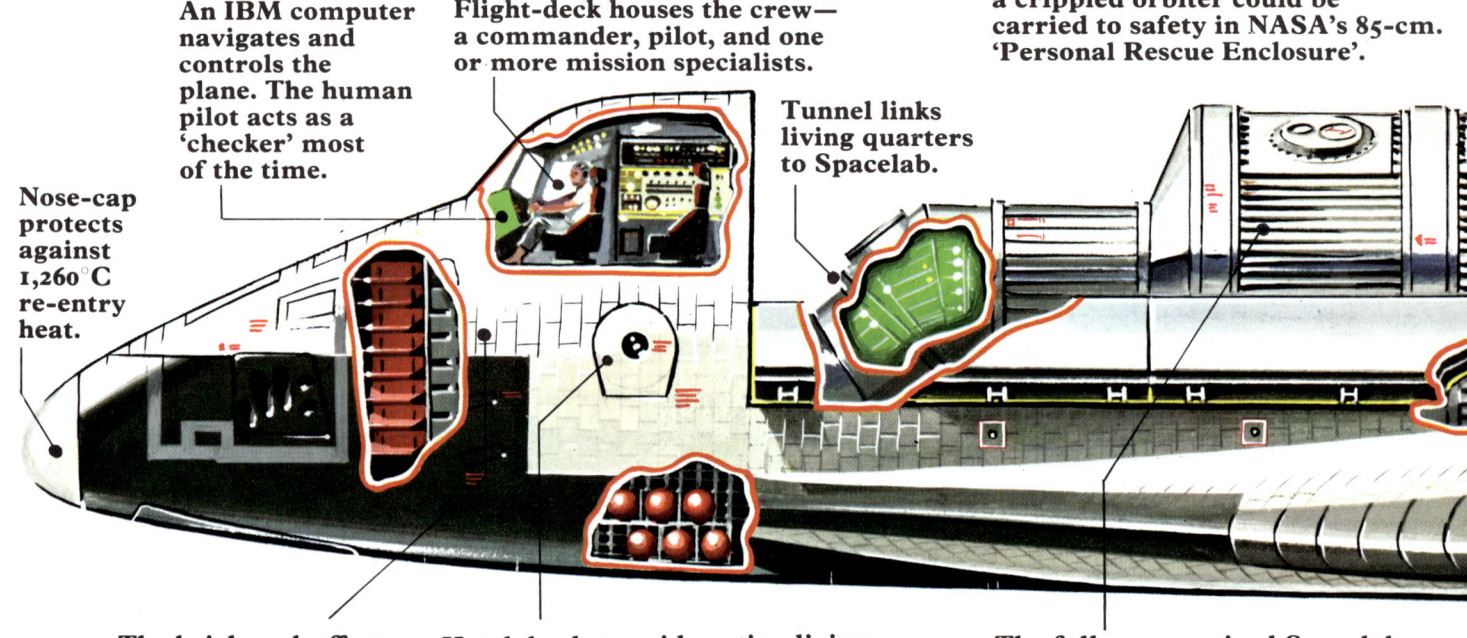

An IBM computer navigates and controls the plane. The human pilot acts as a 'checker' most of the time.

Flight-deck houses the crew— a commander, pilot, and one or more mission specialists.

Tunnel links living quarters to Spacelab.

Nose-cap protects against 1,260°C re-entry heat.

The brickwork effect is caused by heat insulation tiles fixed to the outside of the orbiter.

Hatch leads to mid-section living quarters and to flight-deck. The mid-section has four sleep bays (the crew take turns to sleep), toilet and washing spaces, and galleys with food and water.

The fully-pressurized Spacelab is 4.17 m. in diameter—big enough for four people to work in shirt-sleeve comfort. It allows scientists to work under weightless conditions in orbit.

Flight-testing your Shuttle glider

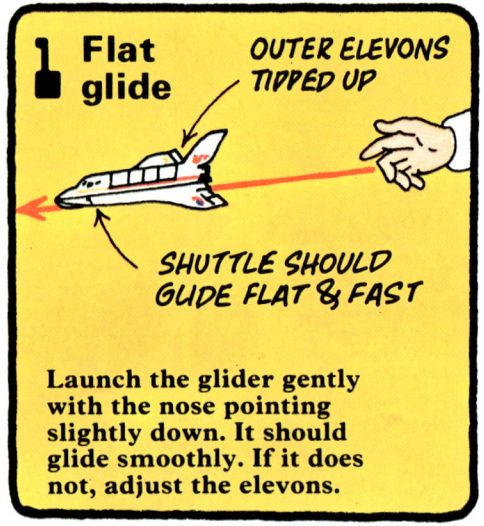

1 Flat glide

OUTER ELEVONS TIPPED UP

SHUTTLE SHOULD GLIDE FLAT & FAST

Launch the glider gently with the nose pointing slightly down. It should glide smoothly. If it does not, adjust the elevons.

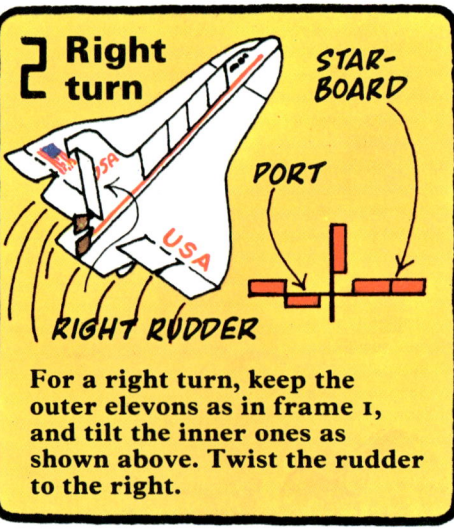

2 Right turn

STAR-BOARD

PORT

RIGHT RUDDER

For a right turn, keep the outer elevons as in frame 1, and tilt the inner ones as shown above. Twist the rudder to the right.

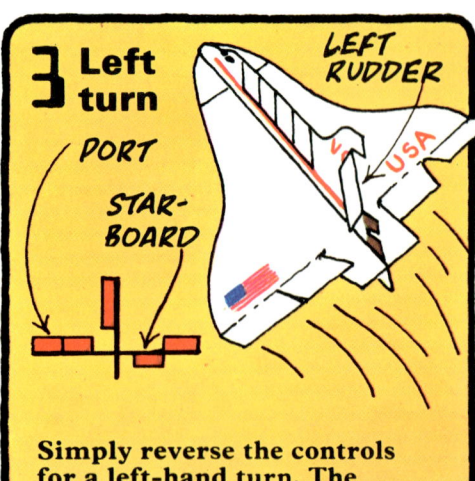

3 Left turn

LEFT RUDDER

PORT

STAR-BOARD

Simply reverse the controls for a left-hand turn. The rudder should point to the left, and the starboard inner elevon should be down.

1980'S

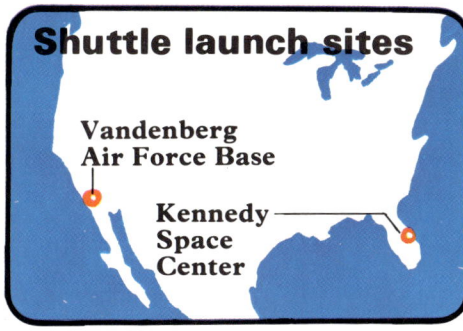

Shuttle launch sites

Vandenberg
Air Force Base

Kennedy
Space
Center

▲Kennedy Space Center will be used for launchings into equatorial orbit. Vandenberg will launch Shuttles going into polar orbit.

This microwave radar scanner, used for studying the ionosphere (see p.39), is typical of the scientific payloads the orbiter will carry.

Two orbital manoeuvring engines—one on each side of the tail—both give 2,722 kg. maximum thrust. They are used to move the space-plane into, during, and out of orbit.

Pallet on which scientific instruments are mounted.

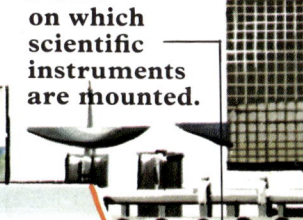

The wings' leading (front) edges are designed to stand temperatures of up to 1,570°C during re-entry into Earth's atmosphere.

Main undercarriage retracted into bay in the wing

The three main rocket engines each give 213,190 kg. maximum thrust. They burn for eight minutes after the launch, and can be used 55 times before being overhauled.

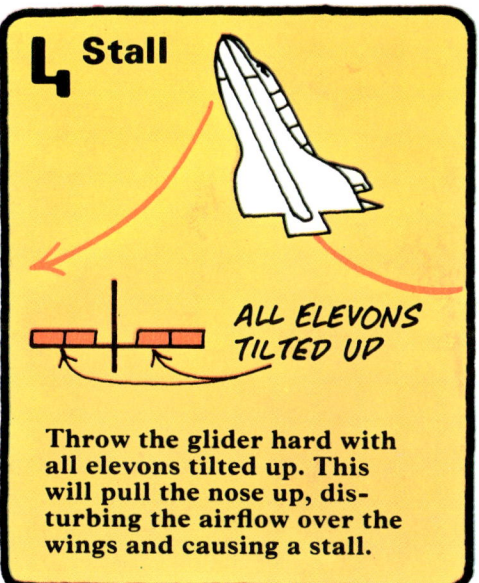

4 Stall

ALL ELEVONS TILTED UP

Throw the glider hard with all elevons tilted up. This will pull the nose up, dis-turbing the airflow over the wings and causing a stall.

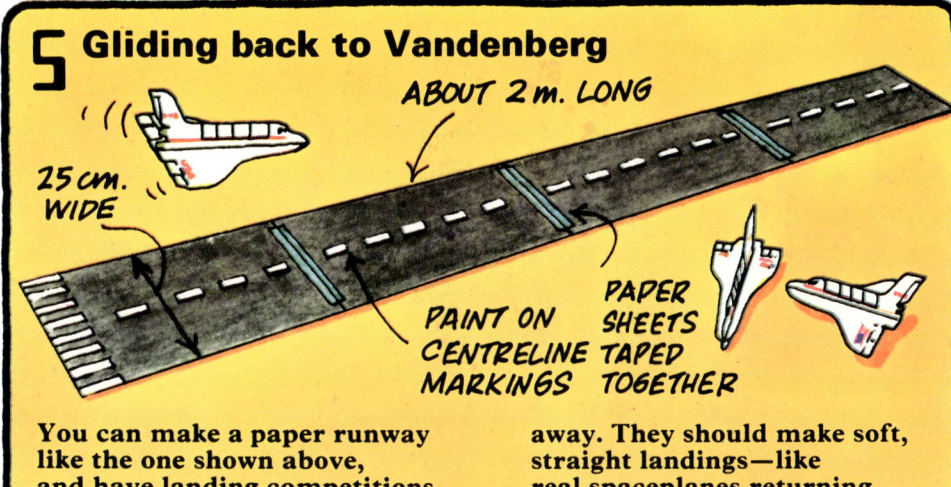

5 Gliding back to Vandenberg

ABOUT 2 m. LONG

25 cm. WIDE

PAINT ON CENTRELINE MARKINGS

PAPER SHEETS TAPED TOGETHER

You can make a paper runway like the one shown above, and have landing competitions with your friends. Launch the gliders from about 4 m. away. They should make soft, straight landings—like real spaceplanes returning to Vandenberg Air Force Base from missions in polar orbit.

INTO THE DEPTHS OF SPACE

Spacemen may not go beyond the Moon this century, but robot craft are increasing our knowledge of other planets by leaps and bounds. Not only are they cheaper to build than manned ships; they can also be abandoned if they break down.

We can fly to the Moon in three days, but reaching the planets is much more difficult. Interplanetary spacecraft must swing right round the Sun. They can only be launched when the planets themselves are in the right positions in their orbits. Journeys of this sort last for months or even years.

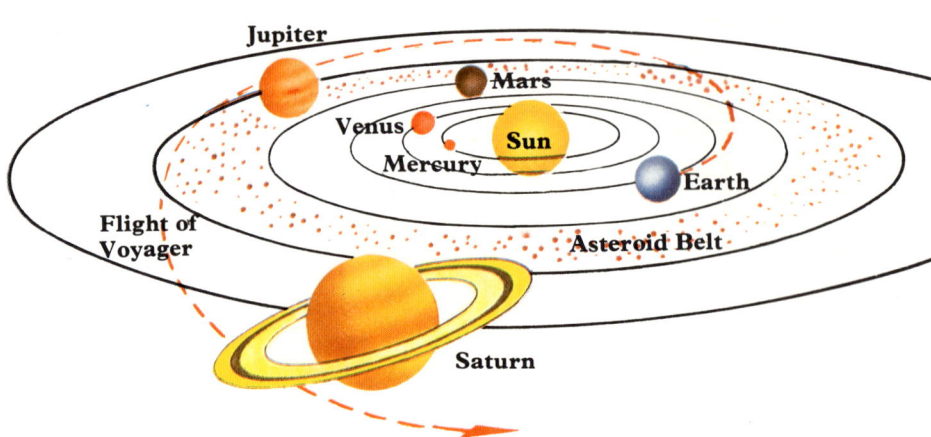

▲ All the planets shown above have been visited by space probes. America's Mariner 2 was the first craft to fly past Venus, in 1962. Mariner 9 looked at Mars from orbit, and Mariner 10 passed Mercury on its way from Venus in 1974. Voyagers 1 and 2 passed Jupiter in 1979 before flying on to the ringed planet Saturn. Voyager 2 is now on its way to Uranus, which it will reach in 1986, and Neptune in 1989. Both Voyagers will eventually leave the solar system, like Pioneers 10 and 11 before them.

▲ The photographs that Mariner 10 took of Mercury show a Moon-like world of craters, mountains and valleys. The planet has a diameter of 4,828 km. and spins very slowly. It is baked by the Sun by day and is freezing cold at night.

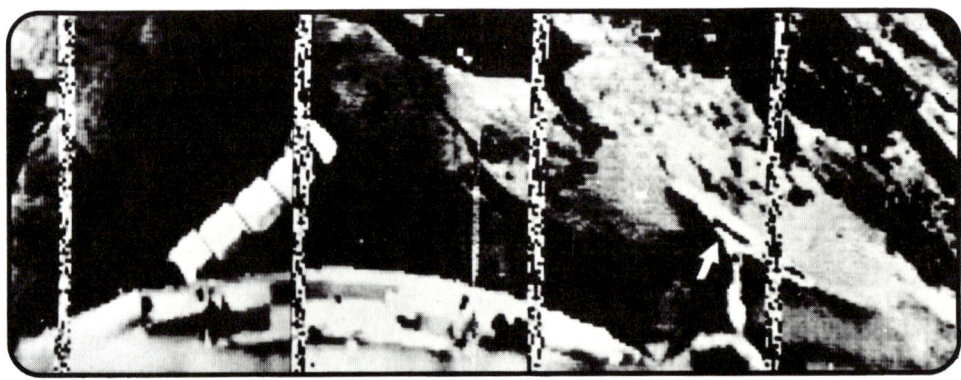

▲ Before Russia's Venera 9 and 10 swung into orbit around Venus in 1975, they sent landing capsules through its thick carbon dioxide atmosphere. Each one sent a panoramic picture by television to Earth. The first showed sharp-edged rocks, the second (above) a view showing rocks that looked like huge pancakes. The surface temperature was far above the melting point of lead, and the atmospheric pressure 90 to 100 times that of Earth.

▲ Saturn and its rings were photographed in 1980 by Voyager 1. The rings are made of swarms of ice-covered lumps of rock all orbiting the planet like tiny moons. Voyager found 1,800 kph winds among Saturn's clouds, and photographed a moon called Titan.

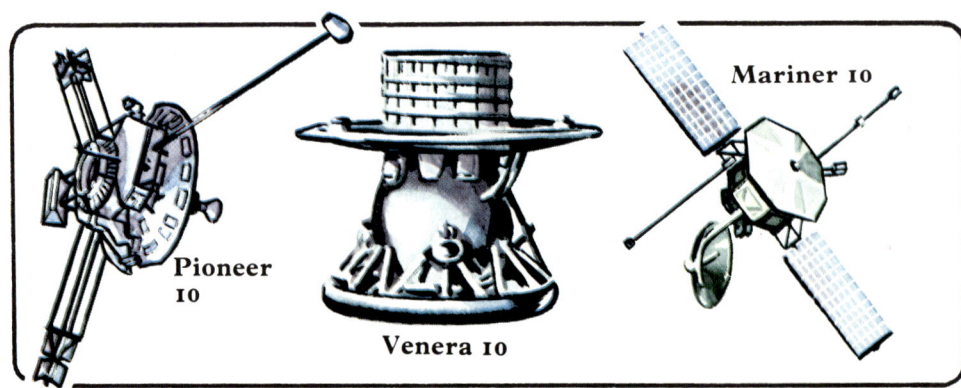

▲ Pioneer 10 flew within 81,006 mi (130,360 km) of Jupiter in December 1973 after an 18 month journey. It confirmed that the planet has powerful radiation belts, many thousand times stronger than the Earth's Van Allen Belts. Venera 9 and 10 were identical. They sent the first pictures from the fiercely hot surface of Venus.

Mariner 10 made a grand tour of the inner Solar System in 1973–74. On its way it photographed the Earth, Moon, Venus and Mercury.

The Viking mission to Mars

Moon

Earth

Deimos ·

Phobos ·

Mars

Scale
0   6,400   12,800 km.

◀▲ The diagram (left) shows the Earth and Moon to scale with Mars and its two tiny moons, Phobos and Deimos. When Mariner 9 went into orbit around Mars in late 1971, dust storms raged on its surface. When the dust cleared, the craft's cameras revealed mountains, canyons, and features looking like dried-up river beds. Nix Olympica (above), the highest known peak in the Solar System, rears 24 km. above a flat plain. Its lava covers an area more than 1,000 km. across.

Mars 1976: Viking's landing sequence

1 11 months after take-off from Earth, the orbiting mothercraft releases the lander. The entire landing sequence takes about 10 minutes.

2 After rocket braking, the vehicle plunges into the thin Martian atmosphere, protected by a heatshield called the aeroshell.

3 When the lander is about 5,790 m. above Mars, dropping at roughly 900 k.p.h., the aeroshell is discarded and a parachute opens.

4 The parachute is jettisoned about 1,400 m. up. Viking is then dropping at a speed of 233 k.p.h. Braking rockets allow the vehicle to soft-land at 9.6 k.p.h.

5 After touchdown, the lander's cameras send pictures to Earth by television. Sample and meteorological booms extend, instruments send the data to Earth receiving stations.

Dish antenna transmits information to Earth.

Mechanical scoop with retractable arm digs soil samples for the biological laboratory.

One of three landing rockets

Cameras

Computer-controlled laboratory tests the soil for signs of life.

DRIVING ON ANOTHER WORLD

When astronauts eventually land on Mars, they will want to explore farther afield than they can go on foot. They will need transport for the search for minerals and for ice or permafrost, which could be a source of water and oxygen.

The future Mars Roving Vehicle may well look like the one shown here, which is a development of the Moon Rovers already used successfully for lunar exploration. It is equipped with a pressurized cabin and a laboratory, and is electrically powered by rechargeable storage batteries.

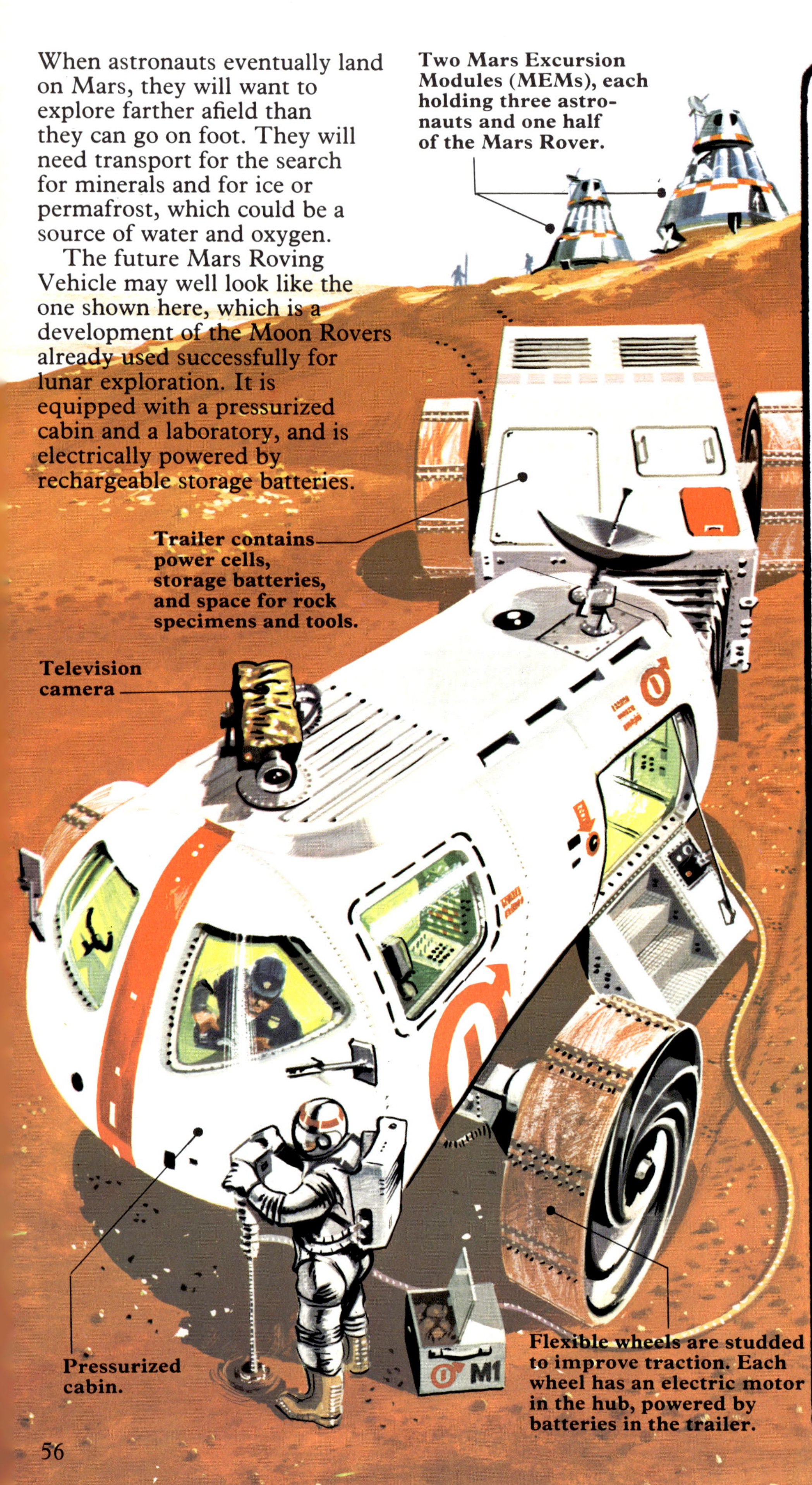

Two Mars Excursion Modules (MEMs), each holding three astronauts and one half of the Mars Rover.

Trailer contains power cells, storage batteries, and space for rock specimens and tools.

Television camera

Pressurized cabin.

Flexible wheels are studded to improve traction. Each wheel has an electric motor in the hub, powered by batteries in the trailer.

1 Build a Mars Roving Vehicle

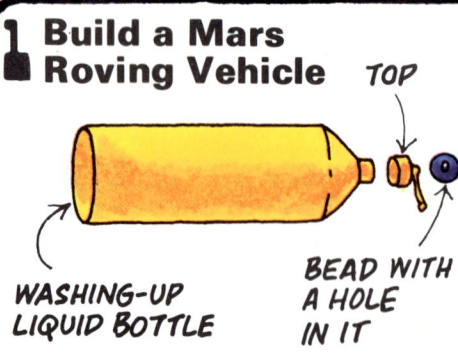

TOP

WASHING-UP LIQUID BOTTLE

BEAD WITH A HOLE IN IT

▲You will need two plastic bottles, some card, a little polystyrene foam, a matchstick, a rubber band, some thick wire, an empty ballpoint pen case, and four beads with holes through them.

5

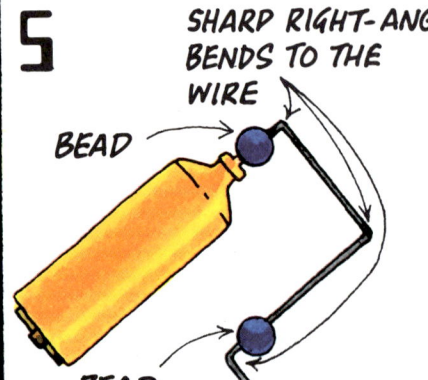

SHARP RIGHT-ANGLE BENDS TO THE WIRE

BEAD

BEAD

▲Holding the band taut, pass the bottle-top and then a bead along the wire. Fit the top back on the neck. Bend the wire to the shape shown above, and fit a second bead onto its trailing end.

9 Testing trials

FOAM STRIPS

▲Lift the body off again, and wind up the driving-wheel wire about 50 times. Replace the body, then test your MRV. If it skids, you can glue two foam strips around the driving-wheel.

Construction note

The sizes of plastic bottles vary, so we cannot give exact measurements. Your MRV can be any size you like, but the proportions of its parts should be as shown in frame 8 below.

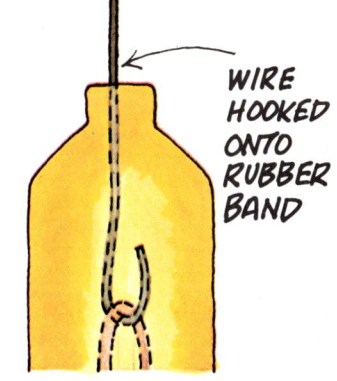

2

HOLE
CUT STOPPER OFF

▲Make a hole in the exact centre of the bottom of one bottle. Ease off the bottle-top. If there is a stopper, cut it off. Select a rubber band that is about two-thirds as long as the bottle.

3

PUSH RUBBER BAND INTO BOTTOM HOLE
RUBBER BAND
MATCH

▲Use the matchstick to push the rubber band through the hole. Once it is nearly all inside the bottle, loop its end around the matchstick. Tape the matchstick to the bottom of the bottle.

4

WIRE HOOKED ONTO RUBBER BAND

▲With a pair of pliers, cut a piece of wire about one-and-a-half times the length of the bottle, and bend one end of it into a hook. Pass the hook through the bottle's neck and catch the band's loose end.

6 Making the body

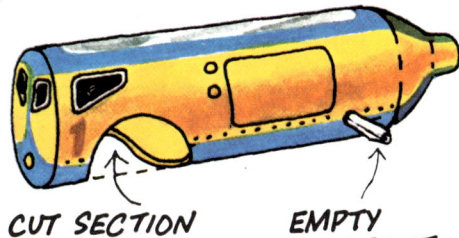

CUT SECTION AWAY FOR DRIVE WHEEL TO REST IN
EMPTY BALLPOINT PEN CASE

▲Make the body section from the other plastic bottle by cutting a circular section into which the first bottle can fit (see above). Cut holes for rear axle, and slide ballpoint pen case through them.

7 Rear wheels

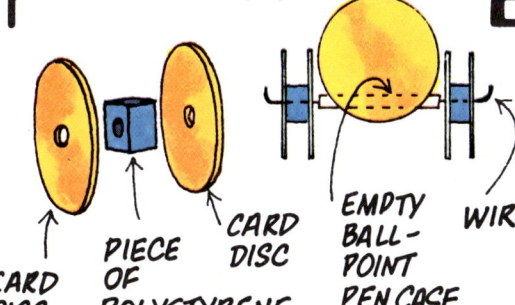

CARD DISC
PIECE OF POLYSTYRENE FOAM
CARD DISC
EMPTY BALL-POINT PEN CASE
WIRE

▲Make each wheel by glueing two card discs cut to the same size around a small square of poly-styrene foam. Pierce centre holes. Attach to the body with wire through the pen case, as shown.

8 The finished MRV

DRIVE WHEEL
BEAD
REAR WHEELS

▲Fit the driving-wheel into the body, with the trailing bead midway between the two sets of wheels. Decorate the top of the MRV with a model TV camera and radio aerial cut out of card.

10

Obstacle course for MRVs

GIANT CARD DISCS SLIPPED OVER WHEELS
CARPET
OLD SHIRT
FLOOR TILES
SAND

▲You will find that different ground surfaces will affect the performance of your MRV. The wide driving-wheel works well on smooth floors, for instance, but not on carpets. Test it over an obstacle course like the one shown above.

One way of making it go better over rough surfaces is to put giant card discs over all the wheels. Cut a hole of the same width as the bottle in the centre of two of the discs. Then slide them over the driving-wheel, one on each side of the body. Pierce a small hole in the centre of the other two, then attach them to the rear axle wire with pliers.

SPACE STATIONS

Factories in space sound like science fiction. But America's Skylab and the series of Soviet Salyut space stations have already taken electric furnaces into space.

This early 21st-century space station revolves to produce artificial gravity in the living quarters. In the control hub, which does not revolve, people are weightless.

The small diagram (right) shows how a 1980s station could be built from modules taken up by the Space Shuttle.

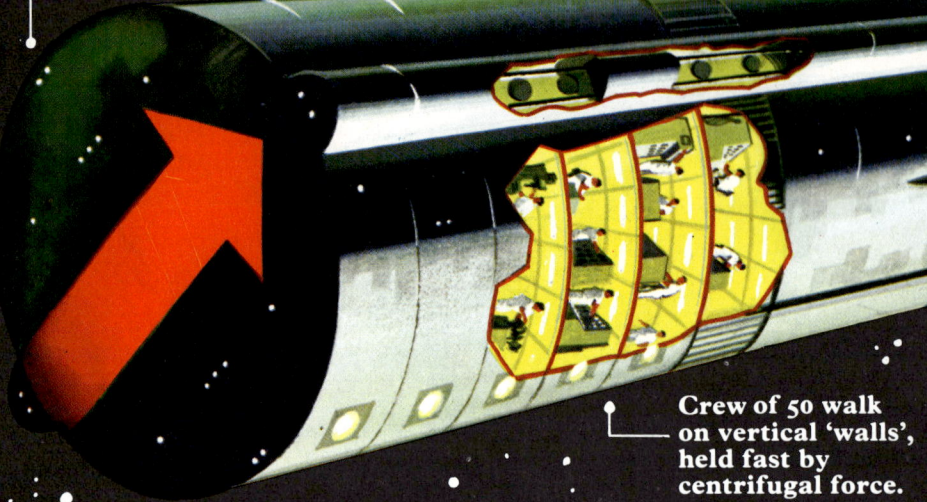

The station revolves 3.5 times a minute to simulate Earth gravity.

Space Shuttle orbiter carries supplies to the station from the Earth.

Lift between floors

Crew of 50 walk on vertical 'walls', held fast by centrifugal force.

Make your own rotating space station

1 LEAVE POWER WIRE BENT OVER

TAPE BALANCE FINS TO SIDE

The space station works in the same way as the Mars Rover (see p.56). You can re-use its driving-wheel if you want. Tape stiff card fins to the base to make the station stand securely.

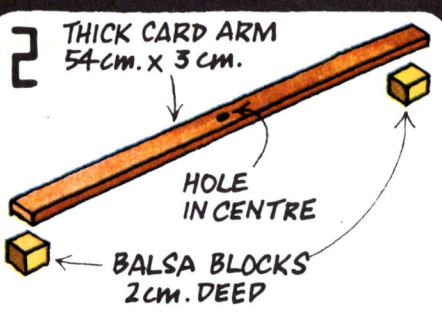

2 THICK CARD ARM 54cm. x 3cm.

HOLE IN CENTRE

BALSA BLOCKS 2cm. DEEP

Cut an arm out of thick card to the size shown. Punch a hole in its exact centre. Glue two balsa blocks, as shown, to the two ends. Make a small hole through the centre of each block.

3 TAPE WIRE FIRMLY

Unbend the power wire, and poke it through the hole in the centre of the arm. Bend it down and tape it firmly to the arm. Wind the arm up a few turns to test that it rotates freely.

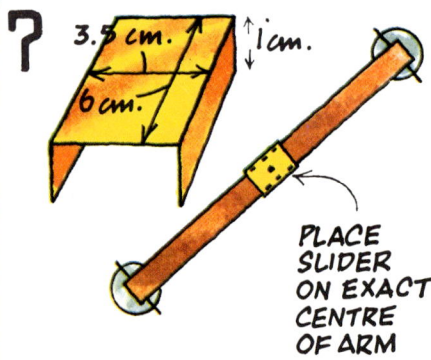

7 3.5 cm. 1cm. 6cm.

PLACE SLIDER ON EXACT CENTRE OF ARM

Cut a slider out of postcard to the dimensions shown. Bend the edges over. Wind the arm up, and put the slider on its exact centre. Let the arm spin. The slider will stay in place.

8 CENTRIFUGAL FORCE

Try it again with the slider a little off-centre. As the arm speeds up, it will move away from the centre hole. This outward momentum is called centrifugal force.

9

MODEL ASTRONAUT

Wind the arm up again. This time put a plastic model astronaut in one tub, balancing the other tub with plasticine. Let the arm speed up gently, as in frame 6.

Nuclear reactor in shielded pod supplies the station with electrical power.

Framework extending from the end of the station supports the power plant.

Part of the central core stays still in space, so that visiting spacecraft can dock easily and safely. Zero-gravity workshops are in this part of the station.

Docking arm

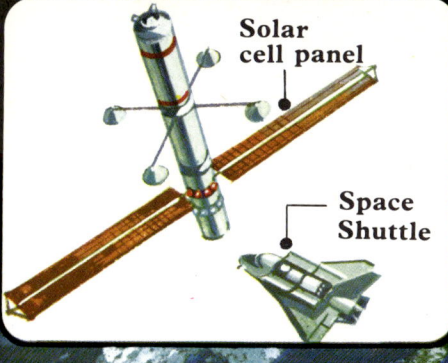

Solar cell panel

Space Shuttle

4

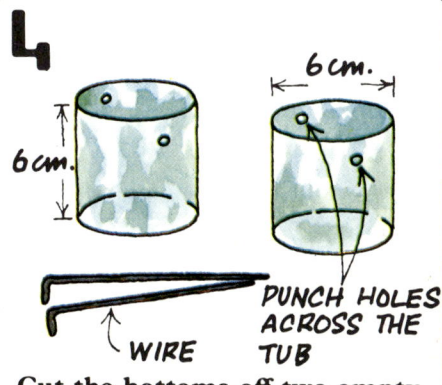

6 cm.

6 cm.

PUNCH HOLES ACROSS THE TUB

WIRE

Cut the bottoms off two empty plastic bottles—transparent ones if possible. Punch two small holes in them, as shown. Cut two lengths of wire, about 1½ times the width of the tubs.

5

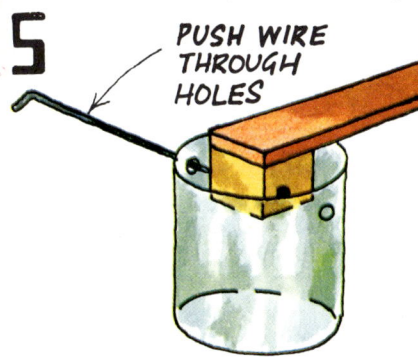

PUSH WIRE THROUGH HOLES

To fasten the tubs to the balsa blocks, thread the wires through the holes as shown Then twist the ends over the rims of the tubs. Check that the tubs can swing freely.

6

WIND UP ABOUT 50 TURNS

HOLD FIRMLY TO TABLE

Testing time! Wind the arm up, then press a finger over its centre to serve as a brake. Keeping a firm hold on the base, ease your finger off. The arm should gain speed gently.

10

ASTRONAUT SHOULD STAY STANDING

The tub will swivel up until it is level with the arm. Yet because of centrifugal force the astronaut will remain on his feet—like those in the space station shown above.

11

WATER

You can do the same trick with almost anything. Try it with water. Fill the two tubs about half full. Make sure there are no leaks. Take care that the arm speeds up at a steady rate.

12

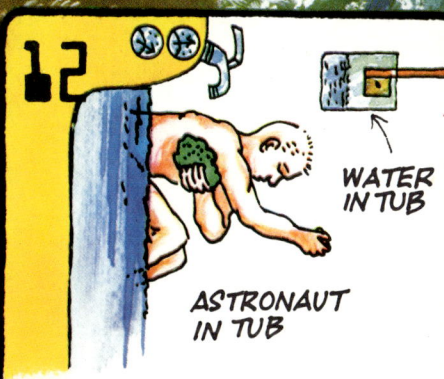

WATER IN TUB

ASTRONAUT IN TUB

Because Skylab did not rotate, there was no force to hold things in it down. They floated weightlessly. But in one that rotated, astronauts could even have baths!

MOONBASE

When astronauts return to the Moon, it will be to set up a colony. An ideal site would be near the Leibnitz Mountains (see map below) at the south pole where the Sun never sets.

Scientists and moonminers will live and work inside pressurized shelters. There will be solar furnaces for smelting lunar ore, and solar cell 'farms' will be used to make electricity from sunlight.

This is how Man's space frontier might look in your lifetime. After the moonbase, the next step will be the planets, and perhaps the stars.

Apollo landing sites

Site of base

▲ Twelve men have walked on the Moon—two each at the six Apollo landing sites shown above. The last manned mission was in December 1972. No new ones are planned at present.

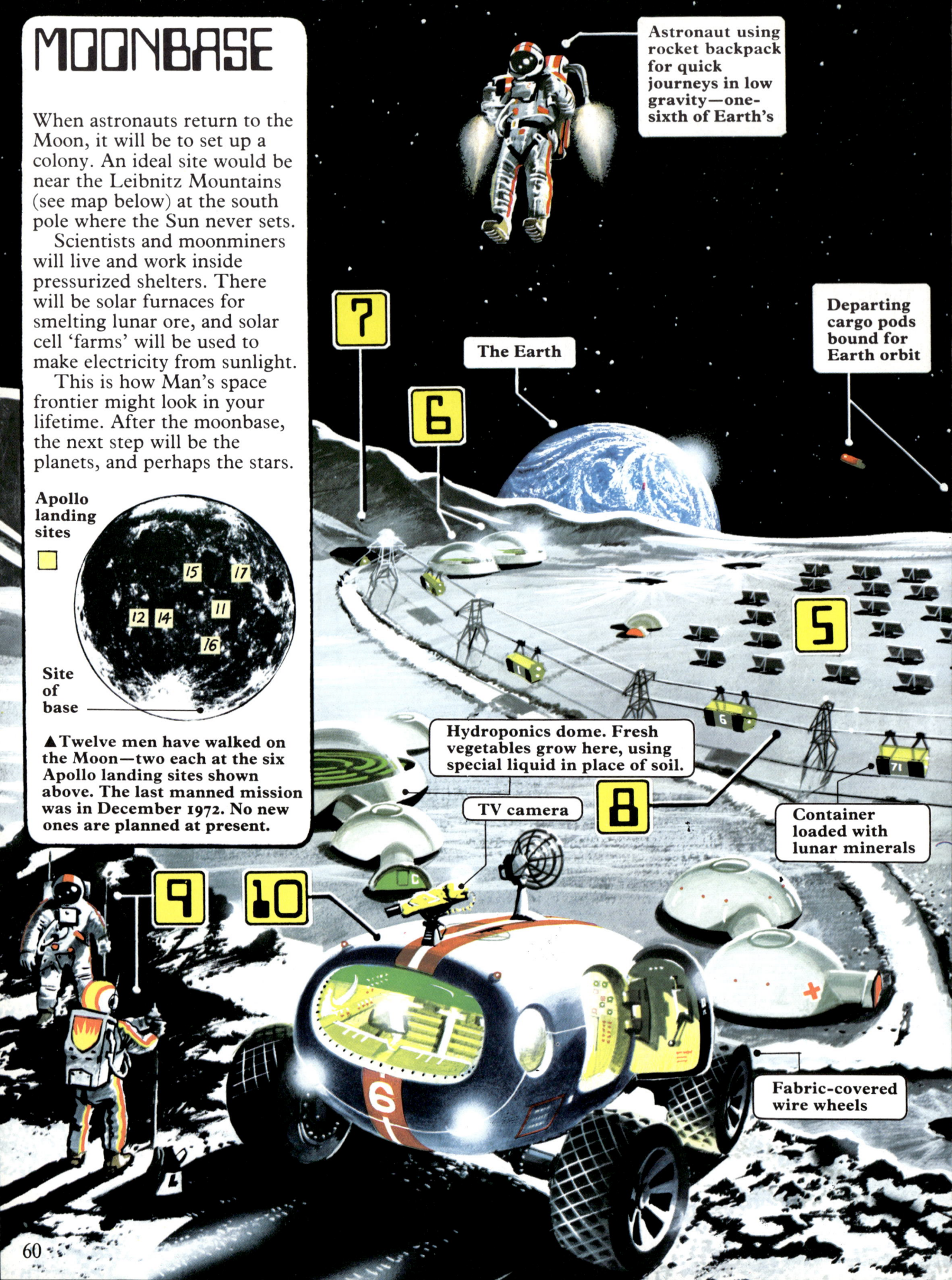

Astronaut using rocket backpack for quick journeys in low gravity—one-sixth of Earth's

The Earth

Departing cargo pods bound for Earth orbit

Hydroponics dome. Fresh vegetables grow here, using special liquid in place of soil.

TV camera

Container loaded with lunar minerals

Fabric-covered wire wheels

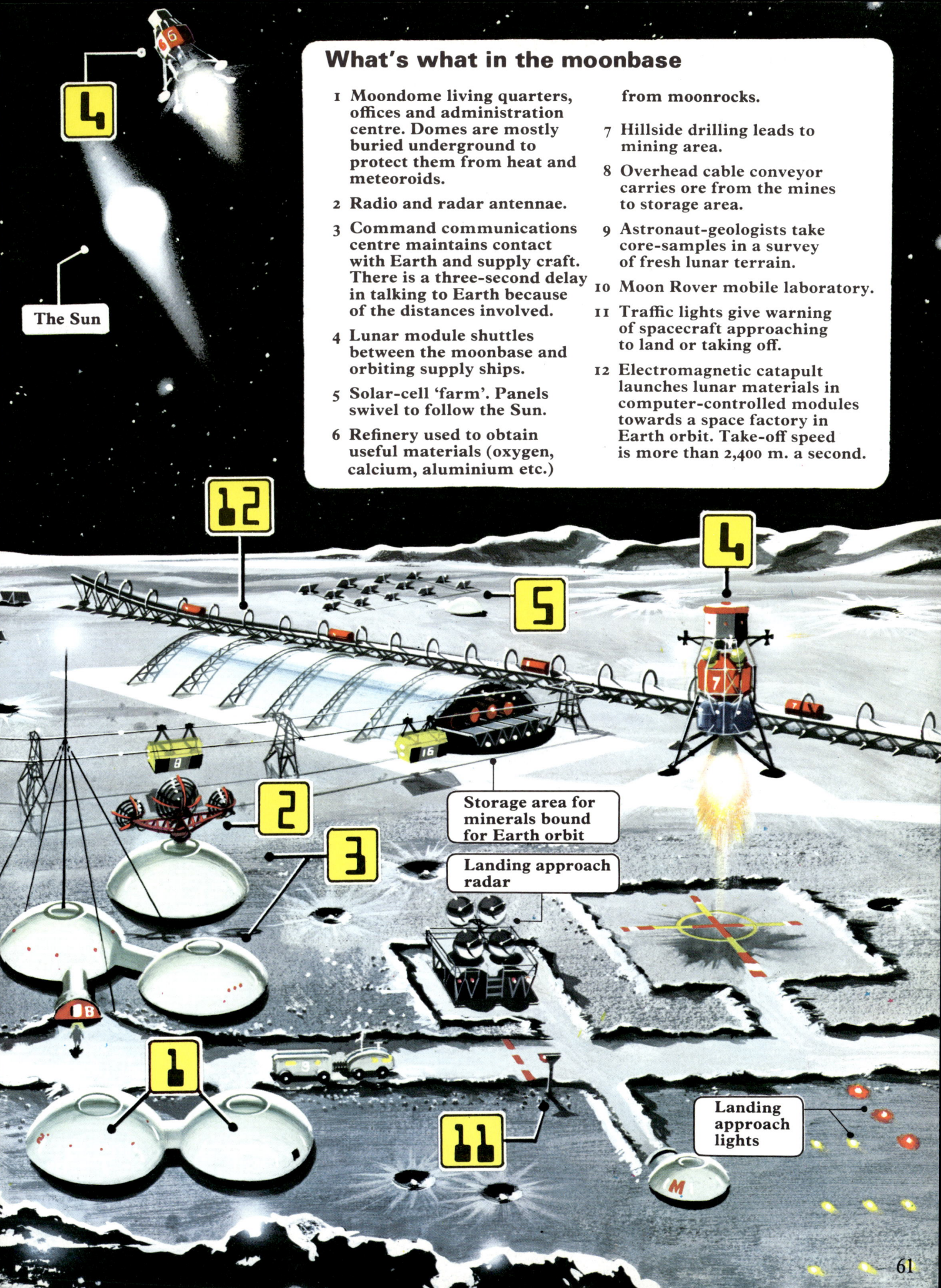

What's what in the moonbase

1. **Moondome living quarters, offices and administration centre. Domes are mostly buried underground to protect them from heat and meteoroids.**
2. **Radio and radar antennae.**
3. **Command communications centre maintains contact with Earth and supply craft. There is a three-second delay in talking to Earth because of the distances involved.**
4. **Lunar module shuttles between the moonbase and orbiting supply ships.**
5. **Solar-cell 'farm'. Panels swivel to follow the Sun.**
6. **Refinery used to obtain useful materials (oxygen, calcium, aluminium etc.)** from moonrocks.
7. **Hillside drilling leads to mining area.**
8. **Overhead cable conveyor carries ore from the mines to storage area.**
9. **Astronaut-geologists take core-samples in a survey of fresh lunar terrain.**
10. **Moon Rover mobile laboratory.**
11. **Traffic lights give warning of spacecraft approaching to land or taking off.**
12. **Electromagnetic catapult launches lunar materials in computer-controlled modules towards a space factory in Earth orbit. Take-off speed is more than 2,400 m. a second.**

The Sun

Storage area for minerals bound for Earth orbit

Landing approach radar

Landing approach lights

61

SPACE FIRSTS

Yuri Gagarin

1903
Konstantin Tsiolkovsky was the first man to suggest using liquid-fuel rockets.

March 16, 1926
Robert H. Goddard launched the first liquid-fuel rocket at Auburn, Massachusetts. It flew for 184 ft (56 m).

October 3, 1942
First successful launching of a V-2 rocket at Peenemünde. It flew for 118 m (190 km).

October 4, 1957
Russia launched Sputnik 1, the world's first artificial satellite.

November 3, 1957
A dog called Laika was the first living thing to go into orbit, in Sputnik 2.

February 1, 1958
The first American satellite, Explorer 1, was launched from Cape Canaveral.

April 12, 1961
Russian cosmonaut Yuri Gagarin became the first man to orbit the Earth, in Vostok 1.

May 5, 1961
Alan Shepard was the first American to enter space when he made a sub-orbital flight in Freedom 7.

February 20, 1962
John Glenn was the first US astronaut to orbit the Earth, in the spacecraft Friendship 7.

June 16, 1963
Valentina Tereshkova of the USSR became the first woman to go into orbit, in Vostok 6.

March 18, 1965
Cosmonaut Alexei Leonov made the first space walk. He spent a total of 20 minutes outside Voshkod 2.

February 3, 1966
Soviet probe Luna 9 made first soft landing on the Moon.

March 16, 1966
Neil Armstrong and David Scott aboard Gemini 8 made the first space docking, linking with an Agena target vehicle.

January 27, 1967
Virgil Grissom, Edward White and Roger Chaffee died in a fire on the Kennedy Space Centre launch pad. They were the first (and so far the only) casualties of the American space program.

April 24, 1967
Vladimir Komarov was the first Russian cosmonaut known to have died on a mission when Soyuz 1's landing parachute tangled.

July 20, 1969
The Apollo 11 astronauts Neil Armstrong and Edwin Aldrin were the first men to land on the Moon.

April 19, 1971
Russia launches the 20.4 ton (18.5 tonne) Salyut 1, the first manned space station.

May 14, 1973
Skylab, the first American space station, was launched. Skylab was the heaviest-ever spacecraft, weighing 75 tonnes.

July 17, 1975
First Russian-American space link-up, between an Apollo carrying Tom Stafford, Vance Brand and Deke Slayton, and a Soyuz with Alexei Leonov and Valeri Kubasov aboard.

July 20, 1976
US Viking 1 made the first landing on Mars to look for life, though none was found.

December 24, 1979
First launch of European rocket Ariane.

April 12, 1981
First flight of the American Space Shuttle, carrying John Young and Robert Crippen.

SPACE FACTS

One of the most amazing things about the coming of the Space Age was the speed with which it arrived. Only 27 years passed between the V-2's first flight and the landing of manned spacecraft on the Moon.

Man's knowledge of space has grown almost as fast. Here are some of the odder facts, events and theories to have come out of the years of discovery.

Because there is no wind or rain on the Moon to erase them, the footprints of the Apollo astronauts should, if left undisturbed, last for millions of years.

The most conspicuous features of the Earth as seen from space are its clouds. A visitor from space with eyesight similar to a man's would not see any sign of human life until he came within 250 km. of the surface.

At the beginning of 1980, a total of 1,019 satellites which provide (or once provided) information were in orbit around our planet. In addition, about 3,500 pieces of debris were being tracked by ground radars. This debris ranges from burned-out rocket stages to tiny metal fragments. By the start of 1980, a total of 2,308 satellites had been launched.

Because the gravitational pull of the Moon is only one-sixth of that of Earth, athletes in a pressurized lunar stadium could (in theory) jump six times higher than they could on Earth. They might even be able to strap on wings and fly like birds!

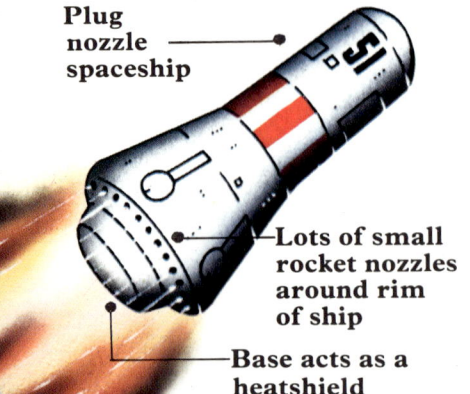

Plug nozzle spaceship

Lots of small rocket nozzles around rim of ship

Base acts as a heatshield

A new type of re-usable space rocket has been designed in America. Called the plug nozzle spaceship, it could take off and land vertically. This wingless single-stage rocket concept has a heatshield cooled by liquid hydrogen, surrounded by a ring of small rocket engines, which are used to drive it into orbit.

When it comes back to Earth, the heatshield protects it and the rockets fire backwards to brake it down gently to land.

Pioneer 10 is expected to become the first man-made object to leave the Solar System. It is due to

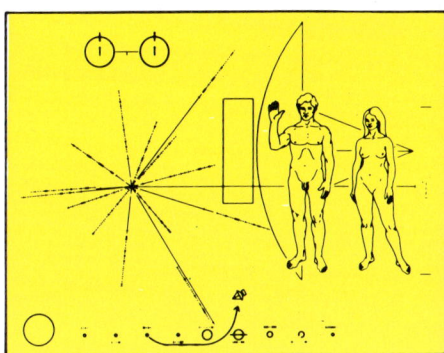

Message plaque carried aboard Pioneer 10

cross the orbit of Pluto in 1987. After that it will disappear into the depths of space. It carries a message plaque bearing drawings of a man and a woman and coded information about the Earth for the benefit of any alien beings who may discover it. It should reach the neighborhood of the giant star Aldebaran in the constellation of Taurus after 1,700,000 years.

On July 20, 1969, Houston Mission Control put through the longest-distance telephone call in history. It connected Richard Nixon, then President of the United States, with the first men on the Moon. At the time, Neil Armstrong and Edwin Aldrin were setting up a base on the Sea of Tranquility some 238,618 mi (384,000 km) from Earth.

The Apollo spacecraft which carried astronauts to and from the Moon had nearly two million working parts. A large motor car has less than 3,000.

SPACE WORDS

This glossary only includes words that are not fully explained anywhere else in the book.

You will find other rocket words explained on pages 36 and 37. Satellite terms are covered on pages 48 and 49, and space Shuttle words on pages 50 to 53.

Centrifugal force
Outward movement caused when an object moves around another. When a satellite is in orbit, its outward, centrifugal force is exactly balanced by the inward pull of gravity.

Docking
Mechanical linking of two or more craft in space.

Elevons
Control surfaces on aeroplanes or spacecraft which can operate both as elevators (to make the craft climb or dive) or as ailerons (to make it bank left or right).

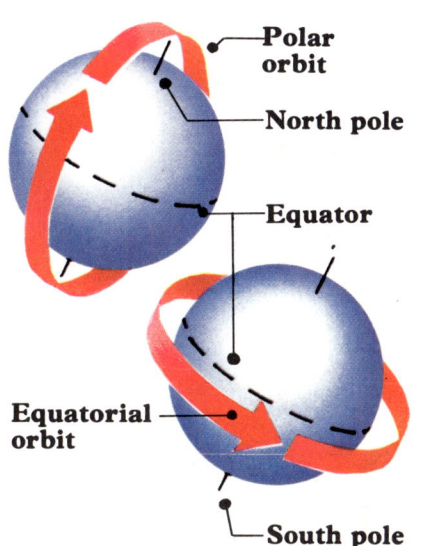

Polar orbit
North pole
Equator
Equatorial orbit
South pole

Equatorial orbit
Orbit around the equator. Polar orbit is an orbit which passes over the poles.

Fairing
Covering to protect inside parts of a rocket or satellite while it is passing through the atmosphere.

Heat insulating materials
In spaceflight terms, materials used to protect parts of spacecraft from extremes of heat and cold.

Hydroponics
Way of growing plants in water treated with nourishing chemicals instead of in soil.

Module
Section of a spacecraft.

Pallet
Platform for carrying research instruments.

Payload
The useful load launched by a rocket into space.

Permafrost
The part of a planet's surface that is frozen all the time.

Propellant
The fuel and oxidizer of a rocket.

Re-entry
The return of a spacecraft into the Earth's atmosphere.

Retro rockets
Direction of flight

Retro rockets
Rockets which fire against the direction of flight to slow down a spacecraft.

Sensory ring
Base of a satellite or space probe used for mounting cameras and other sensors—information-gathering instruments.

Soft-landing
Slow-speed landing, after braking by parachute or retro rocket.

Synchronous orbit
An orbit in which satellites 35,880 km. up keep pace with the Earth's turning, staying above a fixed point on its surface.

Thrust chamber
The combustion chamber of a rocket engine, in which fuel and oxidizer are burned.

Zero gravity
Condition of spaceflight in which astronauts and loose objects float weightlessly.

FIRST FLIGHTS

All these rockets have been drawn to the same scale, so their sizes can be compared at a glance.

You can see how the Russians made their early advances in space by launching the first Sputniks with a large military missile (2)—at a time when the Americans were limited to the tiny Vanguard (3) and Juno 1 (4).

Now compare these early launchers with the huge Saturn 5 rocket (10) which the Americans later built to send the first men to the Moon.

1 **A4/V-2 (1942)**
2 **Sputnik (1957)**
3 **Vanguard (1958)**
4 **Juno 1 (1958)**
5 **Vostok (1961)**★

6 **Mercury-Atlas (1962)**★
7 **Gemini-Titan 2 (1965)**★
8 **Soyuz (1967)**★
9 **Saturn 1B (1968)**★
10 **Saturn 5 (1968)**★
11 **Ariane (1979)**
12 **Space Shuttle (1981)**★

★ **First manned flight**

Europe

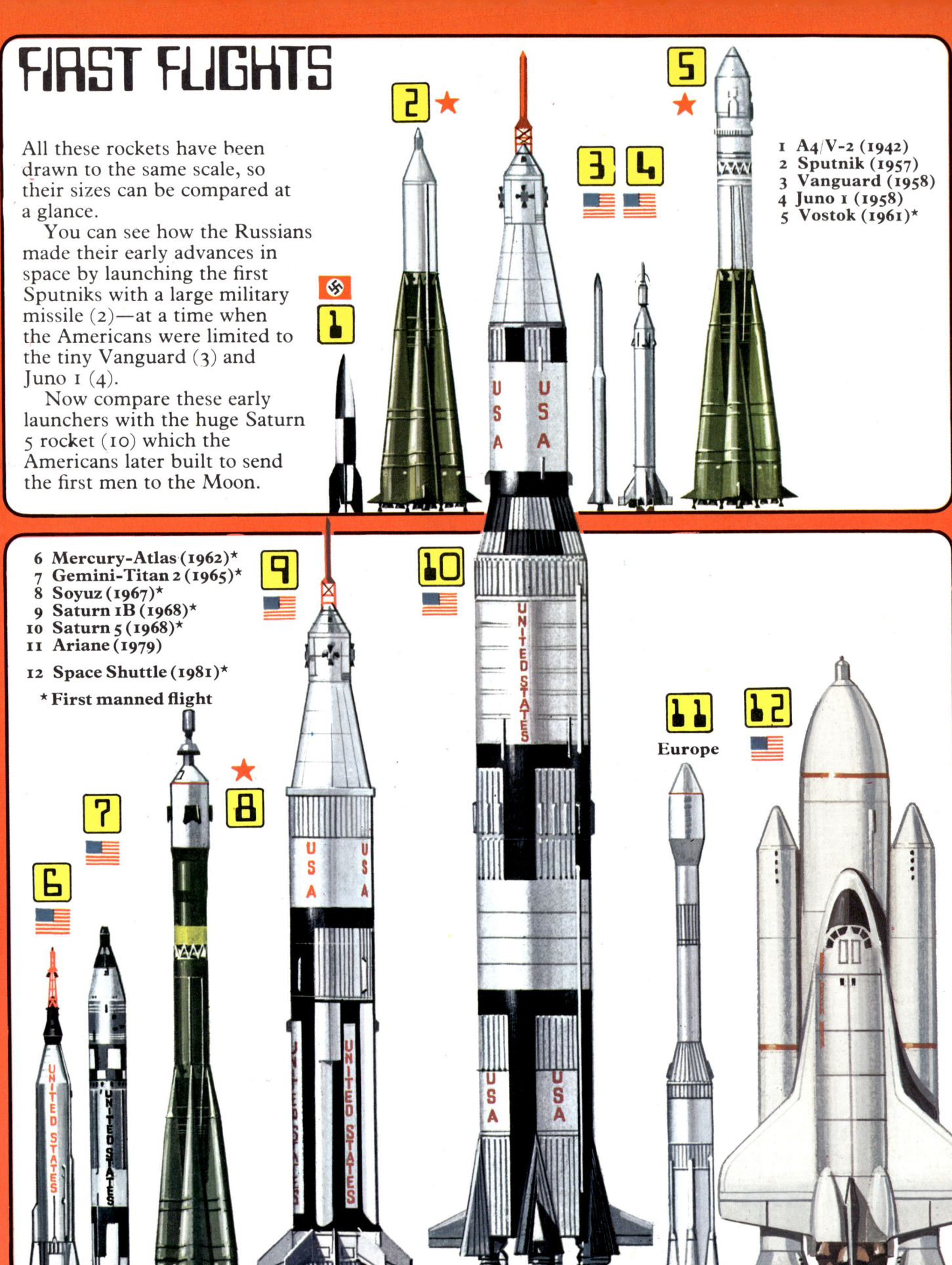

PART 3: ELECTRICITY

Electricity is one of the most widely used yet most mysterious sources of power. Here are just some of the ways you can see it at work.

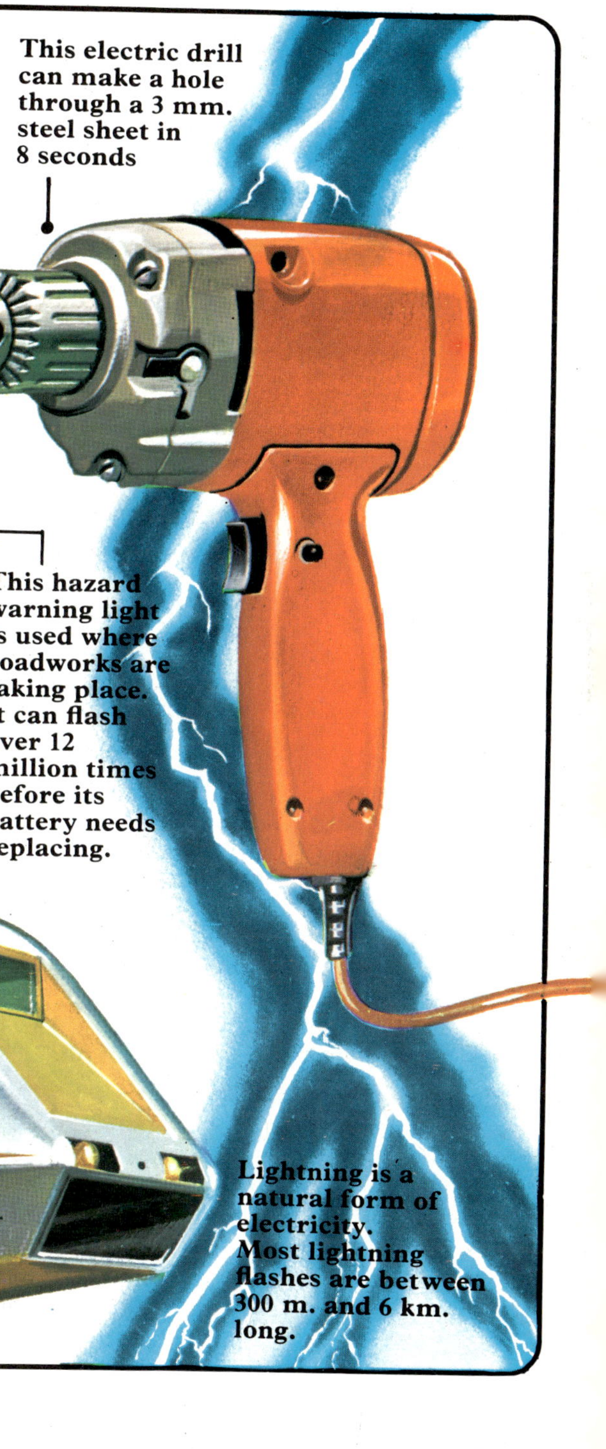

This electric drill can make a hole through a 3 mm. steel sheet in 8 seconds

The motor-driven cutting blades of an electric shaver vibrate from side to side 3000 times a minute

This hazard warning light is used where roadworks are taking place. It can flash over 12 million times before its battery needs replacing.

This special type of electric cooker will cook a joint of meat in 20 minutes

The latest electric passenger train can travel at speeds of 220 k.p.h.

Lightning is a natural form of electricity. Most lightning flashes are between 300 m. and 6 km. long.

CREDITS

Written by
Philip Chapman
Art and editorial direction
David Jefferis
Educational adviser
Frank Blackwell

Illustrators
Roland Berry
Sydney Cornford
Malcolm English
Phil Green
John Hutchinson
Malcolm McGregor
Michael Roffe

The weird looking machinery on this page is the transformer equipment in a power station.

THE EXPERIMENTS

All the experiments in this book are absolutely safe if you always use a 4.5 volt battery.
NEVER play with electricity from the mains.

Here is a list of equipment you will need.

General equipment

Four 6 volt bulbs in bulbholders
Two 4.5 volt batteries with screw-down connections
About 5 m. of connecting wire
Sticky tape
Scissors
Glue
Compass
15 m. of fine insulated wire
Paper clips
12 cm. long nail
Wire cutters
Two magnets
Plasticine

For special experiments

Current detector (p.77):
Saucer
Water
Small cork
Needle

Motor (p.79):
15 × 17 cm. sheet of balsa wood
50 cm. of 5 × 5 mm. balsa wood strip
Balsa cement
Ten 3 cm. long pins
15 cm. long knitting needle
Two drawing pins

The battery we have chosen for all the experiments in this book supplies electricity at 4.5 volts. Not all batteries supplying this voltage look the same, so get ones looking like either of the two shown below.

The battery with screw-on terminals is best because you can fix the wires very easily. You can use the battery with springy terminals but you will have to wind the wires onto them.

BATTERY WITH SCREW-ON TERMINALS

Large cork
Two horseshoe magnets
Two aluminium milk bottle tops

Turbine (p.85):
15 cm. long knitting needle
Sheet of stiff paper about 10 cm. × 10 cm.

Telegraph set (p.90):
Sheet of cooking foil
Length of 3-core cable
Large sheet of cardboard

WEIGHTS AND MEASURES

All the weights and measures are metric. Here are some imperial equivalents.

mm. = millimetre
(1 inch = 25.4 mm.)

cm. = centimetre
(1 inch = 2.54 cm.)

m. = metre
(1 yard = 0.91 m.)

km. = kilometre
(1 mile = 1.6 km.)

k.p.h. = kilometres per hour
(100 m.p.h. = 160 k.p.h.)

sq. km. = square kilometre
(1 square mile = 2.59 sq. km.)

kg. = kilogram
(1 pound = 0.45 kg.)

A tonne is 1000 kg.
(1 ton = 1.02 tonnes)

1 litre is 1.76 pints

M means one million
(1 MW = one million watts)

k means 1000
(1 kW. = 1000 watts)

°C. = degrees Centigrade
(Water freezes at 0°C. and boils at 100°C.)

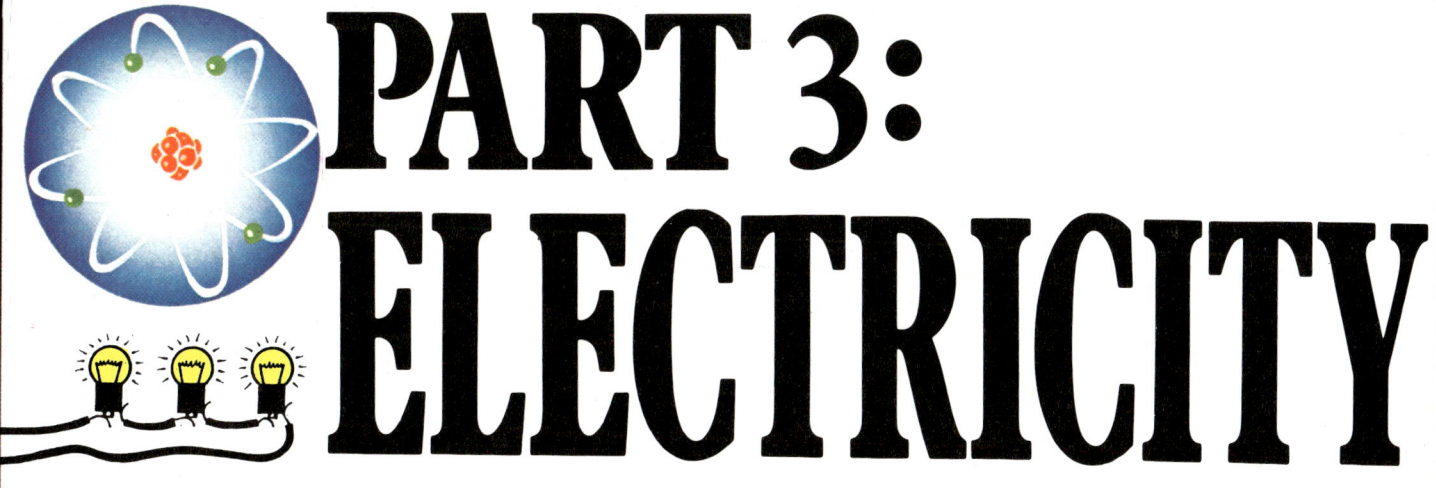

PART 3: ELECTRICITY

ABOUT ELECTRICITY

Do you know why an electric light bulb shines or how a battery works? Have you ever wondered how electricity is made in a power station or how an electric motor works?

Part 3 explains in simple terms what electricity is, and how it works and how we use it. It tells the story of how electricity is made, transmitted around the country, and finally reaches our homes, offices and factories.

A series of safe and simple experiments easily carried out on the kitchen table shows you how to construct simple circuits, including working models of an electromagnet, an electric motor and a two-way telegraph system.

CONTENTS

INSIDE THE ATOM

The atom

Everything is made up of atoms. The air you breathe, the pages of this book, your own body—all are built up from millions of invisibly small atoms. They are so small that ten million of them lined up side by side would measure only one millimetre!

At the centre of each atom is a nucleus containing tiny particles called protons. Even smaller particles called electrons move round the nucleus. They orbit round the nucleus like planets round the Sun, and there are always as many electrons as protons.

Each electron has a negative electric charge; each proton has a positive electric charge.

This ⊖ sign means negative and this ⊕ sign means positive.

Electron

Electron

Electron

Electron

Electron

Electron

The atom's nucleus is made of protons (red) and neutrons (black)

Electron

Electron

Electron

Electron—these all have a negative charge.

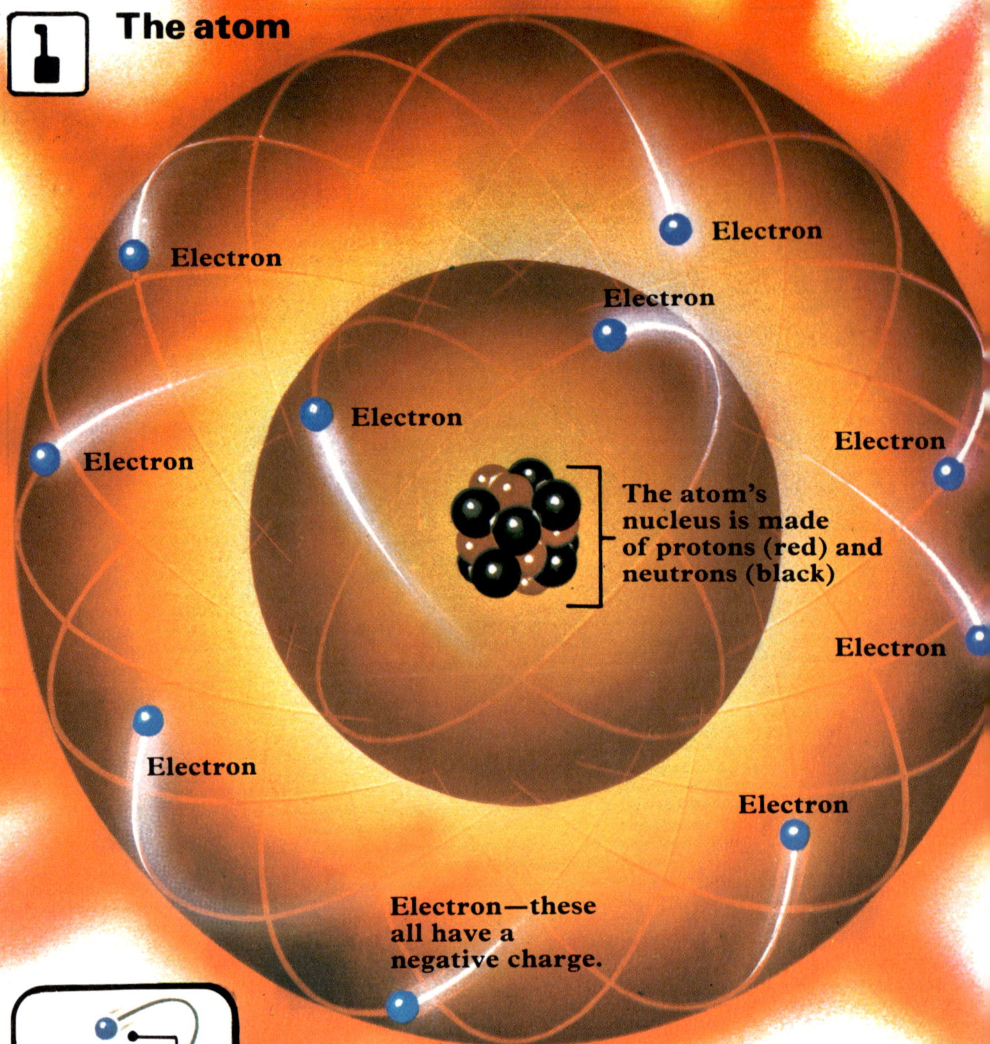

▶ Hydrogen is the simplest atom. It has only one proton and one electron. All the other atoms are more complicated. They have other particles called neutrons, but these have no electric charge at all. The big picture shows you the important parts of an atom.

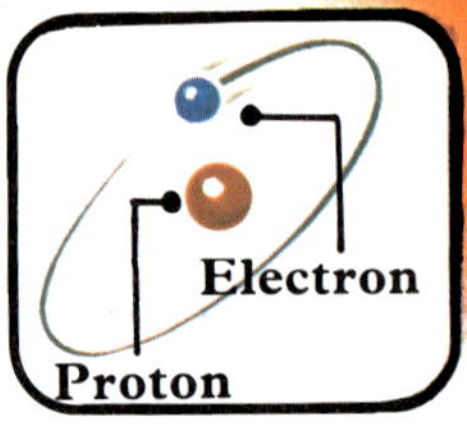

Electron

Proton

Electric circuits

SECOND WIRE WILL ACT AS A RETURN PATH

BULB GLOWS

BULB

WIRE CONDUCTOR

▲ To light a bulb using a supply of electricity from a battery, the bulb must be connected to the battery. An electrical conductor such as a wire provides an easy path for the electrons to follow.

▲ But simply connecting a single wire from the battery to the bulb will not light it. A second wire must be connected to the battery's other terminal. This makes a path for the electrons to flow back to the battery.

▲ This unbroken path is called a circuit. The second wire has completed the circuit, and the bulb lights up. The electrons flow through the bulb but are not used up in it. They pass through and return to the battery.

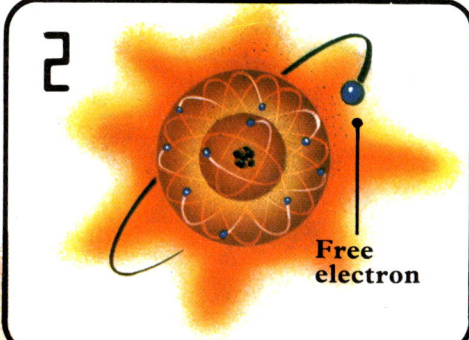

2

Free electron

▲ An electrical conductor is something that allows electricity to pass through it easily. A good conductor has one 'free' electron orbiting outside the others. It can be separated from its atom.

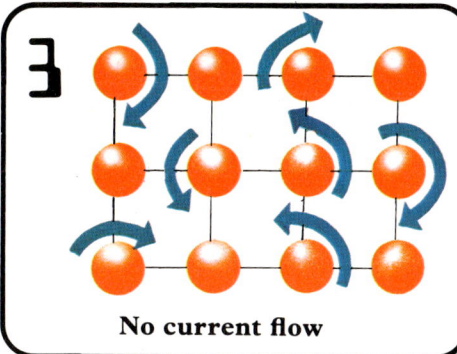

3

No current flow

▲ In metals, the atoms form a regular pattern. This gives metals their strength. The free electrons do not orbit round their own atoms, but can wander from atom to atom through the metal. The red arrows above show them moving.

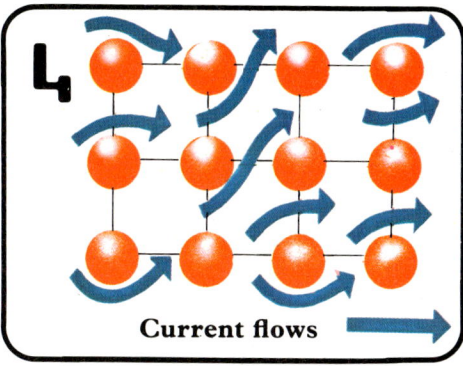

4

Current flows

▲ When a metal wire is connected to a battery, the free electrons in the wire start to drift from one end to the other, passing from atom to atom. This drift of electrons is called an electric current.

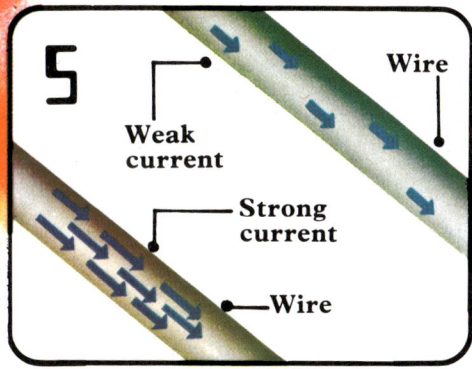

5

Wire

Weak current

Strong current

Wire

▲ The strength of an electric current flowing in a wire depends on the number of free electrons passing along it. Lots of free electrons mean a strong current, a few mean a weak current is flowing.

6

Filament

▲ When you switch on a light in your home, this lets the electric current flow through the bulb. About 3 million million million free electrons are passing through the filament in the bulb every second!

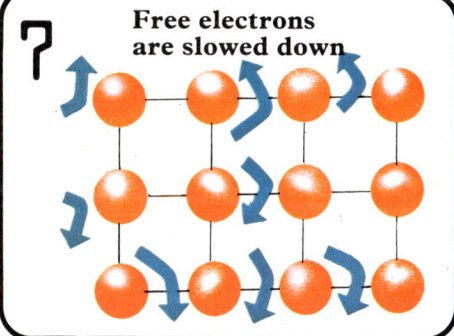

7

Free electrons are slowed down

▲ Free electrons do not pass along a wire smoothly. They bump into the atoms of the wire and their progress is slowed down. This slowing-down effect is called resistance. The better the conductor, the lower its resistance.

Instant electricity

The free electrons drifting along a wire move quite slowly—only a few millimetres a second. This mini-experiment shows you why you do not have to wait when you turn on an electricity supply.

Get some marbles and line them up between two books. Push the left-hand marble a little way to the right. See how all the other marbles move as well, even at the far end. Like marbles, electrons all begin to move at the same time, but they do so only when their circuit is completed—so they have a return path back to the battery.

ALL THE OTHER MARBLES MOVE AS WELL

PUSH THIS MARBLE

NATURE'S ELECTRICITY

A lightning storm is one of nature's most dramatic shows of strength. Flashes of electricity leap down from thunderclouds in the sky.

Although men have known about thunderstorms for thousands of years, exactly what causes them is still not very clear.

Scientists say that lightning is the releasing of electricity that has built up inside the clouds. It is probably like the electricity that is built up when you comb your hair on a warm dry day. You can sometimes hear a crackling noise as the teeth of the comb pass the strands of hair.

Lightning conductors are strips of metal running down the side of a building. They provide an easy path for the electricity to follow and so keep the lightning away from the building itself.

Lightning will strike a tree rather than go direct to the ground because the tree gives the lightning an easier path to earth. Why? Because the tree-top is nearer to the cloud than the ground.

1 Making electricity with a comb

Things sometimes get charged with electricity just by rubbing. Have you ever felt a small shock when you touch a door knob after walking across a thick pile carpet? This is because electrons have been rubbed off the carpet and onto your body. This 'static' charge then escapes suddenly as you touch the door knob, and you feel a tingling shock.

Here are two experiments you can do to show the effects of static electricity.

CLEAN DRY HAIR

▲ Comb your hair with a plastic comb. As the comb's teeth pass the strands of your hair, electrons are transferred across, and the comb becomes charged with static electricity. Make sure you comb your hair vigorously.

▲ Hold the comb a little way from some small scraps of paper. You will see the pieces of paper jump up to the comb and stick to it. The static electricity in the comb is attracting the pieces of paper.

Electricity may flash across between two clouds. This is the most common type of lightning. It appears as a bright flash across the sky.

Lightning strikes direct to the ground are quite rare. The lightning normally strikes a tree or building as these provide an easier path for the electricity to follow.

▲ The skin of an electric eel conceals hundreds of tiny cells all acting like miniature batteries. The cells charge up to a voltage of more than 600 volts which the eel then uses to stun its victim.

▲ Glow worms are light-producing beetles. Their pale yellowish-green glow is made by a chemical process in the rear part of their bodies. They can flash their lights in special rhythms to attract each other.

▲ Your own body is one of the most complicated electrical systems. All information from the senses—sight, sound, touch, taste and smell—is passed to the brain along nerve fibres. The information is passed along as an electric signal. This footballer's brain receives all the information needed for him to aim and kick the ball. His brain then sends out electric signals along nerve fibres to tell his muscles when and where to kick the ball.

4 PIECES OF PAPER FALL

▲ After a minute or two, the electricity in the comb leaks away through your body, and the scraps of paper will fall off. You can repeat the experiment if you comb your hair again to recharge it with static electricity.

5 SLOW AND STEADY FLOW

▲ Another static electricity trick is bending water. Turn on a water tap and adjust it carefully until a slow, steady stream of water is flowing. Comb your hair again and hold the comb near the stream of flowing water.

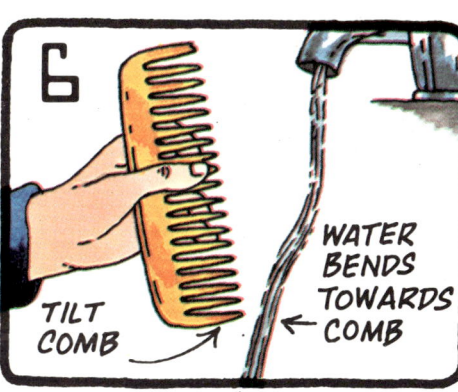

6 TILT COMB   WATER BENDS TOWARDS COMB

▲ You will see the water bend towards the tip of the comb. The static electricity in the comb is attracting the water towards it. Again the charge leaks away through your body. As it does so, the water flows normally again.

HOW BATTERIES WORK

Electric current is the movement of electrons through a wire. They won't travel along the wire by themselves, so a force is needed to push them along. This force is produced by a battery and is called the electromotive force.

The strength of the force is measured in volts, named after Alessandro Volta, the inventor of the first battery.

Batteries are not as powerful as the electricity supplied to our homes, but they can be carried about from place to place or used as an emergency supply during a power cut.

▲ In 1800, Count Volta, an Italian scientist, made the first battery. A supply of electric current was now available to experimenters who until then had used static electricity which lasts for only a few seconds at a time.

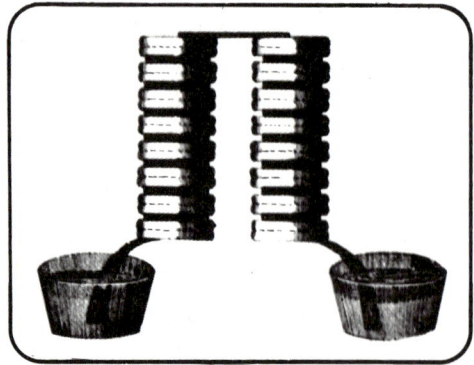

▲ The voltaic pile, as Volta's battery came to be known, was made of lots of silver and zinc discs separated by damp fabric pads. The electric current made by the voltaic pile could be used for lots of long-lasting experiments.

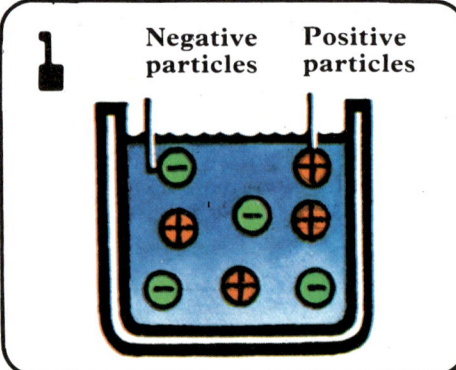

1 Negative particles Positive particles

▲ This is how a battery works. It is made of lots of cells and one of them is shown above. In the cell is a liquid called the electrolyte. It is made of billions of positive and negative particles.

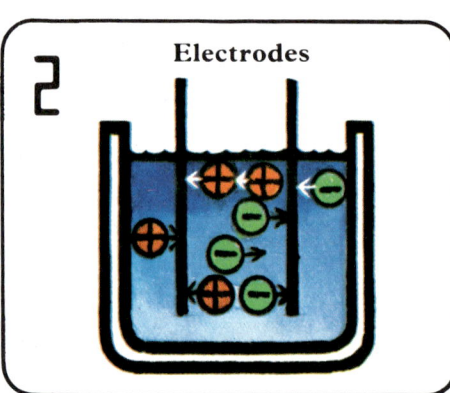

2 Electrodes

▲ Two rods made of different materials are submerged in the electrolyte in each cell. These are called electrodes. A chemical reaction in the electrolyte sends positive particles to one electrode, negative particles to the other.

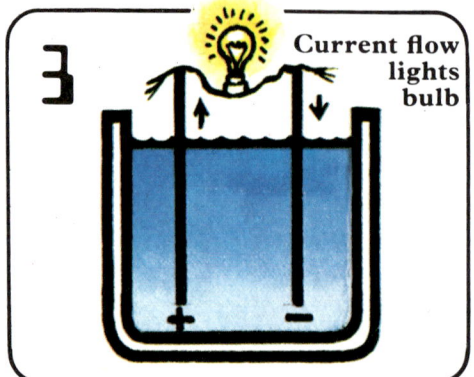

3 Current flow lights bulb

▲ When a wire is connected to the two electrodes, current flows along the wire. This can be used to light a bulb like the one shown above. When the chemicals in the cell are used up, the current stops flowing.

Dry cells

Liquids can easily spill out so special dry batteries are made for things like torches. There are still two electrodes, the carbon rod and the zinc case, but the cell has a paste electrolyte sealed into its leakproof case.

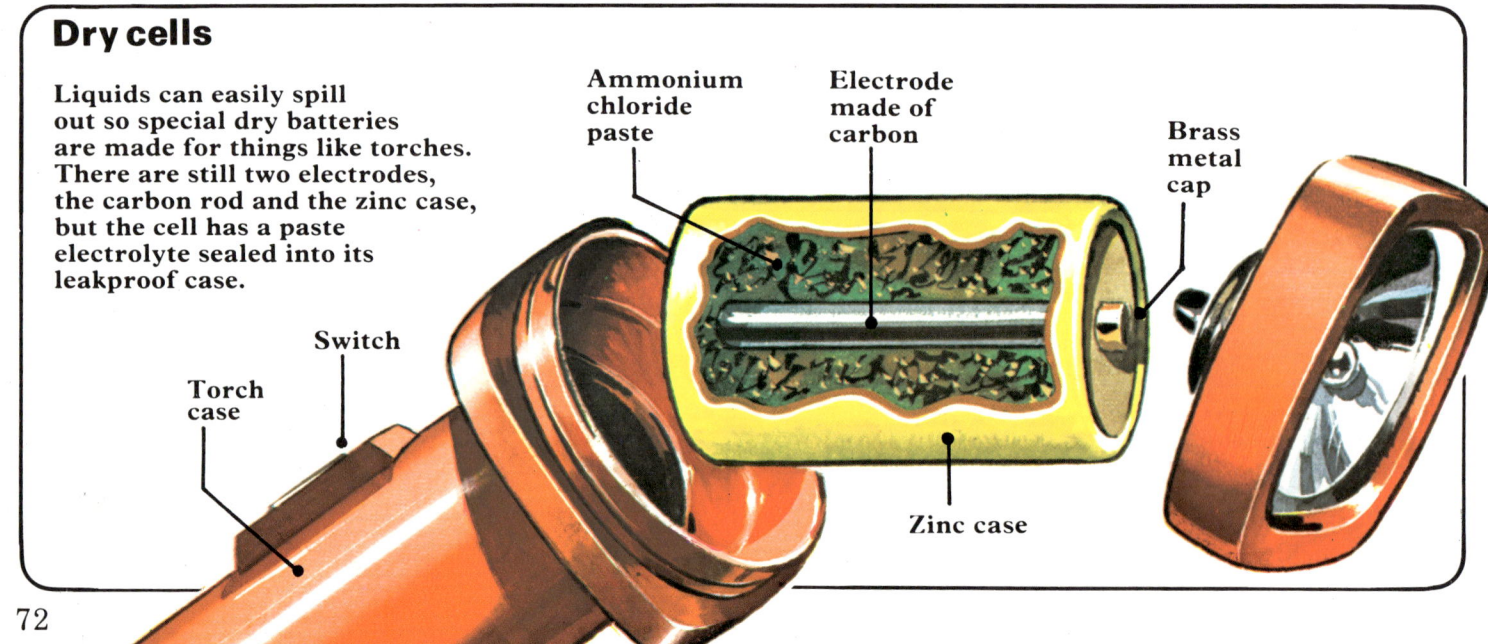

Ammonium chloride paste

Electrode made of carbon

Brass metal cap

Switch

Torch case

Zinc case

Rechargeable power for the motor car

A modern car uses many small electrical machines: starter motor, heater motor and fan. They would soon wear out an ordinary battery so special car batteries are made. These are designed so that they can be recharged with electricity.

A small electric generator is driven by the car engine. The power it produces when the engine is running is fed back into the battery to replace that used by the starter motor in starting the car.

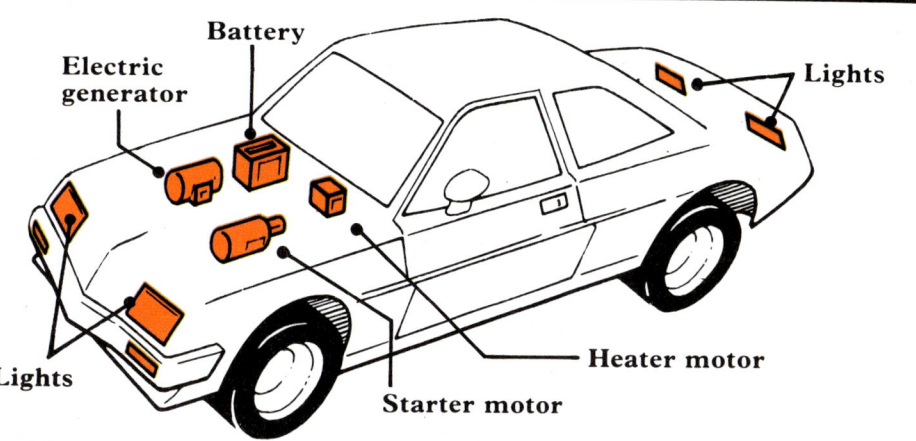

This picture shows just some of the things in a car which use up the battery's electricity supply. You can also see the generator which recharges the battery. Almost all car batteries provide a 12 volt power supply.

Non-polluting power of the future

Two electric cars draw up at 1997's clean version of our filling station. The driver on the right has just inserted his credit card (1). Robot machinery underground slots in a newly charged battery module (2) under the driving compartment. The old battery is pushed out of the other side of the car by the new module. It passes into the automatic receiving bay (3) to go for recharging. Once recharged, (4) it glides along a conveyor belt to be used again (5). A 30 second 'fill-up' gives another 1000 km. driving.

TURNING POWER INTO LIGHT

American inventor Thomas Edison

Thomas Edison produced the first electric light bulb in 1879. He sealed a fine cotton thread into a glass bulb. After pumping out the air he saw that the thread glowed brightly when a current was passed through it.

The thread had a high resistance because it was so fine. The electrons passing through it kept bumping into the atoms of the thread. This heated it up so much that it glowed white hot.

If you look at a new light bulb in its cardboard packet, you will see a number—60W or 100W This tells you how much power the bulb uses and how brightly it glows. The bigger the number the brighter the glow. The W stands for watt, the unit of power named after James Watt the Scottish inventor.

Length and resistance

Current flow

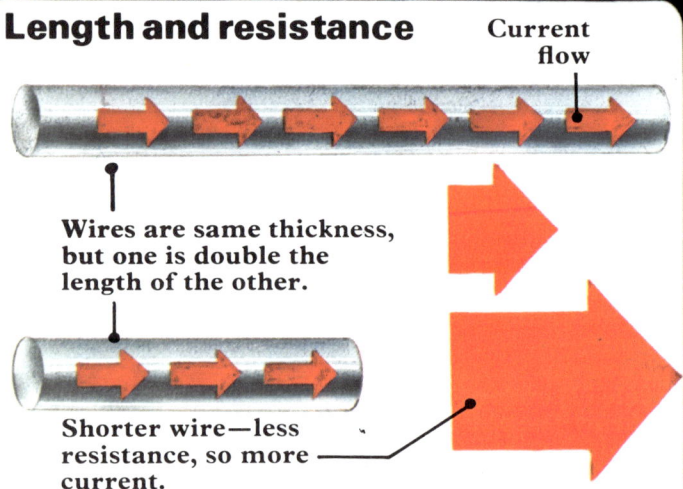

Wires are same thickness, but one is double the length of the other.

Shorter wire—less resistance, so more current.

Good conductors of electricity allow electrons to flow easily. Sometimes they bump into atoms in the wire. This slows them down. The braking effect is called the wire's resistance. Halving the length of the wire halves the resistance.

Width and resistance

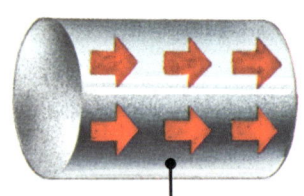

Wires are the same length, but one is twice as thick as the other.

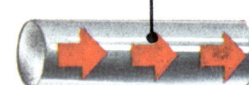

Thick wire—less resistance, so more current.

A thick wire has a lower resistance than a thin wire. There is a greater area of wire for the electrons to pass through. It is like a wide three-lane motorway that can carry far more traffic than a narrow single-lane country road.

Current and resistance

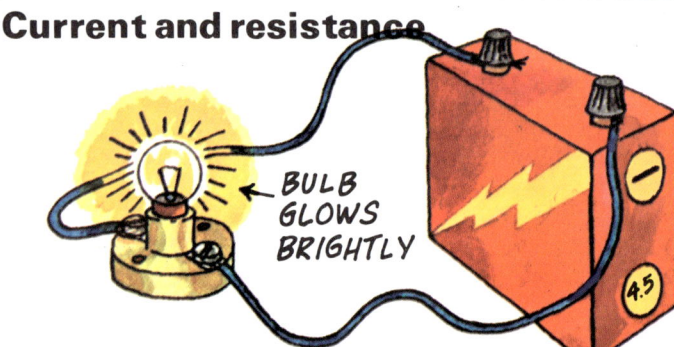

BULB GLOWS BRIGHTLY

DIM GLOW

▲ Connect a wire from the ⊕ terminal of a battery to a bulbholder terminal. Then wire the other bulbholder terminal to the ⊖ of the battery. The battery forces current round the wire and through the bulb.

▲ Now connect up the second bulb to the first and complete the circuit to the battery. The bulbs glow less brightly now. By connecting up the second bulb you have doubled the resistance so less current flows.

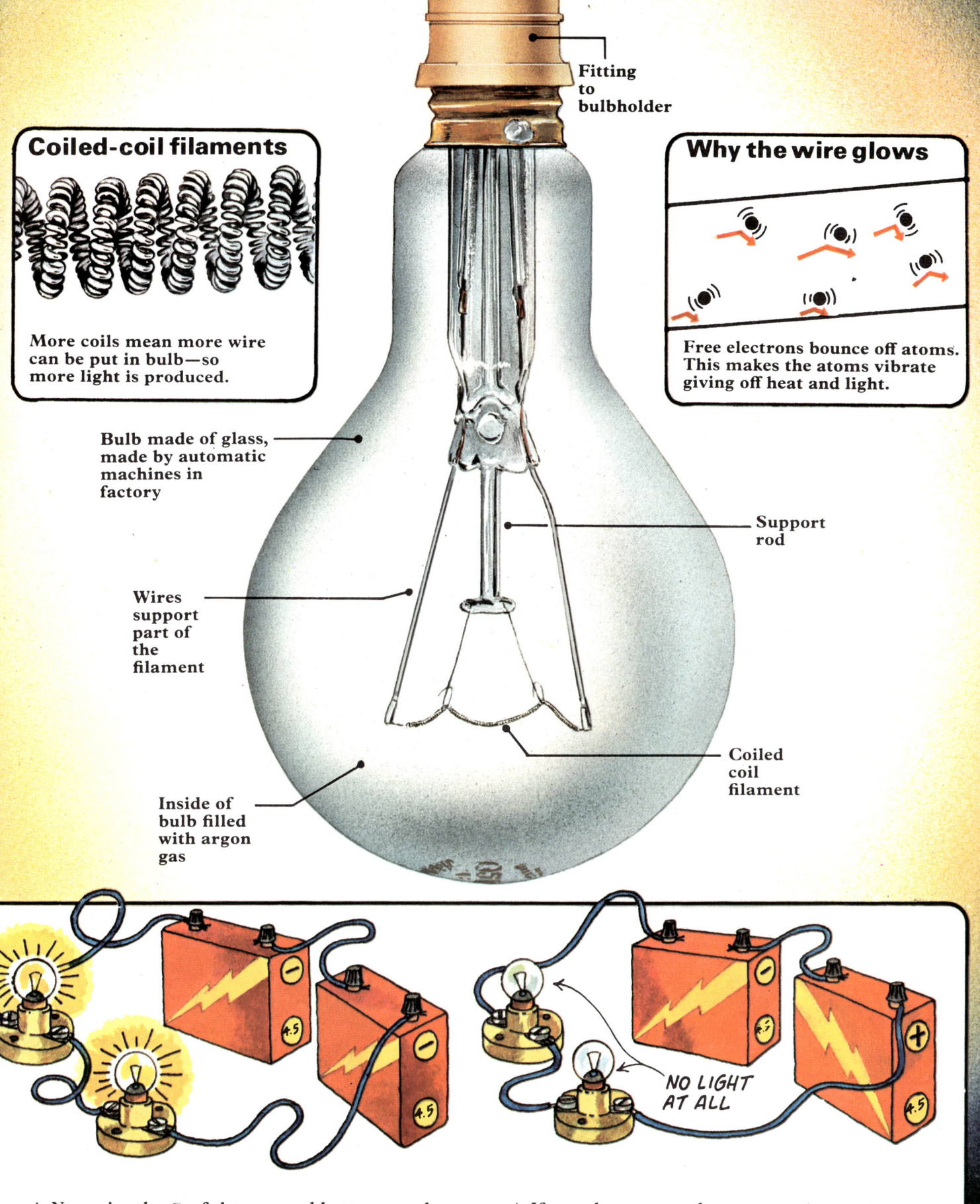

Coiled-coil filaments

More coils mean more wire can be put in bulb—so more light is produced.

Why the wire glows

Free electrons bounce off atoms. This makes the atoms vibrate giving off heat and light.

Fitting to bulbholder

Bulb made of glass, made by automatic machines in factory

Support rod

Wires support part of the filament

Coiled coil filament

Inside of bulb filled with argon gas

NO LIGHT AT ALL

▲ Now wire the ⊕ of the first battery to the ⊖ of a second battery. The bulbs glow brightly again. By connecting the second battery you have doubled the voltage. Twice the current flows and the bulbs shine brightly again.

▲ If you change over the connections to one of the batteries, the bulbs will not light up. The first battery tries to send current in one direction and the other tries to send it the other way. The result is no current flow at all.

MAGNETISM AND ELECTRICITY

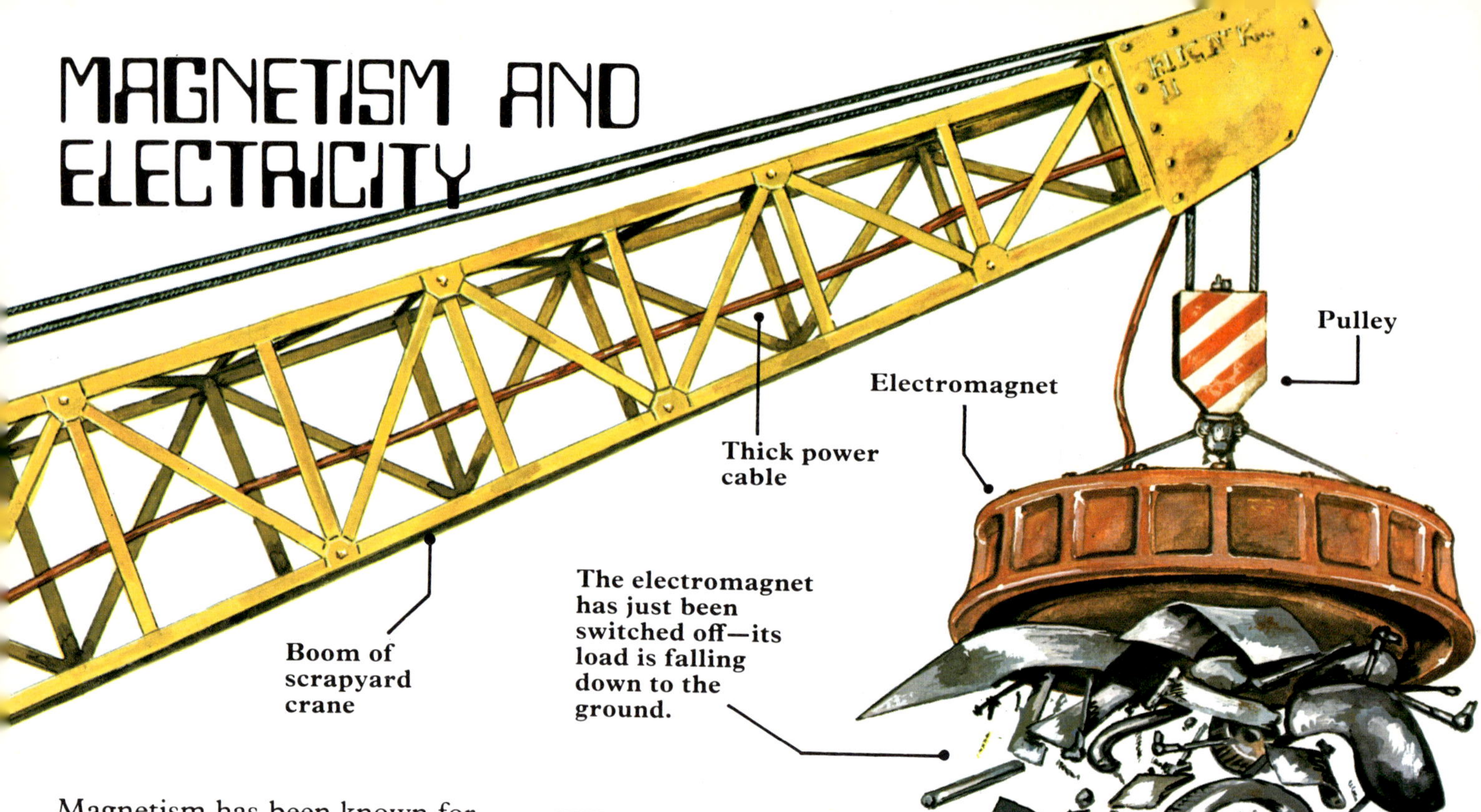

Pulley

Electromagnet

Thick power cable

Boom of scrapyard crane

The electromagnet has just been switched off—its load is falling down to the ground.

Magnetism has been known for thousands of years, and scientists have puzzled over it for just as long. The strange invisible force that attracts pieces of iron and steel to a magnet is still not fully understood.

A magnet affects only certain materials, and then only when they are close to it. They must be within its magnetic field.

Magnetism has been put to good use. Giant electromagnets like the one above lift very heavy loads, and for centuries sailors have used the compass for navigation.

Needle points north

▲ A compass needle is a small magnet, and it always points to the Earth's north pole. All magnets are therefore said to have magnetic poles. The north-seeking pole is the north pole and the other is the south pole.

N S   S N — Unlike poles attract

N S   N S — Like poles repel

▲ When a pair of magnets are placed close together, they attract one another if a north pole faces a south pole. Two north poles or two south poles face to face repel one another.

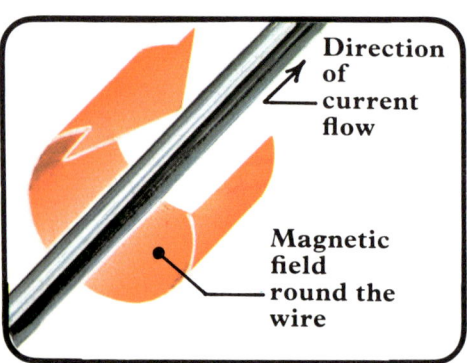

Direction of current flow

Magnetic field round the wire

▲ When a wire carries an electric current, a magnetic field is produced round the wire. The field is present along the whole length of the wire, and if the current is increased the field gets stronger.

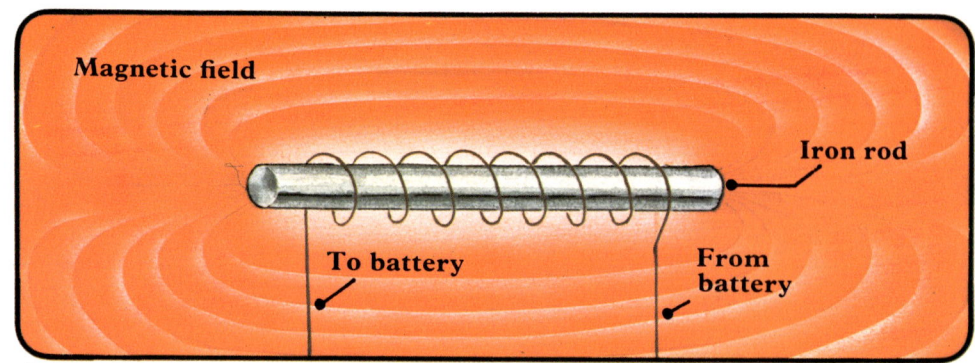

Magnetic field

Iron rod

To battery

From battery

▲ Simple and small magnets like horseshoe-shaped ones are not very powerful. A stronger magnet is produced when a coil of wire is wound round an iron bar. As soon as the current is switched on the bar becomes a very

powerful magnet that can be switched off simply by stopping the current flow. Giant electromagnets like the one above are used in scrap metal yards and lift huge loads of metal at a time.

Make an electromagnet

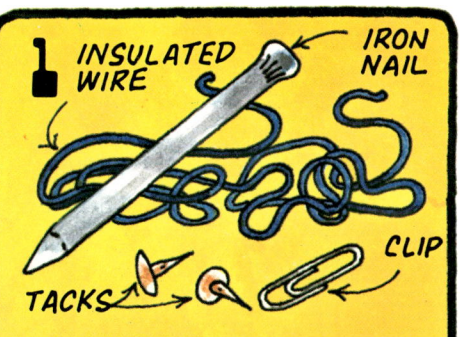

1 INSULATED WIRE — IRON NAIL — TACKS — CLIP

To make an electromagnet you need a nail about 12 cm. long, 3 m. of wire and a battery. Wind 60 turns of wire around the nail. Put sticky tape on to stop it unwinding.

2 60 TURNS — BATTERY

Remove about 2 cm. of the plastic insulation from each loose end of the wire. Wind one end of the bare wire around the ⊕ terminal of the battery. Make sure that the wire will not slip.

3 NAIL PICKS UP TACKS AND CLIPS — WIRES TO BATTERY

Touch the other end of the wire onto the ⊖ terminal of the battery. The electromagnet will now pick up nails, paperclips and other small objects with iron in them.

Detect electric currents

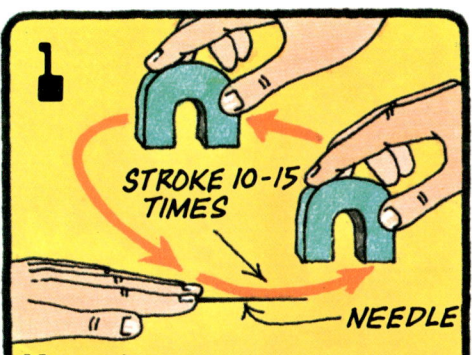

1 STROKE 10-15 TIMES — NEEDLE

Magnetise a needle by stroking it with a magnet. Make sure the return path of the magnet is well away from the needle, otherwise the needle will be very poorly magnetised.

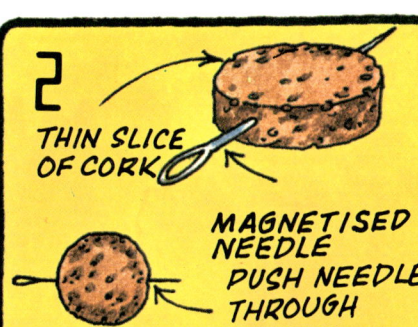

2 THIN SLICE OF CORK — MAGNETISED NEEDLE PUSH NEEDLE THROUGH MIDDLE

Cut a slice of cork about 1 cm. thick. Push the needle through the cork, making sure it passes through the centre so that it will float properly when you put it into a dish of water.

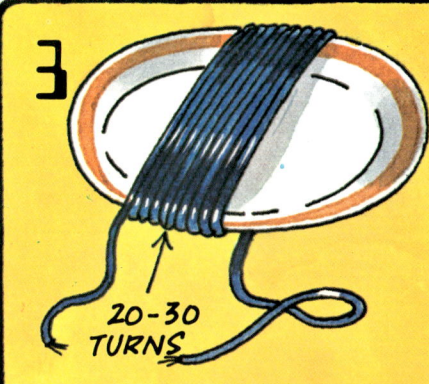

3 20-30 TURNS

Now wind 20 to 30 turns of wire around the dish. Keep the wire in place with sticky tape. Place the dish well away from electrical appliances, and pour in enough water to float the cork.

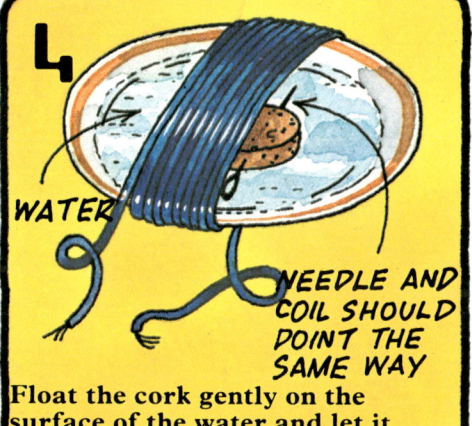

4 WATER — NEEDLE AND COIL SHOULD POINT THE SAME WAY

Float the cork gently on the surface of the water and let it come to rest. It will settle with one end pointing northwards. The needle must be able to float without scraping against the wire.

5 TOUCH WIRE TO TERMINAL — SCREW WIRE TO TERMINAL — NEEDLE KICKS WHEN CIRCUIT IS COMPLETED

Remove 2 cm. of insulation from the ends of the wire. Connect one end to the ⊖ terminal of the battery. Touch the other wire to the ⊕ terminal. The needle will give a 'kick' and spin round.

This is because the coil round the dish produces a magnetic field when a current flows through it. The needle then turns round to line itself up with this field.

77

THE ELECTRIC MOTOR

English scientist Michael Faraday invented the first electric motor in 1831. He could hardly have known at the time just how revolutionary this discovery would turn out to be.

Now industry all over the world uses electric motors to make everything from pins to spacecraft.

Motors drive inter-city and underground trains, and kitchens throughout the world would come to a halt without motors to drive food mixers, refrigerators, washing machines and other gadgets.

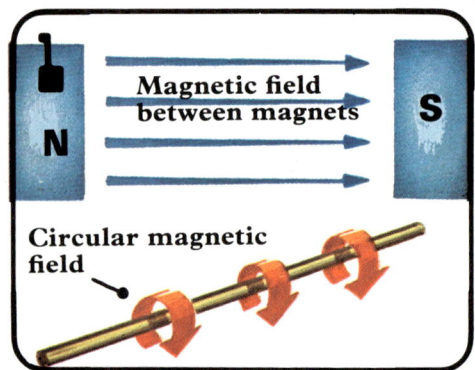

▲ The force that makes an electric motor turn round is produced when two magnetic fields meet. The first is the field between two magnetic poles and the second is the one round a wire carrying an electric current.

Inside an electric motor

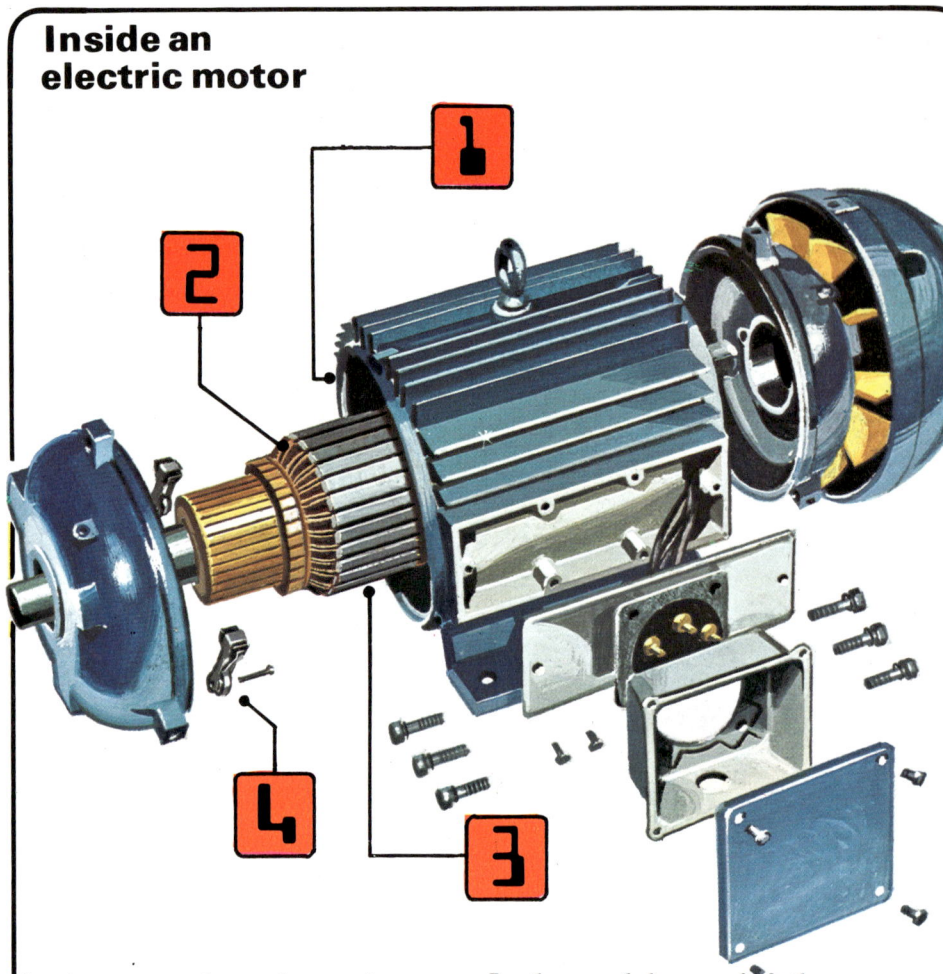

In the motor shown here, the magnetic field is produced by electromagnets (1), the coils carrying the current (2) are wound round the armature (3). The current goes to the coils through brushes (4).

In the model opposite, the magnetic field is produced by two horseshoe magnets, the armature is made from coils wound round a cork, and the current is passed to them using milk bottle tops as brushes.

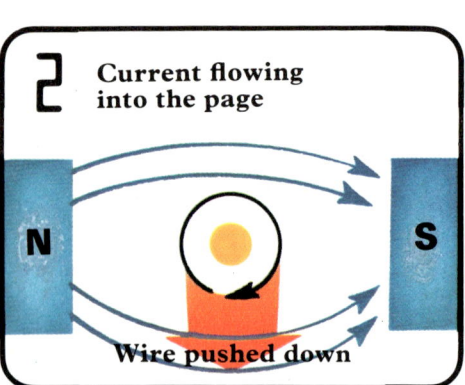

▲ In an electric motor, a wire is put between two magnets. (The circle in the picture above is an end-on view of the wire.) When the current is flowing along the wire, into the page, the wire is pushed downwards.

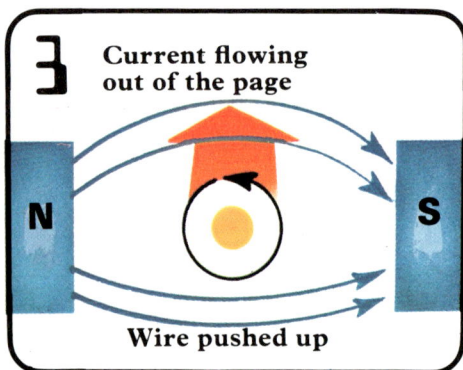

▲ If the current in the wire is travelling the other way—out of the page in this picture—the push on the wire changes as well. The wire is now pushed upwards instead of downwards.

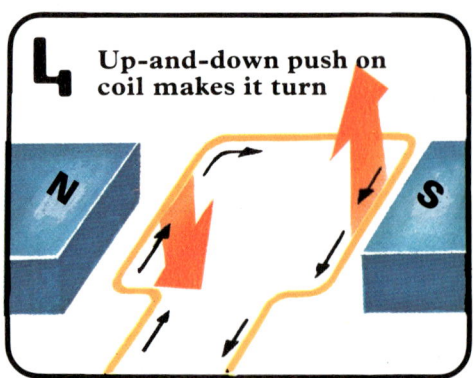

▲ Using a coil of wire means that the current flows first into, then out of, the page. So one part of the wire is pushed downwards and the other pushed upwards. Putting the coil on a shaft lets it spin round.

Make your own electric motor

You can make an electric motor that works just like the real one shown opposite. You will need the following pieces of equipment:

Sheet of balsa wood 15 cm. × 17 cm.
50 cm. of 5 mm. × 5 mm. balsa strip
Balsa cement
Two horseshoe magnets
Large cork
15 cm. knitting needle
15 m. of fine insulated wire
Three 30 cm. lengths of wire
Two drawing pins
A milk bottle top
Two 4.5 volt batteries
Ten 3 cm. long pins
Sharp knife
Sticky tape

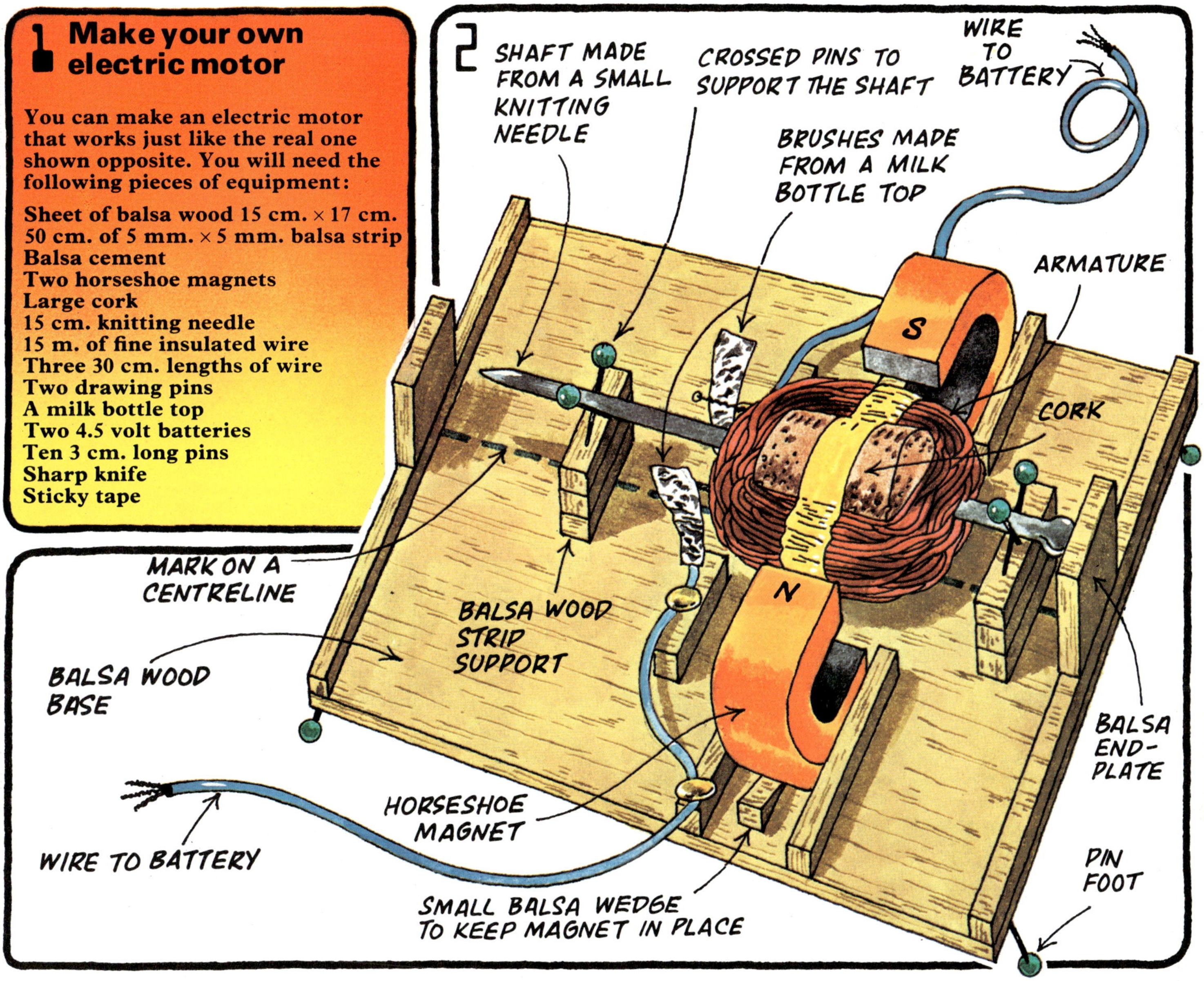

2

SHAFT MADE FROM A SMALL KNITTING NEEDLE

CROSSED PINS TO SUPPORT THE SHAFT

WIRE TO BATTERY

BRUSHES MADE FROM A MILK BOTTLE TOP

ARMATURE

S

N

CORK

BALSA END-PLATE

PIN FOOT

BALSA WOOD STRIP SUPPORT

MARK ON A CENTRELINE

BALSA WOOD BASE

WIRE TO BATTERY

HORSESHOE MAGNET

SMALL BALSA WEDGE TO KEEP MAGNET IN PLACE

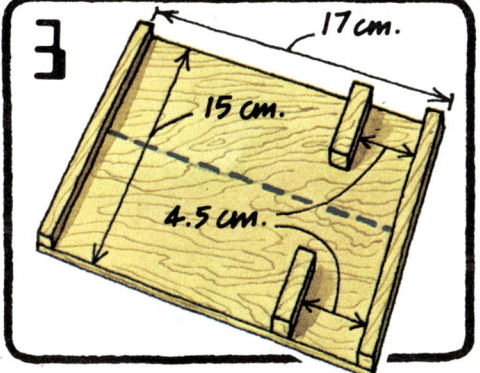

3

17 cm.

15 cm.

4.5 cm.

▲ First make the baseboard. A 15 cm. × 17 cm. sheet of balsa is about the right size. Draw in the centreline as shown above. Glue down the end strips and the first two magnet guides 4.5 cm. from one end of the baseboard.

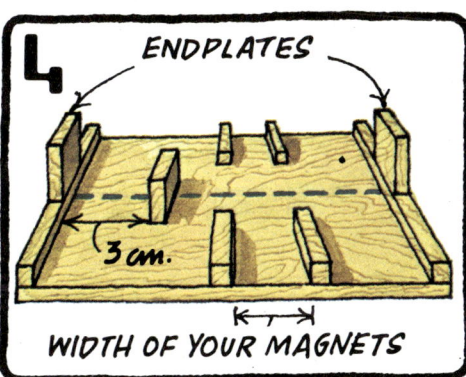

4

ENDPLATES

3 cm.

WIDTH OF YOUR MAGNETS

▲ Glue the next pair of magnet guides. The magnets should slide smoothly in the channel you have made. Stick down the endplates across the centreline. These will keep the motor in place when it goes round.

5

1 cm.

BALSA WOOD SUPPORT

▲ The supports for the bearings should be made from three layers of the balsa wood strip.

Continued next page

Make your own electric motor

continued from p.79

6 CROSSED PINS

▲ Use crossed pins to support the armature shaft. They do not need plastic ends like the ones shown, but they should be at least 3 cm. long. Push them very firmly into the wood, so they will not come loose when the motor is working.

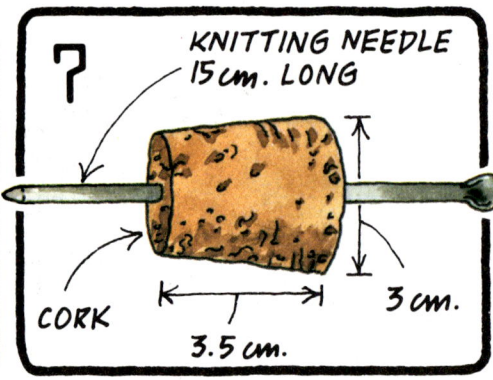

7 KNITTING NEEDLE 15 cm. LONG
CORK
3.5 cm.
3 cm.

▲ Push the knitting needle into the centre of the cork. If there is already a hole in the cork, fill up the space with plasticine to make a tight fit. Make sure there are about 5 cm. of knitting needle sticking out of each side.

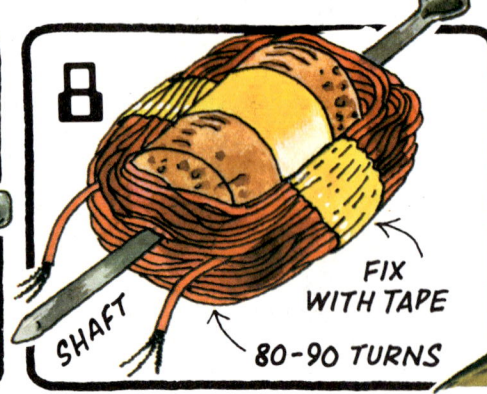

8 FIX WITH TAPE
80-90 TURNS
SHAFT

▲ Wind 80-90 turns of fine wire round the cork. Stick in two pins (see 9 below) which should be the same distance from the shaft. If you find this difficult, stick the pins into the cork before winding on the wire.

9 PIN
WRAP WIRE ROUND PIN

▲ Remove 4 cm. of insulation from the loose ends of the wire. Wind one of the bare wires round a pin. Repeat for the other wire and pin. Make sure they are firmly in place. Place the shaft on its crossed-pin supports.

10 FOLD OVER
5 cm.

▲ Take two 30 cm. lengths of the thicker wire. Remove the insulation from one end of each wire for a distance of about 5 cm. Place half a milk bottle top over the end and fold it over to make a 5 cm. long strip.

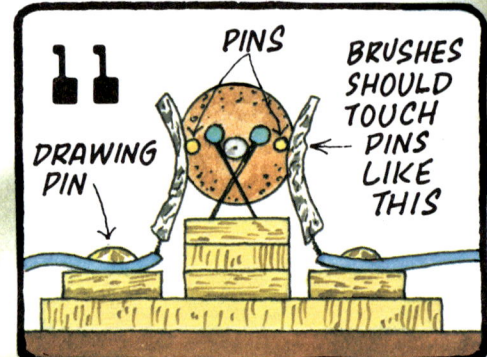

11 PINS
BRUSHES SHOULD TOUCH PINS LIKE THIS
DRAWING PIN

▲ Pin the thicker wires to the baseboard so that the flexible bottle top brushes touch the pins at the same instant when the shaft turns. These wires will be connected to the batteries when the motor is ready to run.

12 MAKE SURE POLES OF MAGNETS ARE LIKE THIS
N   S

▲ Place the magnets in position. Make sure that the two poles facing each other are opposite poles (test this by seeing that they attract one another). The armature should lie directly between the two poles.

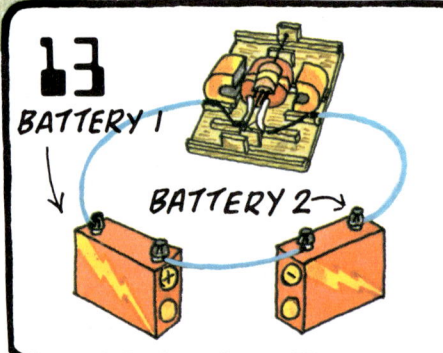

13 BATTERY 1
BATTERY 2

Connect the ⊕ of battery 1 to the ⊖ of battery 2 with the third length of wire. Then connect the brush wires to the ⊖ of battery 1 and the ⊕ of battery 2. A gentle push should start the motor spinning round.

14 Troubleshooting!

No matter how much care you take, your motor might not work first time. Points to check are:

1 Make sure the armature is free to turn.
2 Keep the magnets as close as possible to, but not touching, the armature.
3 When the armature is horizontal it should lie between the poles of the magnets.
4 Make sure the brushes touch the pins at exactly the same instant.
5 The brushes should just stroke the pins as they pass.

HOW ELECTRIC MOTORS ARE USED

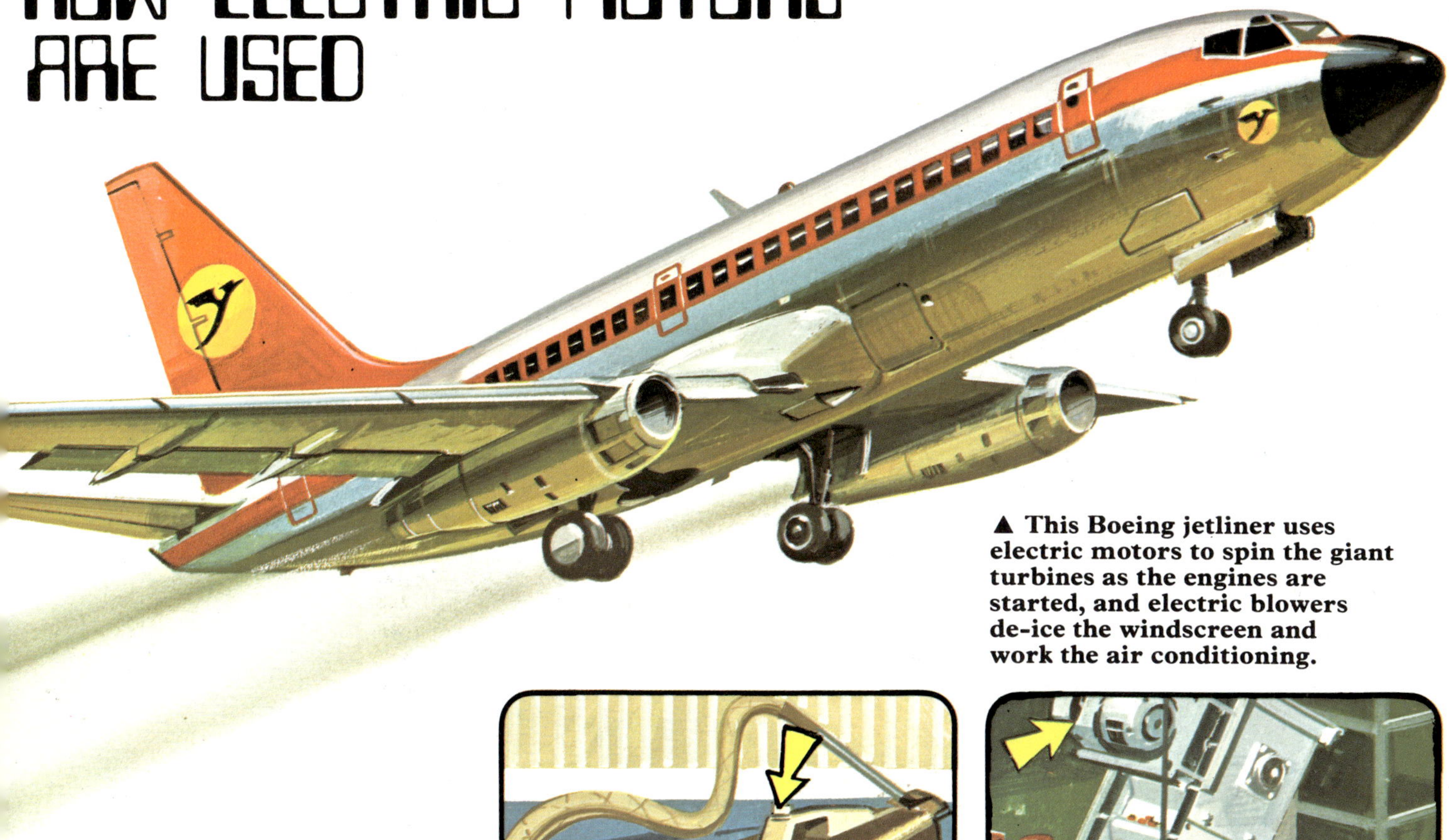

▲ This Boeing jetliner uses electric motors to spin the giant turbines as the engines are started, and electric blowers de-ice the windscreen and work the air conditioning.

Electricity is used to drive all sorts of things—from huge locomotives to electric clocks.

The combination of great power and high precision has led to the widespread use of electric motors in the home as well as in factories.

You will probably be surprised at the number of gadgets in your home that use motors. Try making a check list of all the things in your house that have one.

▲ The vacuum cleaner is a useful tool in the home. The motor turns a high speed fan which produces a suction effect in the flexible pipe. Dust and dirt sucked in are trapped in a disposable paper bag.

▲ The motor shown here is lifting sweets from a conveyor belt into a container that weighs out the right quantity and packs them automatically. The motor lifts over 100,000 sweets every day. That's a lot of sweets!

▲ As motor-cycles get bigger, the old fashioned kick starter is being replaced by an electric starter motor like those used in motor cars. The rider simply presses a button on the handlebars to set the engine going.

▲ Manufacturers have to use more and more motors to speed up production in factories. In this picture aerosol cans full of fly killer are passed along a motor-driven belt ready to have their labels stuck on.

▲ Motor-driven machines can do many jobs much better and faster than people. All the pages in this book were stitched together by machines like the one above. If you look carefully, you can see this page in the picture above.

ALTERNATING CURRENT

The electricity supplied by a battery flows in one direction and is called direct current.

The other sort of electricity, made in power stations, is called alternating current. The electrons move to and fro in the wire instead of in one direction. But they produce the same effect as electrons drifting only one way.

▶ To make alternating current, power stations use generators that have coils like an electric motor. As each coil is turned between the two magnets, current is made—the exact opposite of an electric motor. But the amount of current varies as the coil turns round.

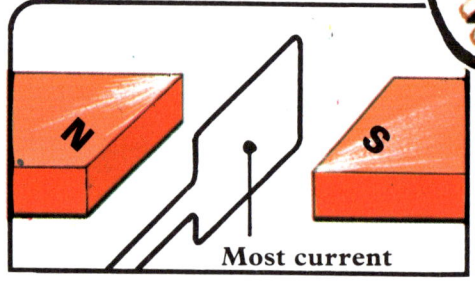

Most current

No current

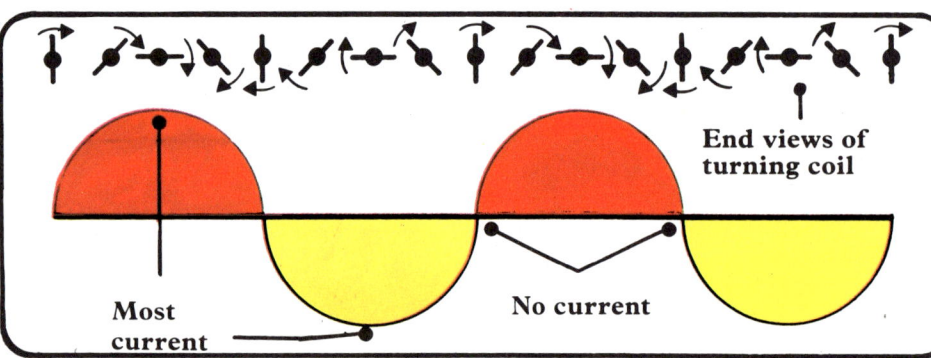

End views of turning coil

Most current

No current

▲ The picture above shows you how the amount of current varies as the coil turns. The turning coil is shown end-on along the top of the picture. You can see that when the coil is upright, no current is made at all. As it turns the current flow begins to increase, but soon the flow gets smaller again. After the coil has turned half a circle, the current starts to flow the other way. Power stations produce 50 of these two-way cycles every second.

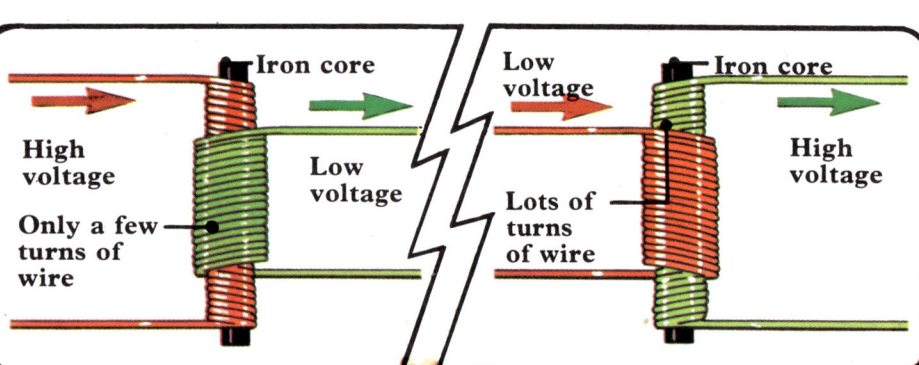

Iron core

High voltage

Only a few turns of wire

Low voltage

Low voltage

Iron core

High voltage

Lots of turns of wire

▲ Alternating current is useful because its voltage can be changed by using a transformer, which is simply two coils of insulated wire wound round an iron core. Although there is no electrical connection between the two coils, any voltage in the first coil sets up a voltage in the second coil. This effect is called induction. Larger or smaller voltages—whatever is needed—can be set up by varying the number of turns in the two coils.

Transformers like this one are used in power stations all over the world.

These insulators are several metres long. They keep the very high voltages away from the metal tank.

The transformer coils and core are kept in this thick metal tank.

Increasing the voltage is called stepping up. Making it smaller is called stepping down.

High voltage power lines enter and leave the transformer through large insulators.

Oil flows round the coils keeping them cool.

1 How induction works

The current flow in a transformer's second coil is set up by a magnetic effect called induction. Induction only works when a current is getting bigger or smaller, not when it is a steady flow. This is why power stations use alternating current which varies all the time as the coils in a generator spin round. Turn your battery on and off to provide the varying current you need.

FIX WITH TAPE

WIND 50 TURNS OF WIRE ROUND NAIL

▲ You will need a large nail and enough wire to make 100 turns of wire round it. Cut the wire in half and wind 50 turns round the nail. Use sticky tape to stop it unwinding. Leave 10 cm. of wire free at each end.

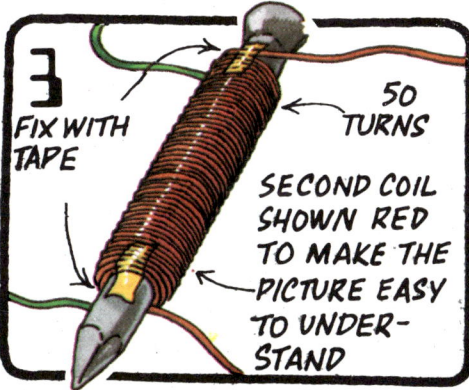

FIX WITH TAPE

50 TURNS

SECOND COIL SHOWN RED TO MAKE THE PICTURE EASY TO UNDER-STAND

▲ Wind the rest of the wire over the top of the first coil. Tape it down so it does not unwind. Leave about 1 m. of wire free at the ends of this coil. Strip off 2 cm. of insulation from the ends of the two coils.

NORTH

30 TURNS

▲ More wire and a compass needed! Wind 30 turns round the compass and tape it firmly. The wire coil should line up with the compass needle. The needle will kick sideways when any electric current flows in the wire round it.

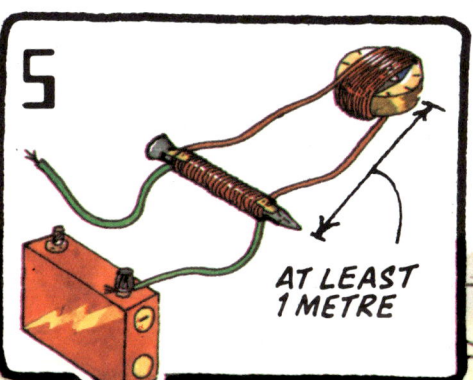

AT LEAST 1 METRE

▲ Connect the compass wires to the second coil wires. Make sure the compass is 1 m. away from the coil. This is because the compass might point towards the nail when you switch the current from the battery on.

TAPE COMPASS TO TABLE

COMPASS WILL KICK, THEN SINK BACK. KICK AGAIN WHEN YOU SWITCH OFF

▲ Connect a wire to one of the battery terminals. Touch the other wire to the other terminal. The needle will kick, then sink back. Switch off and the needle will kick again in the other direction.

INSIDE A POWER STATION

Although electricity appears naturally as lightning, it is impossible to turn this to our own use. Even if the power of lightning could be used there is no way to know when or where it would strike.

The electricity used for lighting, warming homes and running industry is completely man-made.

It is difficult to store large amounts of electricity, so power stations are designed to produce electricity at the time that it is needed.

▲ Power stations use turbine wheels (which are rather like propellers on a ship) to turn the coils in their generators. One way to spin turbines is to use fast flowing water, so rivers are dammed to provide the water.

▲ Most power stations use coal or oil. The fuel burns and boils water. The steam from the boiling water is passed through pipes to spin turbines which turn the generator coils. Most modern power stations are very clean.

A giant turbine generator

Power stations burn coal or oil, or use nuclear fuel, to heat water up to make high pressure steam. The steam spins turbines, and a generator attached to the turbine shaft produces hundreds of megawatts of electricity. A megawatt is a million watts— enough to light 10,000 powerful light bulbs.

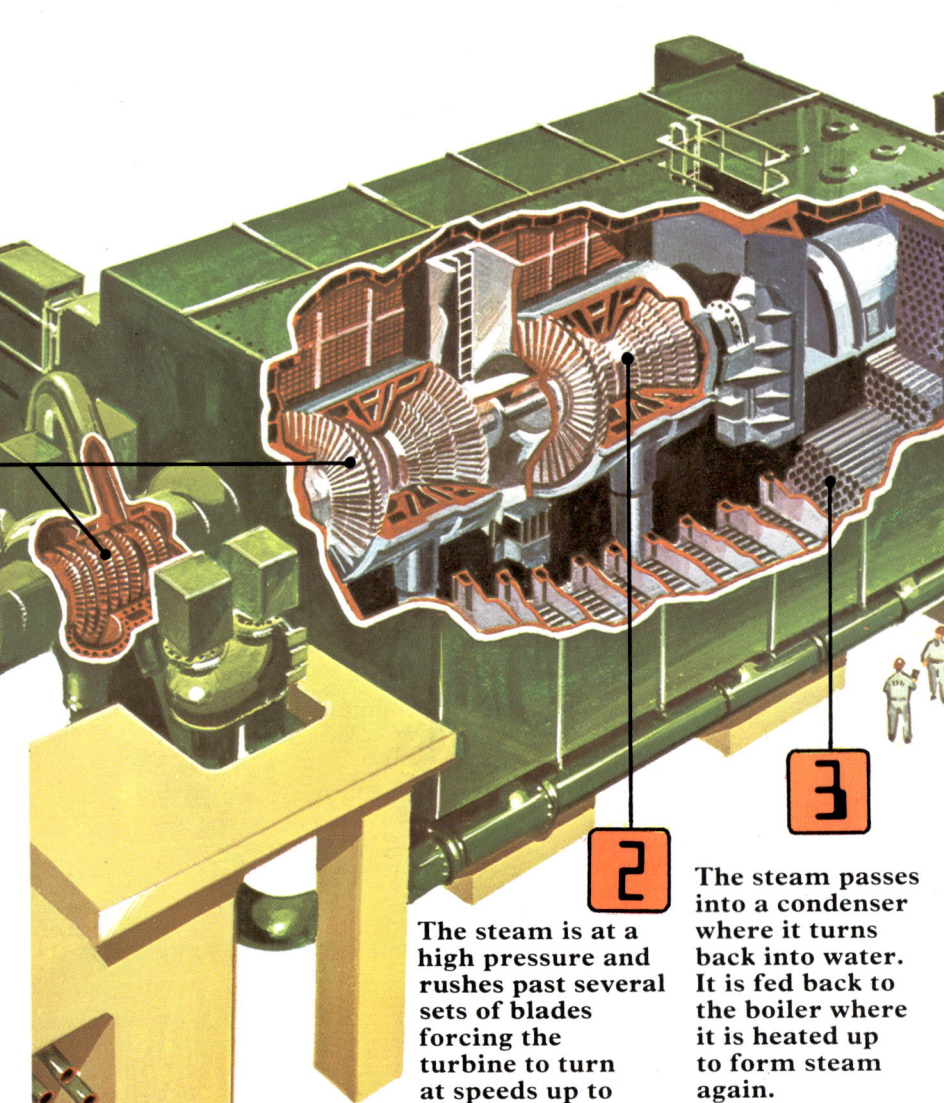

 Steam produced by the boiler is fed into cylinders containing the turbines.

2 The steam is at a high pressure and rushes past several sets of blades forcing the turbine to turn at speeds up to 3000 times a minute.

3 The steam passes into a condenser where it turns back into water. It is fed back to the boiler where it is heated up to form steam again.

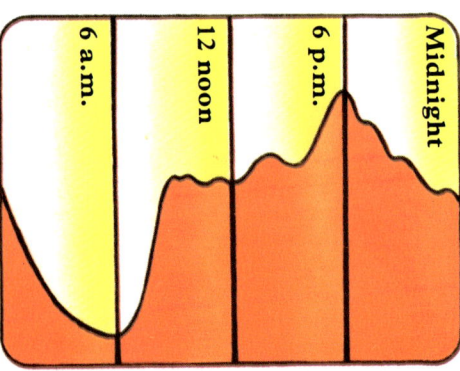

▲ This chart shows when power is most needed. There is a steep increase in the morning as people wake up and put on the kettle at breakfast time. There is another peak at 6 p.m. when they return from work.

▲ The power behind the atom bomb can be used peacefully, and nuclear power stations are producing more and more of the world's electricity. But one problem is the dangerous radioactive waste produced.

4

An electrical generator attached to the end of the turbine shaft turns round with it and produces power.

1 Make a spinning turbine wheel

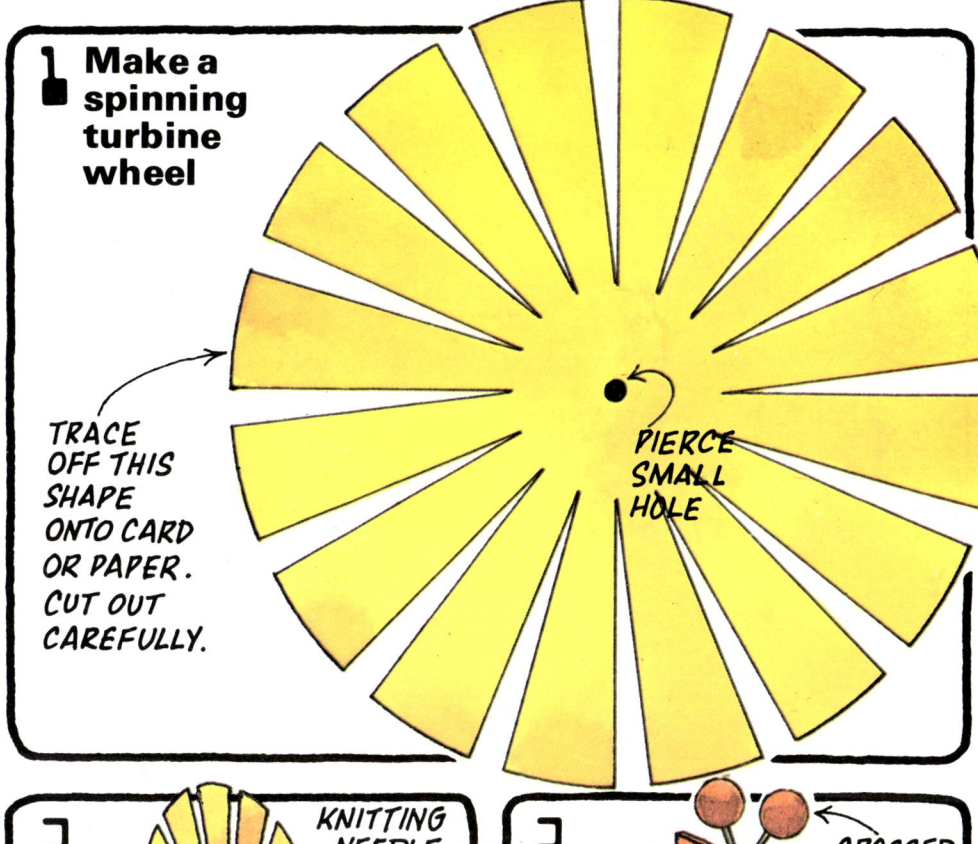

TRACE OFF THIS SHAPE ONTO CARD OR PAPER. CUT OUT CAREFULLY.

PIERCE SMALL HOLE

2

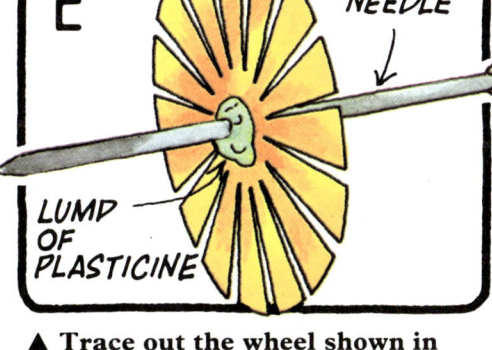

KNITTING NEEDLE

LUMP OF PLASTICINE

▲ Trace out the wheel shown in 1 above onto thin card. Cut it out, and pierce the middle with a knitting needle as shown here. Fix two lumps of plasticine on either side to keep it steady, otherwise it will not work.

3

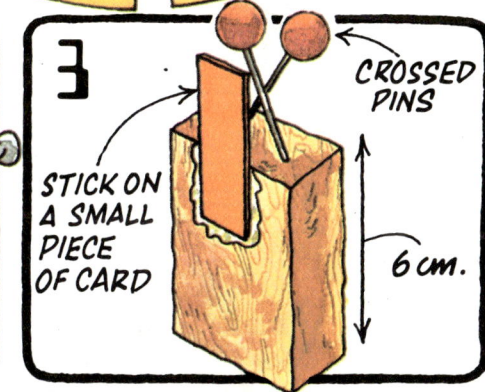

CROSSED PINS

STICK ON A SMALL PIECE OF CARD

6 CM.

▲ Two crossed pins stuck into a block of balsa wood are the bearings. A small piece of card stuck on the back will stop the needle sliding through the crossed pins. Make two sets of bearings.

4

BEND BLADES

▲ Carefully twist each of the blades at a small angle. This will make the turbine spin round when you blow through it. You will have to experiment to find the angle which will spin the wheel round fast.

5

BLOW GENTLY

FIX WITH PLASTICINE

▲ Place the balsa blocks on a table. Place the needle on the crossed-pin bearings. Using your breath just like the steam in a power station, blow along the needle. The turbine will spin round just like the real thing.

POWER LINES ACROSS THE COUNTRY

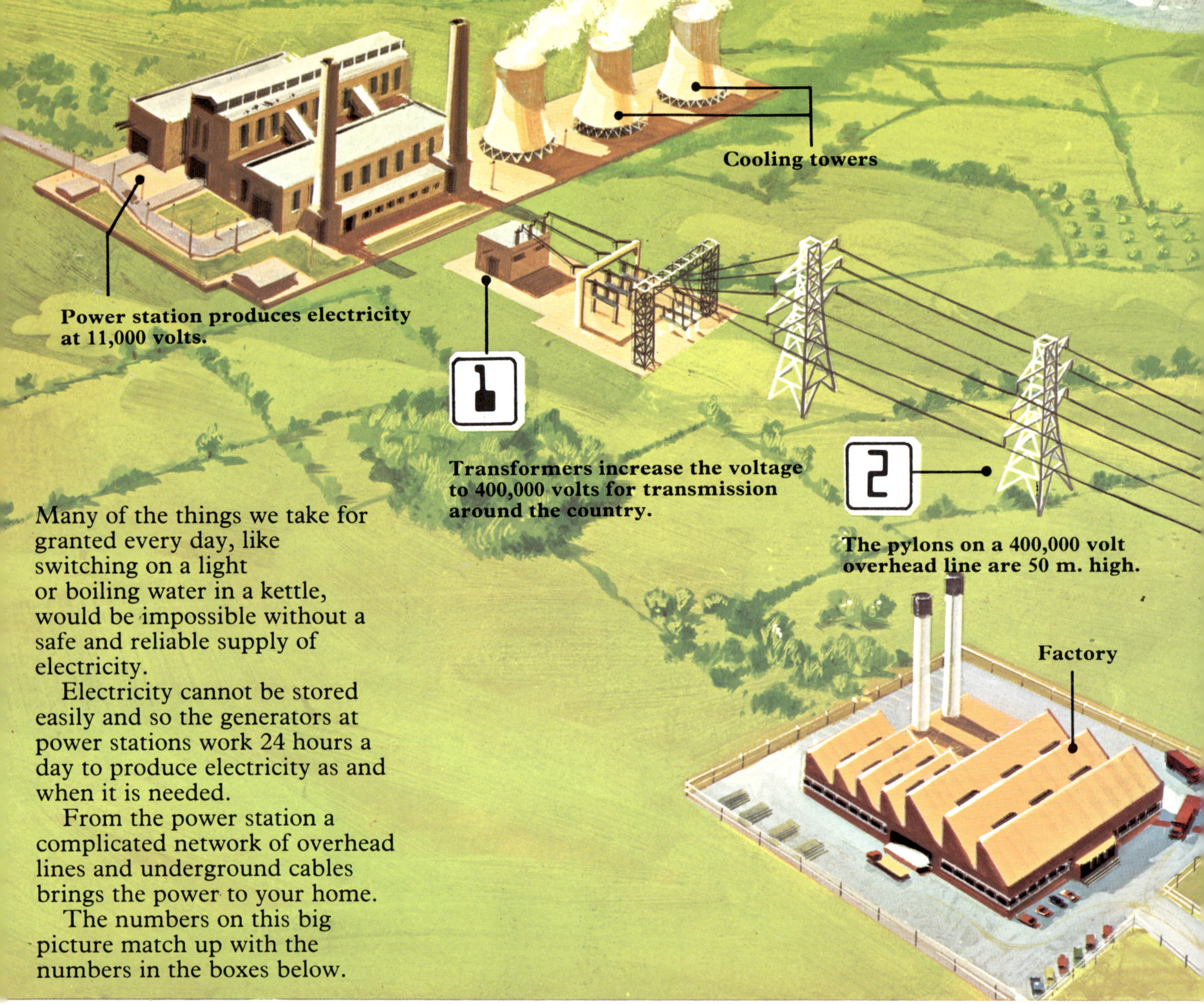

Cooling towers

Power station produces electricity at 11,000 volts.

1

Transformers increase the voltage to 400,000 volts for transmission around the country.

2

The pylons on a 400,000 volt overhead line are 50 m. high.

Factory

Many of the things we take for granted every day, like switching on a light or boiling water in a kettle, would be impossible without a safe and reliable supply of electricity.

Electricity cannot be stored easily and so the generators at power stations work 24 hours a day to produce electricity as and when it is needed.

From the power station a complicated network of overhead lines and underground cables brings the power to your home.

The numbers on this big picture match up with the numbers in the boxes below.

▲ Power station generators make electricity at 11,000 volts. To deliver electricity with as little waste as possible a very high voltage must be used. So transformers at the station step up the voltage to 400,000 volts.

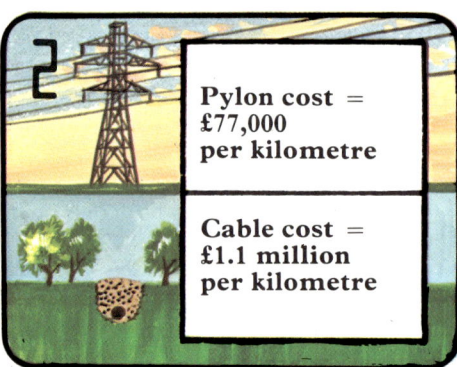

Pylon cost = £77,000 per kilometre

Cable cost = £1.1 million per kilometre

▲ Electricity can be carried over the countryside on overhead lines or underground cables. Pylons over the ground are ugly but they are much cheaper to make and erect than underground cables as you can see above.

▲ When lightning strikes an overhead line, switches called circuit breakers cut off that section of the line. Users on the 'dead' part are left without electricity until the fault is put right.

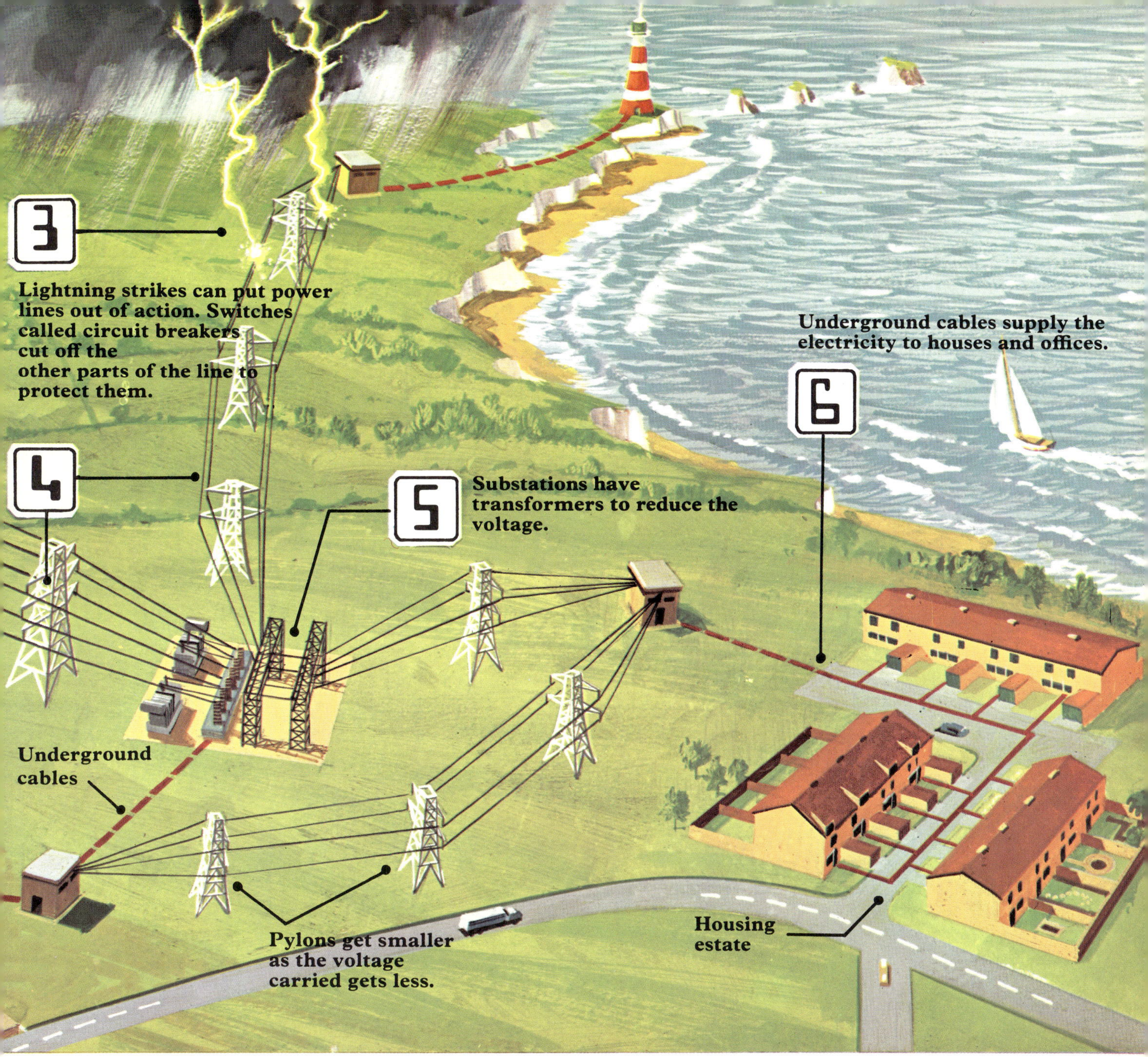

3 Lightning strikes can put power lines out of action. Switches called circuit breakers cut off the other parts of the line to protect them.

4

Underground cables

5 Substations have transformers to reduce the voltage.

Pylons get smaller as the voltage carried gets less.

Underground cables supply the electricity to houses and offices.

6

Housing estate

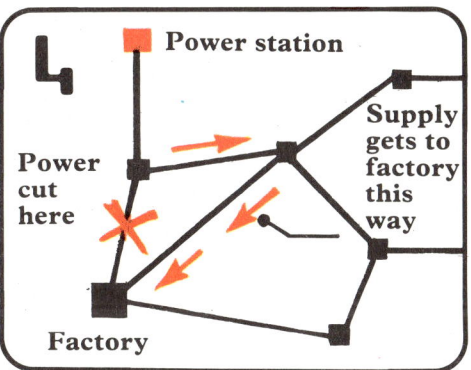

▲ To avoid power cuts caused by lightning, electricity supply lines are arranged in an inter-connecting grid. If one of the supplies to a factory is cut off, it can still get its supply from another line.

▲ When the electricity reaches the main substation, it is still at a very high voltage. Step-down transformers in the substation reduce the voltage to a lower level which is carried on smaller, lighter pylons.

▲ The final link in the chain from power station to home. Underground cables are used in towns because overhead lines would be dangerous. They pass beneath the pavement and feed the power to your home.

INSIDE THE HOME

Once the power has come into your home, the many gadgets and appliances are fed by several different circuits. There are usually 5 circuits. One for the downstairs wall sockets, one for those upstairs, one each for the downstairs and upstairs lighting circuits, and one for the electric cooker.

The wires carrying the power are run in metal or plastic tubes hidden in the walls and ceiling, or under the floor, so they can't be touched. This picture shows some of the uses for electricity in your home.

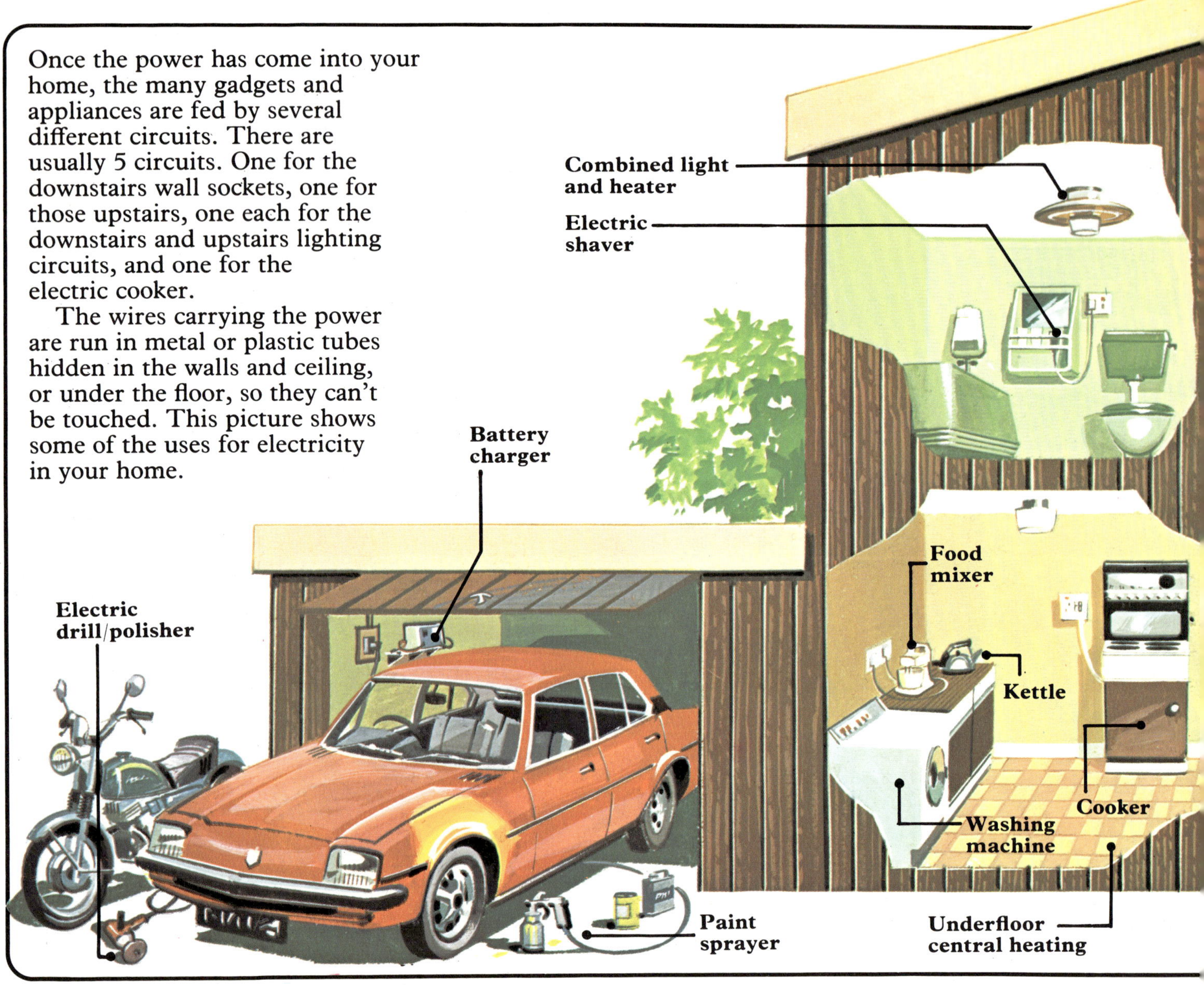

Combined light and heater

Electric shaver

Battery charger

Food mixer

Kettle

Cooker

Electric drill/polisher

Washing machine

Paint sprayer

Underfloor central heating

Using electricity

Different appliances use different amounts of electricity. They all work at mains voltage but use different amounts of current. The energy used by a 100 watt bulb in 10 hours keeps an electric clock going for 3 months.

Boil 7 litres of water

Drill holes for 4 hours

Watch the clock for 3 months

22 14 19

Light a 100W bulb for 10 hours

Have a 40W strip light on for a day

Immersion
heater

Radio

Electric
blanket

Fuse protection

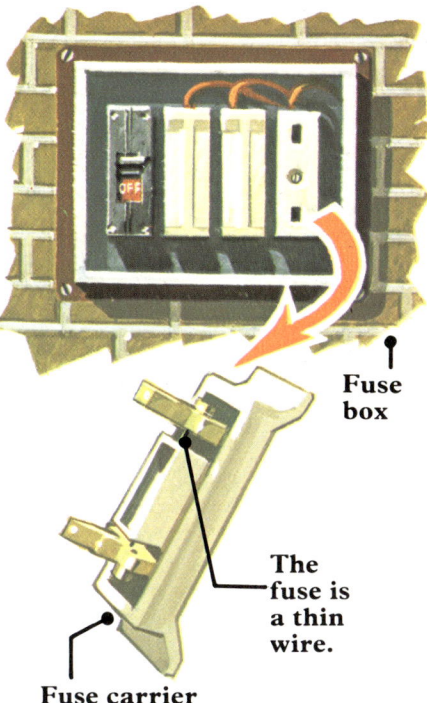

Fuse
box

The
fuse is
a thin
wire.

Fuse carrier

Fuse box   Doorbell   Television   Vacuum cleaner

▲ The current flow to each circuit
in a house passes through a fuse,
which is a strand of wire held in
a plastic carrier. If a fault in
the circuit makes a high current
flow, the fuse heats up and breaks,
cutting off the power supply.

The fault must then be put right
and the fuse replaced.

Some new houses have circuit
breakers instead of fuses to cut
off the power supply.

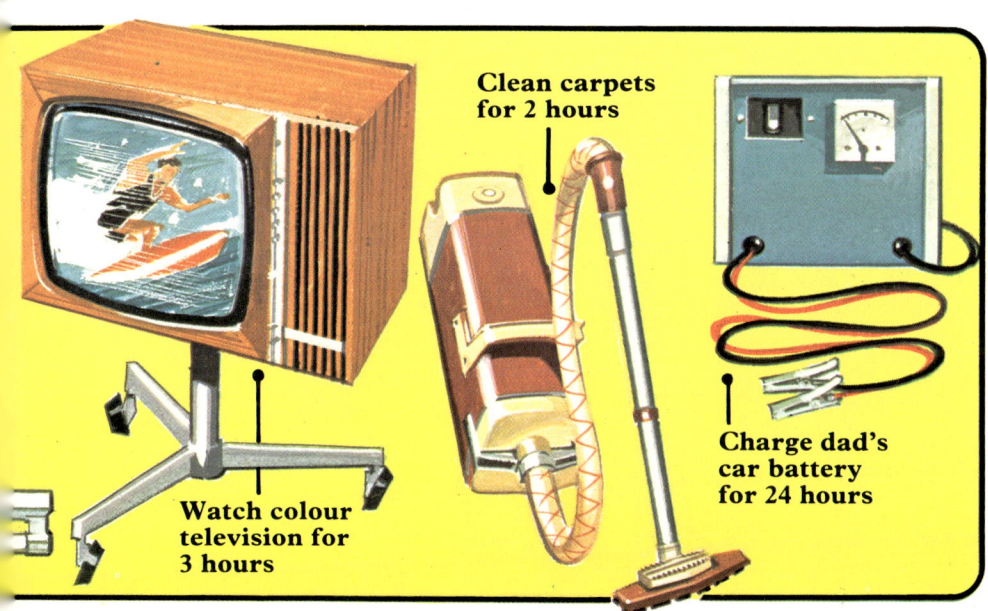

Clean carpets
for 2 hours

Charge dad's
car battery
for 24 hours

Watch colour
television for
3 hours

MAINS ELECTRICITY IS DANGEROUS

The electricity in your
home is at a very high
voltage. It can easily
KILL people.

This is why all the
wiring in a house is
built into the walls,
ceilings and floors.

NEVER play with plugs,
sockets or anything
connected to the mains
supply.

TELEGRAPH AND TELEPHONE

The invention of the electric telegraph in 1838 enabled people to communicate directly with one another over long distances. The only connection between then was the wire which carried the message.

Before Bell invented the telephone in 1876 it was not possible to talk over a telegraph wire. So the message had to be coded into a series of long and short electrical currents which were passed along the wire and decoded at the receiving station. This is why a telegram is sometimes called a 'wire'.

▲ You will need two 4.5 volt batteries, two 6 volt bulbs in holders, a sheet of cardboard and a sheet of cooking foil. Decide where to put the two telegraph stations. Get enough 3-core flex to join the two.

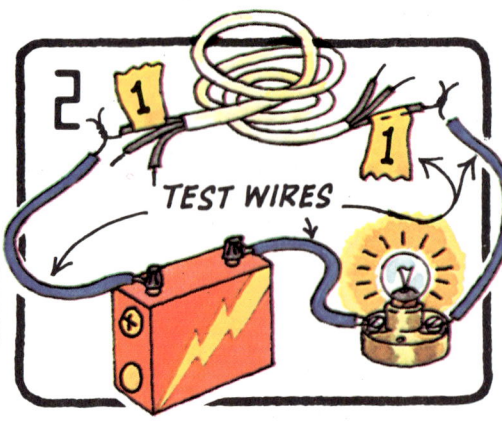

▲ To find out which wire is which, wire up a battery and bulb as shown. Connect a test wire to one of the flex wires. Touch the other wires until the bulb glows. Mark the wires and repeat for the others.

▲ To make station B, wire 3 of the flex's other end is connected to the ⊕ terminal of the other battery. Wire 2 is connected to the other bulbholder. Join the holder's other terminal to wire 1 with a spare wire. Fix the other spare wire to the battery ⊖ terminal. Double-check all the connections you have made so far, to avoid mistakes—the wiring is quite complicated and if you make a mistake, you might have to start all over again!

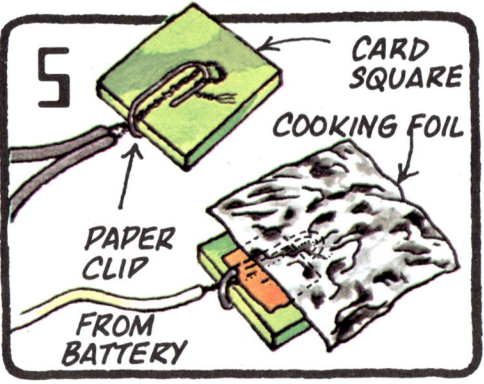

▲ You need four Morse tappers. One on each of the spare wires from a battery, and one on each pair of twisted-together wires. Clip the wires to squares of cardboard with paper clips, and glue cooking foil over the top.

A century of telephones

"Mr. Watson, come here, I want to see you." Alexander Graham Bell's historic call to his assistant in 1876 was the first time speech had been transmitted over a wire.

Bell realised the importance of his new invention and set up a telephone company to satisfy the sudden demand for telephones.

Within two years of this first demonstration thousands of telephones had been installed in offices in America, and within five years Bell retired from the business a famous and wealthy man.

Bell's first telephone, 1875

Gower-Bell wall hanging model 1880

Station A

▲ To make station A, attach wire 1 from the flex to the ⊖ terminal of a battery. Connect wire 2 to a bulbholder. Connect a piece of spare wire to the bulbholder's other terminal, twisting its other end with wire 3.

The second spare wire should be attached to the battery's ⊕ terminal. Remember that these details are to show you how to wire up the telegraph system properly. The wire lengths depend on where you put the stations.

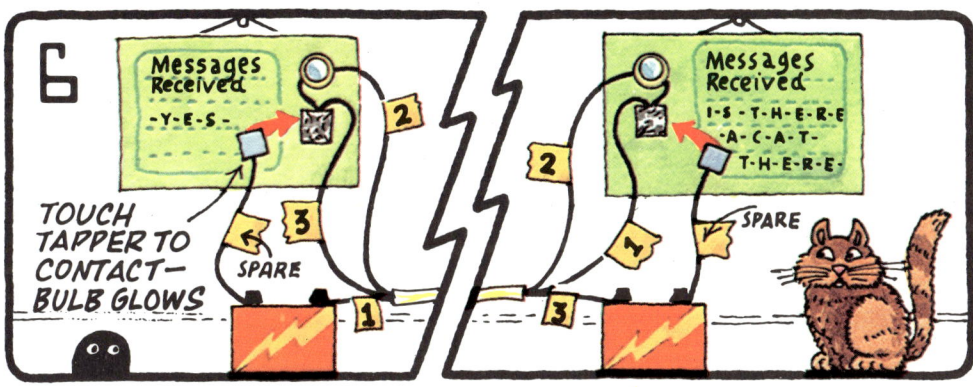

TOUCH TAPPER TO CONTACT— BULB GLOWS

▲ Fix each bulbholder and one of the tappers to a sheet of card that will hang on the wall of Station A. Do the same for Station B. It's a good idea to have a pad of paper there too to write down messages as they come

in. Unless you already know the Morse Code, you will need to use the one we have printed here to code any message you want to send, or to decode messages that come in. Once you get the hang of it, see how fast you can decode Morse!

Table model 1920's

Push button model 1970's

Before messages can be sent over a telegraph wire they must be coded into electrical signals at the sending end. In the code invented by Samuel Morse the 26 letters of the alphabet are represented by 26 different combinations of long and short dots and dashes. Remember that to be exact, your dashes should be three times as long as your dots.

A	● ▬
B	▬ ● ● ●
C	▬ ● ▬ ●
D	▬ ● ●
E	●
F	● ● ▬ ●
G	▬ ▬ ●
H	● ● ● ●
I	● ●
J	● ▬ ▬ ▬
K	▬ ● ▬
L	● ▬ ● ●
M	▬ ▬
N	▬ ●
O	▬ ▬ ▬
P	● ▬ ▬ ●
Q	▬ ▬ ● ▬
R	● ▬ ●
S	● ● ●
T	▬
U	● ● ▬
V	● ● ● ▬
W	● ▬ ▬
X	▬ ● ● ▬
Y	▬ ● ▬ ▬
Z	▬ ▬ ● ●
1	● ▬ ▬ ▬ ▬
2	● ● ▬ ▬ ▬
3	● ● ● ▬ ▬
4	● ● ● ● ▬
5	● ● ● ● ●
6	▬ ● ● ● ●
7	▬ ▬ ● ● ●
8	▬ ▬ ▬ ● ●
9	▬ ▬ ▬ ▬ ●
10	▬ ▬ ▬ ▬ ▬

21ST CENTURY ELECTRICITY

If we go on using coal, oil and gas as fast as we do now, they will be used up in under 100 years. So scientists are looking for other ways of producing electricity.

One idea shown here is for an orbiting solar collector that turns sunlight into electricity and then sends it down to Earth.

Another possibility is a nuclear fusion reactor. The fuels needed for fusion are found in sea water, so the world's oceans could one day produce almost limitless supplies of energy.

The solar collector picks up the sunlight and converts it into electricity using solar cells like the ones which power many of today's satellites. The bigger it is the more electricity it produces. This one measures 8 km. by 8 km. which is as large as 13,000 football pitches.

The Sun

Sun's rays caught by the collector.

The power transmitter is connected to the solar collector, and the pair orbit the Earth. They stay in orbit above the receiving station on the Earth's surface 35,880 km. below.

The sunlight reaching the Earth's surface has been filtered through the atmosphere, but the solar collector out in space catches all the direct rays of the Sun. It produces far more electricity out in space than it would do on Earth.

Superspeed railways

The 21st century railway train will be very different from today's model. It will be driven by linear electric motors and will glide along a track at speeds up to 400 k.p.h. Wheels will not be used because the train will be suspended a few centimetres above the track by powerful magnetic fields.

Passenger cabin

Power coils

Train floats just above the track

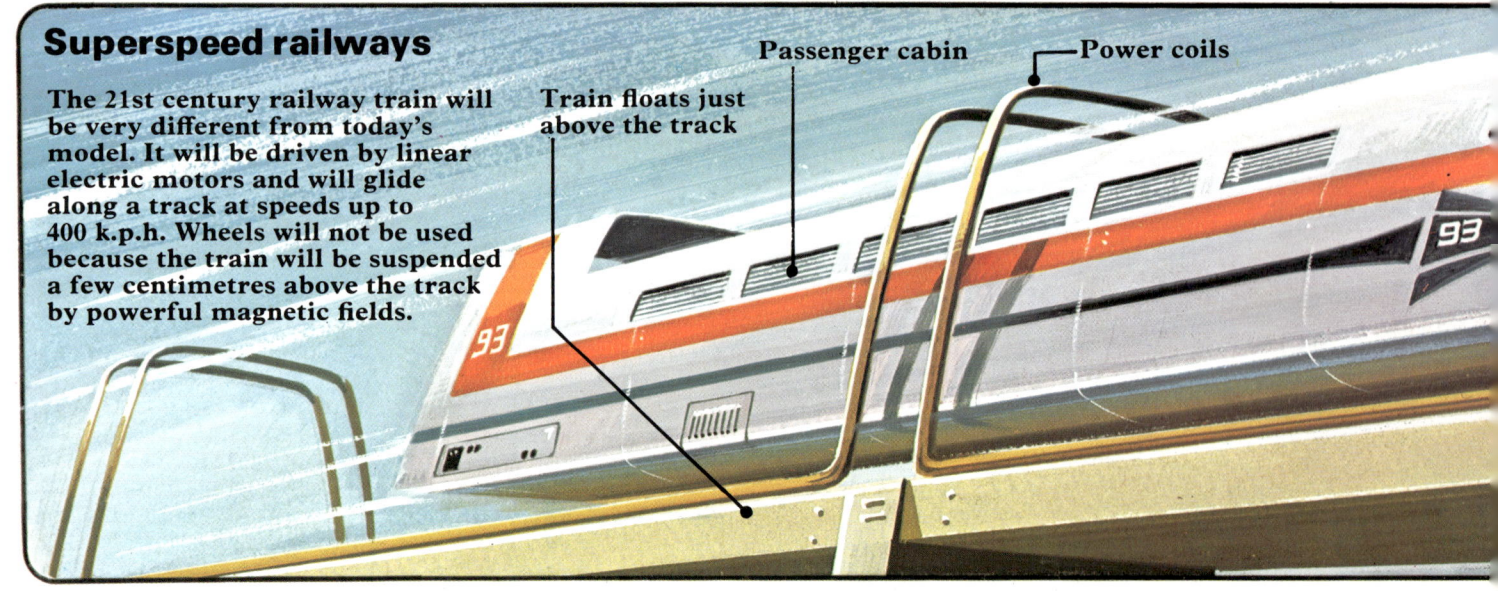

Power beam to Earth

To collect the power beamed down from the orbiting collector, a large collecting area is needed. Each receiving station collects enough power to supply one major city with electricity.

Driver's cabin

Power from the atom

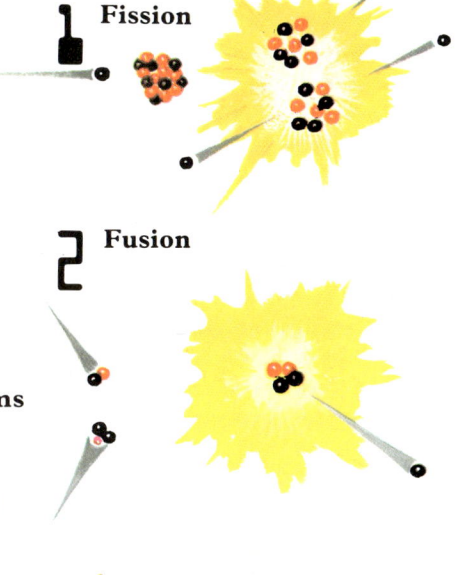

1 Fission

2 Fusion

Today's atomic power stations are all fission reactors. Atoms are split in the reactor and the heat given off is used to boil water for steam. Fission reactors have one major problem—radioactive waste. So scientists are trying to make fusion reactors. A fusion reactor would have little or no dangerous waste.

▶ Fusion is the combining of atoms of deuterium and tritium—both found in sea water. When the two atoms join they give off a lot of energy as heat, which can be used to produce electricity.

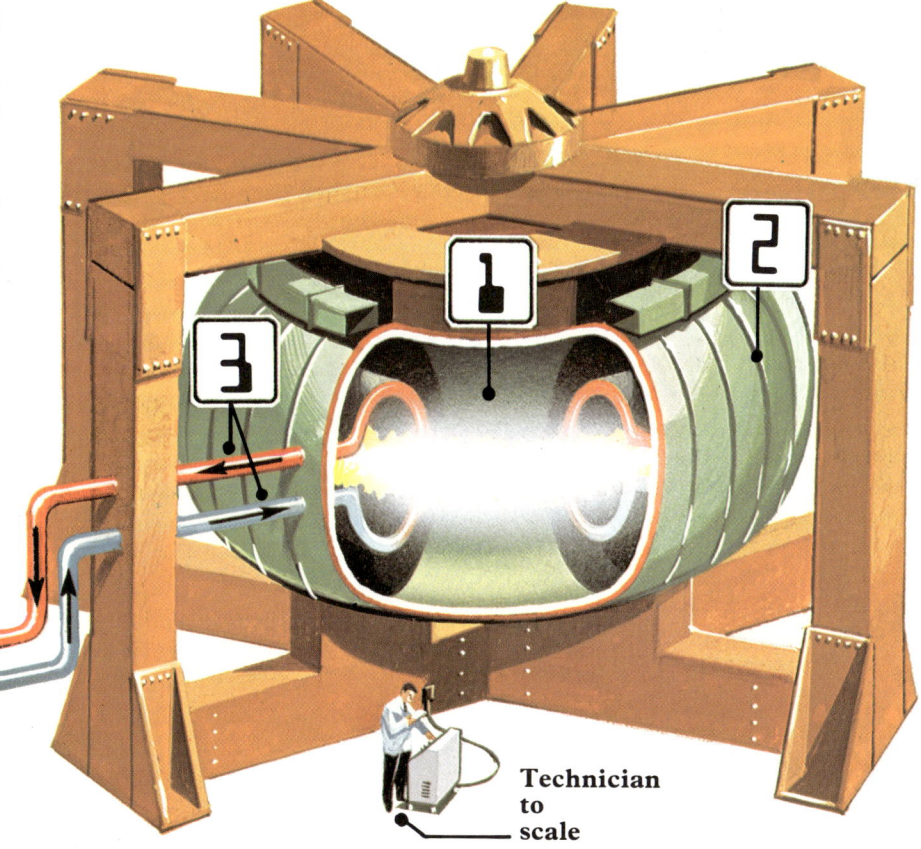

1

2

3

Technician to scale

Tomorrow's fusion reactor

▲ Deuterium and tritium atoms join only at a temperature of 100 million°C. No known material will withstand such a high temperature and the only suitable container for the reaction is a powerful magnetic field (1). The field is produced by a huge electric current flowing through coils of wire embedded in the doughnut-shaped concrete wall (2). Lithium—a metal liquefied by the heat—is pumped through pipes (3) to boil water. The steam given off turns turbines, which turn the coils in a generator.

ELECTRIC FIRSTS

Here are some of the milestones in the development of modern electricity. You will see that some of the inventions have become such an accepted part of day to day routine that it is difficult to imagine what life would be like without them.

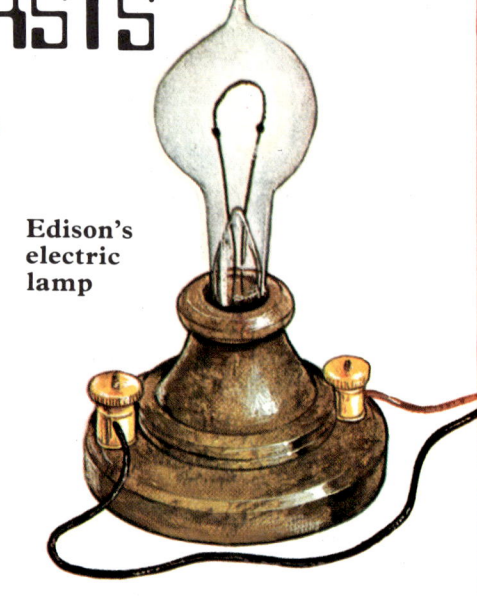

Edison's electric lamp

1600
English scientist William Gilbert published his theory that the Earth had a magnetic field.

1672
Otto von Guericke invented the first electrical machine. A large sulphur ball turned by a handle produced static electricity when a hand was rubbed against it.

1752
Benjamin Franklin showed that thunderclouds are charged with static electricity.

1800
The first electric battery was made by Count Alessandro Volta in Italy.

1831
English scientist Michael Faraday built the first generator of electric current.

1837
The first electric telegraph was built by Samuel Morse in America. The code that bears his name is still used today.

1858
The first transatlantic telegraph cable was laid.

1876
Scottish born inventor Alexander Graham Bell invented the telephone.

1879
The world's first electric railway was opened in Berlin.

Thomas Edison made the first electric light bulb. It glowed for 40 hours before the filament burned out.

1882
Edison set up the first public electricity supply. His Pearl Street station in New York supplied power to shops and houses over an area of 2 square kilometres.

1956
The first power station to produce electricity from the power of the atom was opened at Calder Hall, England. There are now more than 300 nuclear power stations all over the world.

1975
The first production-line built electric car rolled off the assembly line.

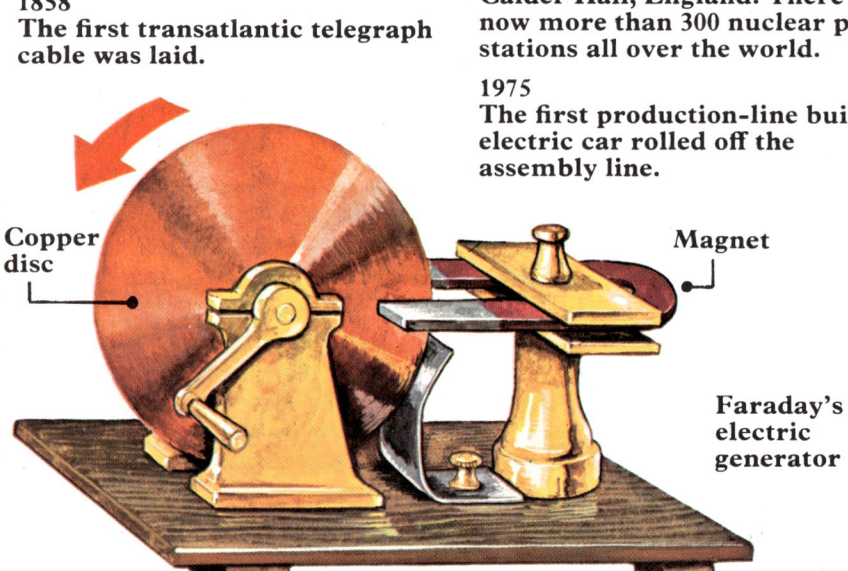

Copper disc

Magnet

Faraday's electric generator

ELECTRIC FACTS

Electricity can be our willing servant or our deadly enemy. It can light an electric lamp or produce a killer thunderbolt. Here are some facts about electricity and how it is used.

The world's biggest power station came into service in 1970 on the Yenisei River in Siberia. It is a hydroelectric station producing more than 6 million kW of power, and the reservoir behind the dam is over 380 km. long. The U.S.S.R. also uses the highest voltages for power transmission. In some areas power lines work at 800,000 volts.

Japan's bullet train

The world speed record for a train running on an ordinary railway track is held by an electric locomotive. In March 1955 the train reached a speed of 330 k.p.h. in France. Electric trains on the Tokaido line in Japan regularly reach top speeds of 255 k.p.h.

The newest transatlantic telephone cable is very thin. It is less than 4 cm. in diameter and can carry more than 1800 telephone calls at the same time. Old fashioned cables had to be very thick to do this.

There are more than 400 million telephones throughout the world. People in some countries can dial direct to as many as 26 others without an operator having to connect the call for them.

The latest communications satellite links Europe, Africa and America. It can relay up to 6000 telephone calls at the same time.

In a modern nuclear power station, 1 kg. of uranium fuel produces as much electricity as 2000 tonnes of coal in a conventional station. When the problems of nuclear fusion are solved, 1 kg. of fuel will produce six times as much electricity again.

The filament of an electric light bulb is made of tungsten, which is one of the best heat resisting materials known. It will withstand temperatures up to 3400°C before melting.

If we could convert into electricity the sunlight falling on a 200 km. square of the Sahara desert, there would be enough power to supply every country in the world with electricity.

The body's nervous system depends on tiny electric currents to pass messages from sense organs to the brain and out again to the muscles. These currents travel at speeds up to 400 km. per hour.

The most powerful flashes of lightning contain enough energy to power a small village for a day. The temperature within the bolt itself is about 30,000°C. The temperature on the surface of the Sun is only 6000°C.

The world's tallest electricity pylons are used to carry power from Italy across the Straits of Messina to Sicily. The pylons tower 220 m. into the air (taller than a fifty storey office block). The distance between the pylons is 3.6 km.

ITALY

Straits
of
Messina

SICILY

ELECTRIC WORDS

Here is a list of some of the technical words used in the book. You will find only those words that were not fully explained on the pages where they appeared.

Armature
The coils in an electric motor that are forced to spin round by the magnetic fields.

Brushes
Conducting pads in an electric motor that pass current to the spinning armature.

Circuit
A path along which electric current travels. Current will not flow until the circuit is complete.

Conductor
A material that allows electric current to flow through it easily.

Condenser
In a power station steam from the turbines is passed into the condenser where it is turned back into water.

Electrodes
The two rods that carry current into and out of the electrolyte in a battery.

Electrolyte
The liquid or paste in a battery. Chemical changes in it produce electricity.

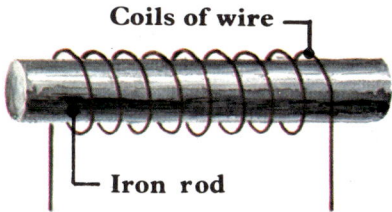

Coils of wire

Iron rod

Electromagnet
An iron rod with many coils of wire wrapped round it. When current is passed through the coils, the iron becomes a very powerful magnet.

Fission
The splitting of uranium atoms by shooting neutrons at them. As the atoms split they release energy that can be turned into electricity.

Fusion
The joining up of two atoms. A lot of energy is given off as they combine.

Tyre

Dynamo

Generator
A machine that produces electric current as it spins round. Generators in power stations produce a.c. Generators that produce only direct current are called dynamos. Bicycles often have a dynamo on the back wheel to power the front and rear lights.

Insulator
Any material that does not allow electricity to flow through it.

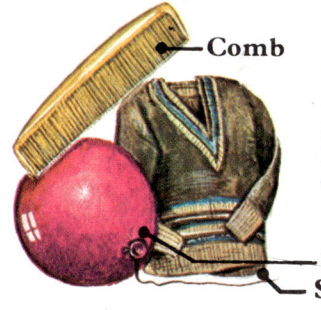

Comb

Things like this produce lots of electricity

Balloon
Sweater

Static electricity
The form of electricity produced when some materials are rubbed together.

Substation
An electricity station where a transformer reduces the voltage of the electricity supply.

Switch
A switch controls the flow of electric current. When the switch is off the circuit is broken and the current flow stops.

Transformer
A device used for increasing or reducing a voltage. Transformers work only with alternating current.

CIRCUITS AND SWITCHES

The experiments in the book have had pictures of bulbs, batteries and so on to show you how to connect them up. But when complicated circuits are drawn it is easier to use symbols. Connect up the circuits on this page using the list of symbols shown on the right.

See the effect of putting a switch in another part of the circuit; check how brightly bulbs glow when two are used instead of one. When you have done these, you can try designing some circuits of your own.

What the signs and symbols mean

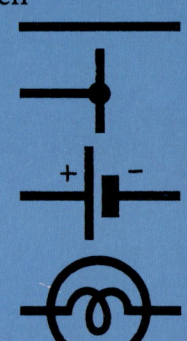

Wire

Connection between wires

Battery

Light bulb

Switch

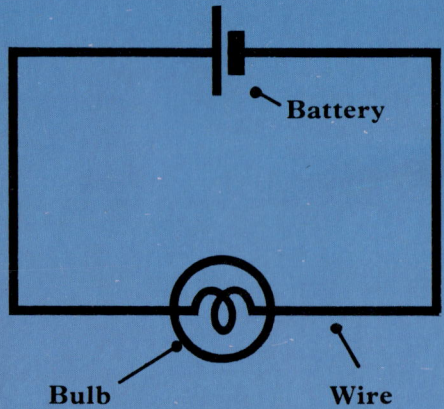

The simplest circuit is a bulb connected to a battery. There must be a wire to take the current out of the battery to the bulb, and another to return it to the battery.

Making a switch

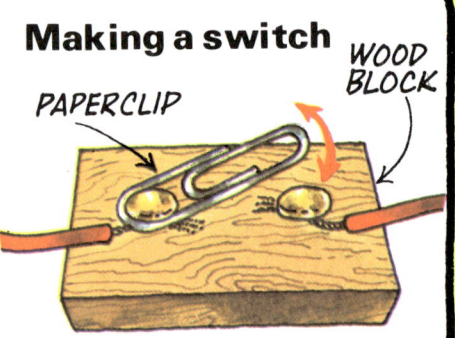

PAPERCLIP
WOOD BLOCK

To help you use these other circuits, you need to make this switch. You need two drawing pins, a small block of wood and a paperclip. Make it up as shown in the picture.

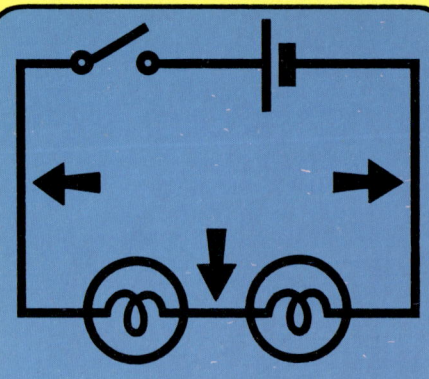

Here the bulbs are connected 'in series'. When the switch is off current will not flow. Try connecting the switch in the other places arrowed. Does it still work?

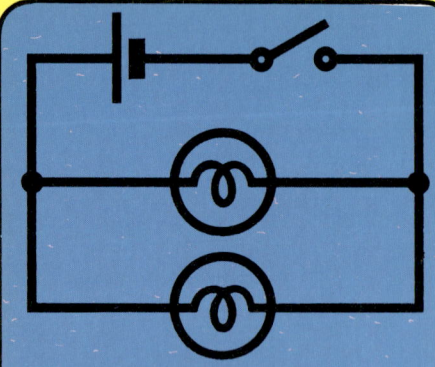

This is a 'parallel' circuit. You can see that when the circuit is completed by turning the switch on, both bulbs are controlled by it.

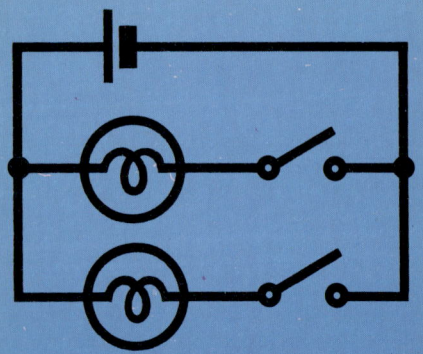

This circuit is very like the one before, but two switches are in the circuit instead of one. How many bulbs does each switch control when you turn it on?

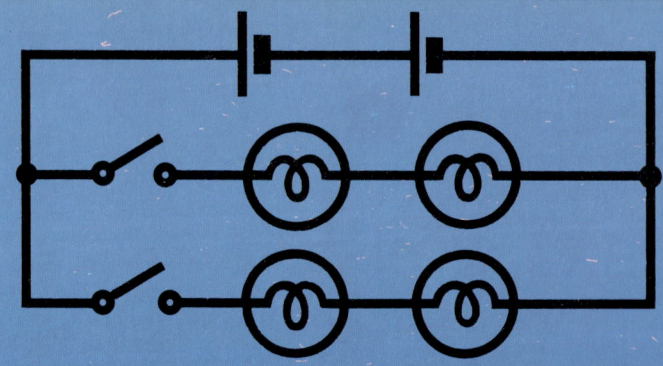

It is possible to connect batteries in series or parallel too—just like the bulbs earlier on. But remember to connect the ⊖ of the first battery to the ⊕ of the second. This means that the voltage in the circuit is twice that of each 4.5 volt battery, making a total of 9 volts. Each switch in this circuit controls two of the four light bulbs.

INDEX